WINGIN' IT

Best Wishes

[signature]

WINGIN' IT
THE **MARK WALTERS** STORY

MARK WALTERS WITH JEFF HOLMES

First published by Pitch Publishing, 2018

Pitch Publishing
A2 Yeoman Gate
Yeoman Way
Worthing
Sussex
BN13 3QZ
www.pitchpublishing.co.uk
info@pitchpublishing.co.uk

A CIP catalogue record is available for this book
from the British Library.

ISBN 978-1-78531-440-7

Typesetting and origination by Pitch Publishing
Printed and bound in India by Replika Press Pvt. Ltd.

Contents

For my Mum, Ivy Millicent Walters

My Uncle Rupert

And my children, Mischa and Marlon –
my world

Acknowledgements

FIRST of all I'd like to thank Graeme Souness for writing the Foreword to this book and for also acting as a guiding light throughout my career. He was a big influence on me so I was delighted when he agreed to provide the opening words.

I have been fortunate to play for some great teams and have met some wonderful people along the way. It has been quite a journey.

Working on this book has also been a new and exciting experience, and also good for the soul. So much has happened in my life and while there are a few things I might have preferred to forget, the good certainly outweighs the bad. Those twists and turns mirror many of my performances on the park!

I have enjoyed working with author Jeff Holmes. We have worked well together and I'm delighted with the result. That wasn't always something I could say at 4.45 on a Saturday evening! Jeff has also kept me right on a few things I'd forgotten, or didn't believe actually happened until he showed me the proof!

Many people have helped along the way and this book wouldn't have been possible without guys like Alex Boyd and Mark McAdam providing materials for research. And then there is Eddie Watson and Derek McNeill, who put me in touch with my co-author.

Paul and Jane Camillin head up a fantastic team at Pitch Publishing and I thank them for giving me the vehicle to get my story out there. Throughout the process they have kept me fully informed and I'm incredibly happy with the final result.

Football is a great life and I played longer than most, which I'm extremely grateful for, so I would say to anyone who gets the opportunity to make football their career, 'It will be over in a flash, so enjoy it while you can.'

Foreword

WHEN you call time on your career, there are a handful of players you look back on with great fondness and, as far as I'm concerned, Mark falls easily into that category. Apart from his individual brilliance, he was a team player and a real treat to work with. He was certainly 'my player' and I had a lot of faith in him.

As both player and coach, I was fortunate to work with so many talented players and Mark is up there with the best of them because he had so much ability. His team-mates also knew that worth because when things were tight he would come up with a bit of individual magic and win us the game, hence the reason they nicknamed him 'Flash'. Yes, he was that special.

There is a saying in football that you don't know a player until you've worked with him, but it wasn't a worry for me to give Mark his debut against Celtic in a New Year's Day game at Parkhead. You have to remember that he was coming from a big club in Villa, although there is absolutely nothing that prepares you for a Rangers v Celtic game: it is a unique derby and the most intense game you can play in. Of course there was an element of how he would deal with it but that wasn't because it was Mark, it would be the same for any player. You have to play in those games at some point, so when is the best time? The simple truth is, Mark was a great player and I knew he would handle the occasion.

I would put him in the same bracket as Davie Cooper, and that's high praise. Both were the type who could open the door for you with a little bit of magic.

When I joined Rangers I had a lot of knowledge about players in England, as I had spent most of my time down there. I was well aware that Mark was a match winner; I had seen it at close quarters, but I still sought out those who knew him best for their opinion and everything I heard back was extremely positive, so I had no fears about signing him.

There were very few players like him around, and I knew exactly what he was capable of, so when I got the chance to take him to Liverpool I didn't hesitate. When we were at Anfield together it was a troubled time for the club. I went there in difficult circumstances but I think Mark acquitted himself well and I hope he would look back on his time at Liverpool and say he enjoyed himself there.

He definitely had the talent to be a regular for England, but I think he was unlucky that the level of direct competition around at that time was phenomenal, with guys like John Barnes ahead of him in the queue. That said, you could put him up there on ability with any of his contemporaries, because he was a top, top player. Later on, Mark left Southampton just before I got there and I thought to myself, 'How unlucky would he have been, having to play for me three times!'

Seriously, though, I am delighted that I got to work with Mark during my managerial career. He was a real pleasure to be around and the type of player that not only put a smile on the faces of our supporters, but also everyone at the club, myself included.

Mark is also a lovely guy, and that can be so important when you're working with someone day in, day out.

Thank you Mark, it was a pleasure.

Graeme Souness
Former Rangers and Liverpool manager

Chapter One
Humble Beginnings

IF being born with a football attached to your feet was an option, I would've happily left Marston Green Hospital dressed in an Aston Villa babygrow and clutching a size four Mitre. When I was growing up, I didn't need much, and Mum always knew where to find me. If by some strange reason I missed an evening 'curfew' all she had to look out for was the mini Afro on a little guy kicking a ball around under the nearest street lamp. When I was a kid, that scene would've played out in Handsworth, Birmingham. Previously a sprawling inner city – but now apparently a city within a city – it's almost impossible to imagine that once upon a time Handsworth was a rural village in the county of Staffordshire, instead of the thriving Afro-Caribbean community it evolved into a decade or so before I was born.

Thousands of people were invited over to the UK from British colonies in the Caribbean to work in local munitions factories during the Second World War, with many more arriving to assist in the rebuilding of the area once the war had ended: the so-called 'Windrush Generation'. My mum was among those who arrived from Jamaica to take up the post-war offer due to a shortage of British men and women of an employable age. Meanwhile, my father had come over from Nigeria and, unbeknown to each other at the time, they both settled in or around Handsworth, thankfully long before racial tension and rioting in the mid-1980s brought the area to a standstill.

In June 1964 though, Handsworth was just another part of Birmingham and home to me, young Mark Everton Walters, fresh out of Marston Green. Mum was renting a room from relations who had also come over to the UK from their native Jamaica, which is the way it was in 1960s Britain, when families looked after each other, especially those who had made a pretty big sacrifice to start a new and better life almost 5,000 miles from home.

At my cousin's, I shared a room with mum and my brother, Michael, who was two years my senior. At that point, I also had a brother and sister I had never met. They were still living in Jamaica, awaiting the green light to come to the UK. That green light would illuminate when we had our own place. As it was, Michael and I slept in the same bed and we had a potty underneath in case we needed the toilet during the night. It sounds light years away today, but we didn't complain as we had never known anything else. I spent the first five years of my life in Handsworth, and I was very happy. Naturally, memories of the early days are sketchy, but having loads of cousins around meant there was always someone to play with, and any recollections I have of that period are positive.

I hadn't long celebrated my fifth birthday when mum was successful in applying for a flat in Newtown. Soon, Michael and I were joined by our older siblings, Kenneth and Vita. We were super excited but apparently that delight wasn't shared by our Jamaican grandparents who were adamant Kenneth and Vita should remain in the Caribbean. Mum eventually got her way and within a few weeks we were finally a proper family. We were grateful for the help given to us by our extended family, but with four kids vying for a shot at the television or bathroom, or even a place at the kitchen table, having our own place was important.

Newtown was, as its name suggests, a purpose-built housing scheme a few miles from Birmingham city centre. In the late 60s, the local authority created the new community by throwing up loads of high-rise flats and maisonette-type blocks in an effort to ease some of the pressure on areas like Handsworth, which were starting to suffer chronic overcrowding. Our new maisonette flat was close to the tower blocks and I remember there was real drama one night when one of the kids fell out of an open window in the close next to ours. We all rushed to get closer to the action and it wasn't long before a massive crowd had gathered. I was still a kid but recall the police and ambulances, sirens blaring, arriving at the scene and everyone creating a pathway to let the emergency services through. I was driving past that spot recently and when I stopped to have a look, memories of that night came flooding back. But things were very different from the way I had previously imagined them. In my head, the kid had fallen from a great height, probably 40 or 50ft, but the reality was more like ten feet. Luckily, though, the girl was okay as she had tumbled on to a patch of nice soft grass, another slightly important fact my mind had glossed over.

I enjoyed living in Newtown, although the excitement Michael and I had earlier felt about being joined by our brother and sister from Jamaica soon dissipated a little as there was quite an age gap and we struggled to bond, probably because they had outgrown the things Michael and I were now up to. But as soon as we were settled in Newtown, I was off to Hampton Junior School to make new friends and begin my education, although I didn't get off to the best of starts. The group of kids I started to hang around with weren't exactly the nicest. Mind you, two of them, Rohan 'Rocky' Rowe and Taju Forlarin, were pretty cool and we remained friends for a long time. But the others introduced me into their world of devilment, which included something akin to a mini protection racket, which saw a few of us hang around outside the school gates and take lunch money off some of the other pupils as they were heading to class. We would store our ill-gotten gains in a little metal combination safe, which one of the lads would then stash away just in case anyone had the audacity to try and nick it! Looking back, I acted appallingly and I'm ashamed to have been a part of it. I was a bit boisterous at the time but I certainly wouldn't describe myself as a gang member, far less the leader. It was only when I reached seven or eight years old that I realised I was decent at football and had a chance, and that if I didn't behave myself then I wouldn't be allowed to play anymore.

In fact, many years later I met one of the lads we used to 'rob'. His name was Wilf O'Reilly and he had become a really successful speed skater, winning a couple of gold medals at the 1980 Winter Olympics in Calgary, and also the 1991 World Championship. He was part of the commentary team at the 2018 Winter Olympics in South Korea. I was delighted to hear he had been successful.

I suppose I was a bad boy for a little while but it wasn't long until I started concentrating solely on my football, which was the perfect escape from the rocky road I seemed to be travelling down. I can't remember if Mum was ever called up to the school because I was misbehaving. Probably not, as she would have sorted me out without a moment's hesitation. Believe me, I would definitely have remembered that!

My mum, Ivy Millicent Walters, was my rock when I was growing up. She came over to Britain in the 1950s and got a job at the West Midlands transport authority where she cleaned the buses as they arrived back into the depot at night. It was there she met my father, Lawrence Johnson Wabara, a mechanic, and originally from Nigeria. The story goes that when I was born, my father wanted to call me after his favourite Brazilian football team, Santos. He was apparently a big fan of the great Pele, who would also, in time, become a huge favourite of mine, but Mum got her way and they settled on Mark. You might think he then claimed a small victory by including 'Everton' as my middle name, but you'd be wrong. That was also Mum. Everton is a really common West Indian name – almost the equivalent of John – and with Mum having absolutely no interest in football (if anything, she would occasionally watch a bit of cricket) it was a couple of normal names for yours truly.

Sadly, they split not long after I was born so I grew up in a one-parent household, but as the baby of the family I was well looked after by my older siblings, which was some consolation for not having my father around. Mind you, it's not like he had taken off and disappeared into the night. Nope. As I was soon to discover, he was living not more than a mile away; information I stumbled upon while nipping out from school to the shops one lunchtime. I was in Hampton at the time and was ambling along the road towards the local bakery when this car slowed down alongside me. I recognised the man as my father but I felt no paternal connection with him. He asked where I was going and, thinking back, he was eyeing me with a degree of suspicion. I told him I was out to get some lunch and then I was going back to school. He just sort of scoffed and drove off. What I didn't realise at the time was that he was married and had another family. He lived on the same road I'd been walking along when he stopped me, so he probably thought I had been sent to spy on him. I had no idea about his secret life so it had all been a coincidence but I'm sure he didn't see it that way. When I eventually found out about his double life, and where he lived, I had a little chuckle at how uncomfortable I must have made him feel that day, even though I was genuinely oblivious to my incredible detective skills!

But even though he didn't live that far from us, he never once came to see how his 'other' kids were faring, and later in life that really pissed me off. Just because you have a new family doesn't mean you disconnect from your other children, as we hadn't done anything wrong and didn't understand why we were being ignored. There are lots of things you don't get when you're a kid and it doesn't make it any easier when adults keep things from you – especially important things.

One of the earliest memories I have of my father is of him coming to watch me playing in a kickabout with my mates in a field behind a block of maisonettes close to our house. We hadn't long moved to Newtown so he had obviously been keeping tabs on us. It would have suited him better to have tried to be a part of our lives rather than just showing up every once in a while. At the time I didn't know he'd been a bit of a footballer himself, and that he'd played for Nigeria in the 1950s. My mother understandably didn't talk about the positive aspects of his life, so it came as a bit of a shock. Later on, I saw a picture of him playing for Nigeria against England. He was one of the smaller players, so I imagine he might have played up front. He had also, apparently, tried to get a trial with Villa at one point, but had been unsuccessful.

Hampton was one of around a dozen schools in the area which took part in an annual football competition, and I would have loved my father to have come and watch me play. It was a big deal for an eight- or nine-year-old, especially when the parents of all the other boys were there to cheer on their kids. My mum was brilliant and would always try and get to see me playing, but because she was a single parent holding down a number of jobs to try and make ends meet, her time was precious. I loved when she was there, though, and when we ran out of the pavilion before kick-off, we were playing in the World Cup, and the small scattering of parents numbered 50,000!

Growing up, I could count on one hand how many times I saw my father. There was the time behind the maisonettes when we were playing football, and the day he thought I was spying on him. I was told he had been to see me play for Villa Reserves when I was 15, but I hadn't seen him as he'd shot off straight after the game. About two years later, after a home match for the first team, he was standing outside the stadium when I came out of the players' entrance. It felt really strange. When he spotted me, he walked over slowly and it was as though he was plucking up the courage to speak to me. I waited until he had finished and said, 'Don't you think it's a bit late? I've managed without you up until now. I don't need anything from you, least of all your money. I'm not interested,' and I stormed off. To be honest, it was quite a put down and I regret doing it, but I've spoken to a few people in a similar position and they said my response was quite normal. It was simply the way I felt about my situation at that time and was probably a lot of my bottled-up childhood frustrations coming out in a rant.

I'm often asked how I felt about him having another family. As a grown man it doesn't really bother me. I know what it's like. I'm divorced myself and well aware that these things happen. At the time, though, it was different. I'm not gonna lie and say it was easy. It was difficult for me to accept that we lived so close to one another yet I didn't ever get a birthday or Christmas card. Things like that bothered me. I know money was tight, particularly in the 70s, but a card would've been ample and he would've had me for life, so I suppose it was the fact I was being snubbed that took me a while to get over. It wouldn't have taken too much effort from him to be a semi-permanent fixture in my life.

When I was about 13 or 14, Mum and I came into a bit of money. All of a sudden we were £300 richer, which was a lot of money back then. I was chuffed but I didn't know where it had come from. When I found out Mum had been forced to take my father to court to pay some maintenance it disgusted me. When I think about it now, if I had to be forced to go to court to pay something towards the upkeep of my children it would be a sad day. So that was the type of thing that made me bitter towards my father, and I didn't get over that until I had my own children.

My parents never married, but he should still have come up with the money to maintain his children. Apparently during the court proceedings, he even denied he was my father, which really hurt me at the time and if the truth be told, it still does to this day and he has been dead nearly 20 years. That is probably the main reason I told him to get lost when he waited for me that day outside Villa Park.

I later found out that my father owned a café in Aston, but it wasn't just any old café. Johnson's Café was the hang-out – and name inspiration – for the notorious Johnson Crew, who, along with the Burger Bar Boys, ruled Birmingham with an iron fist for many years. A succession of gangland assassinations and shootings culminated in the tragic deaths of teenage girls Letisha Shakespeare and Charlene Ellis in 2003 outside a hairdressing salon in Aston. It was an awful period in the history of my city and eventually leaders of both gangs teamed up to try and bring peace and stability to the black neighbourhoods of Aston and Handsworth.

But the disappointment of my father aside, my childhood was an enjoyable one, and I could normally be found outside with a ball at my feet. Most of my friends also loved football and we would play anywhere, any time. We played mostly in the street, although it wasn't like the present day, when kids get a ticking off for playing there. For starters, there wasn't the same number of vehicles on the road so it was a little safer and there was more room. We would also play in the school yard and have little games of keepy-uppy. In those days everyone watched *Match of the Day*, so we would be trying out some of the moves we had seen on the TV and take turns showing off our new-found skills.

I also enjoyed playing cricket and did so until I was about 12 or 13 but, as we were all getting bigger, faster and stronger, it was becoming quite dangerous, especially if you had a chance of making it in football. I had witnessed a couple of lads getting hit on the head with a cricket ball so I decided to stop playing, largely for my own safety. I still played for the school at cricket but gave that up when I was about 14. I also played a bit of basketball. In fact, I took part in anything sporty at school, and that included athletics. I was one of the quickest at Holte Comprehensive, which came in handy on a number of occasions!

In terms of age, I just missed out on the cut-off for school, which meant I was 11 when I went to secondary, while most of the others were 12, and some even approaching 13. At that age, six or seven months can mean quite a difference in size, sometimes a few inches. In fact, I remember a football survey which reckoned children born from October to December were physically more developed and had more of a chance of getting on in the game because of that. In my age group, clubs always went for the biggest and strongest, so the little ones sometimes got left on the shelf. Thankfully my skills weren't size dependent. I was small, compared to most other lads, but I stood out a bit more because of what I could do with the ball. Sadly, though, the really small ones were getting pushed about a bit. If you look at football nowadays, there are far more big guys around than small ones. Physique certainly counts for a lot in today's game.

I was about ten when Mum was offered a house in Aston, which was only a mile or so from Newtown. It was nicer and bigger and for the first time we had a garden. It was certainly a good move for the family and having some outside space was the icing on the cake. And that house, which my mum still lives in, was the perfect base for a burgeoning young footballer, as the moment you opened the front door you could see the floodlights at Villa Park. Imagine a midweek game early evening in winter and those huge floodlights – with the initials 'AV' carved into them – casting a huge blanket of light over the entire area. It was a magical sight. My secondary school, Holte Comprehensive, which shared its name with the famous terraced end at Villa Park, was now about a mile from our house but that didn't bother me one bit. I would walk to school with a ball at my feet and the extra distance meant I could have fun for longer. And one of the positive things about eventually becoming a footballer was that I was able to buy the house for Mum, as she loved it and still does.

At that time most of the kids at school wanted to play for Villa, and we all had our favourite players – guys that we aspired to be like. *Match of the Day* provided us with our staple diet of football so we got to know a lot of the big-time players. But then I went through a very short phase of craving an alternative career. Can you believe it? I was an avid reader of the little *Commando* comics, which were very popular among young boys in the 1970s, and through reading them I decided I would join the army when I was old enough. The stories in these little comic books were fantastic, and made real heroes of their central characters. For a while I would cut out army recruitment posters from newspapers and magazines and pin them up on my wall. I suppose I was kind of obsessed, until one day a couple of friends came to the house and asked my mum if I was allowed out to play football. She told them I was in my room and to go straight up. My army obsession wasn't something I had spoken of much so very few of my friends knew about it. When the lads walked in, one of them said, 'These posters are really cool, Mark,' while the other was a bit more to the point and offered, 'Do you know you can get killed in the army?' That was all he said, while continuing to eye the information that was plastered all over the walls. That was the moment any aspirations of dressing up in khaki ground to a halt. I quickly realised becoming a footballer was a slightly safer bet, and from the moment I realised I was pretty decent at it, I was determined to do everything I could to try and realise my dream.

I fell completely in love with football again and never missed a game on TV, but even that was no substitute for the real thing – which meant watching Villa play on a Saturday afternoon. The main obstacle to that was cash, or rather the lack of it. Mum couldn't afford to shell out the entrance fee so my friends and I would do our best to sneak in, although, if the worst came to the worst, we would wait until they opened the gates with around 20 minutes to go and dive in. Anything was better than nothing.

Villa Park was a fantastic ground in which to watch football. When I started going there, they always had a big crowd in and the atmosphere was superb. European nights were extra special, as I would hear the crowd the moment I opened my front door. The excitement I felt walking to Villa Park in those days was unbelievable. For a young lad it was quite exhilarating, even if we didn't manage to get inside, in which case we would stand outside listening to the 'oohs' and 'ahs' of 30,000 fans and imagine Villa on the attack, or defending stoutly against the big teams. I suppose if we actually got into the ground it was a real bonus.

We lapped it up and I loved watching guys like Brian Little. He was my favourite at the time. He was a great player, and the type I wanted to become: fast and skilful. When I started my love affair with Villa I reckon Brian was the best player at the club.

One of my earliest memories is of sneaking in to see Villa play Arsenal, and marvelling at the contrast of their bright red kit against our claret and sky-blue. Everyone knew all about Arsenal as they were arguably the most famous name in English football at the time. I was mesmerised watching them play.

Andy Gray was doing well for Villa at that time, and I had the pleasure of playing alongside him when he returned to Villa Park in 1985, after spells at Wolves and Everton. I then teamed up with Andy again at Rangers a few years later. I think Villa bought Andy, the first time round, when Keith Leonard got injured. Keith was another of the first batch of players I enjoyed watching at Villa Park, and he would later become my youth coach.

That was that. I was hooked on football. It had reeled me in and it was the start of a lifelong love affair, perhaps even an obsession. It was time to start pulling on the boots, although there was one pretty big stumbling block to that which left my career almost over before it had started.

Chapter Two

The Monster Within

IN the very early days of my football career Mum was definitely my biggest supporter, and it was a decision she made – one which couldn't have been easy, and, indeed, broke with years of tradition – that allowed me to progress in the game. We were living in Newtown at the time, when the doorbell sounded one night. It was a man asking if I was available to play for his team, Newtown Unity. I was standing at the other end of the hall, tuning in, as Mum listened carefully to everything he had to say. He was telling her about the promise I was showing playing for my school team, and of the glowing reports he had received from his scouts. Everything was positive, and I was excitedly starting to think I might get a chance to play for my first proper youth team, until he mentioned the one word that was taboo in our house – Sunday. That was the moment Mum stopped listening and started talking. 'Your team plays football on a Sunday?' she asked, with that look of disdain, which normally preceded a scolding, or a very definite no.

'That's right, Mrs Walters,' he said, adding, 'We are a very well organised club and we put the wellbeing of our young players at the heart of everything we do.'

The thing is, Mum was deeply religious and Sundays were set aside solely for church. She had even prevented my older brother Michael from playing football on a Sunday and as I couldn't expect to be treated any differently, I quickly dismissed the notion of turning out in the near future for Newtown Unity FC. In my mind, it was back to kicking the ball around in the street with my mates.

But I didn't reckon on this mystery guy possessing such steely determination that when Mum told him it was completely out of the question for me to be playing football on the Sabbath, he replied, 'I completely respect your decision, Mrs Walters, but please give it some thought because Mark does have a special talent and I genuinely feel our club could help him develop and prosper. We also have a number of professional scouts who come to watch our games so his chances of moving on to something bigger and better are excellent, especially if he continues to improve at his current rate.'

With that, the door closed. Mum had said her goodbyes and the gentleman was on his way, hopeful that his parting shot had given her food for thought. As I got ready for bed, I also hoped it might make a difference, although I wasn't overly confident.

The following morning at the breakfast table, Mum told me all about her encounter with the stranger and I acted with great surprise. After recounting the conversation almost verbatim, Mum spoke of how Sunday was sacred and the day for church. So you can imagine my great surprise a few moments later when she gave her blessing for me to join the team. I almost choked on my toast. My overriding emotion wasn't one of elation, because I was in total shock. Had I heard correctly? When the news hit home I wasted little time in jumping up and hugging her because I knew the decision hadn't been taken lightly – and I was terrified in case she changed her mind. I knew this ruling would make me deeply unpopular with Michael but that was a small price to pay for such a watershed moment in my life. Instead of heading to church every Sunday I would now be polishing my boots in anticipation of playing for Newtown Unity. I was delighted because up until then there hadn't been any competition. It was either church or you didn't eat! Mum was such a staunch Christian we had to accompany her whether we liked it or not. It wasn't that I liked church, it was just something I had to do. Most Jamaican families are religious. In fact, per square mile, I believe there are more churches in Jamaica than most other countries. Everybody goes to church; it's a way of life. When I was growing up, Sunday could be a long day as quite often you went to church for a couple of hours, headed home for lunch, and then you might go back again. Visiting the Church of God of Prophecy was just part of our Sunday ritual.

Playing for Newtown Unity was a real education: my first proper lesson in how the game should be played. Up until then the only organised football I had played had been with my primary school, which often consisted of 22 kids running after the ball, regardless of whereabouts on the pitch it was! With Unity, we were organised and were each given different positions. My eyes were opened wide, but I quickly found my nirvana. I was an out-and-out striker in those days and was very greedy on the ball. I would regularly take on every single player in the opposing team if I thought I had the slightest chance of getting away with it. But playing for Newtown taught me a lot and gave my football some sort of discipline, so much so that by the time I was playing for Holte Comprehensive I had taken on board lots of the advice I had been given and become more of a team player. We had a cracking team at Holte, good enough to reach the quarter-finals of the National Schools Cup, which was probably one of the most prestigious schools football tournaments in the country. It was a big deal.

Brian Jones was secretary of the Aston Schools Association and also had connections with Aston Villa. He reckoned Villa had one of the best youth development schemes in the country at that time, and the first name he passed on to the Villa youth department was mine, which I'm still very proud of. There were five schools in the Aston area and I was picked to represent the Aston Schools Association. Brian was a teacher at one of the schools and he did a really good job. He was also a really approachable guy and had a good way with people.

Once I had learned the basics of the game, things started to happen relatively fast for me. The manager at Newtown Unity had started the process, by convincing Mum to allow me to play on a Sunday. There were a few teams wanting me to line up for them, but my greatest individual achievement up to then came one afternoon at Holte. I was called into the headmaster's office and was starting to wonder what I had done wrong, when the headmaster told me to sit down. He was quite a stern looking guy, but when he told me I had been chosen to represent England Schoolboys I was speechless. His face lit up like a beacon and he had a smile stretching from ear to ear. It started to sink in that I could soon be pulling on the white shirt of England, and I was in dreamland. This was all my Christmases rolled into one.

I made my debut for England in a Victory Shield match against Northern Ireland. The match should have been played in Belfast, but it was at the height of the Troubles and so the English Schools' Football Association refused to travel to the province and the match took place at Brunton Park, Carlisle. It was a tough game and with the likes of Norman Whiteside in the Northern Ireland side we were happy enough with a 0-0 draw. That year I also represented England against Wales – another draw – and that game was played at Wembley, which was an incredible experience for a 15-year-old boy. Everything about that day was special. From arriving in London, seeing the twin towers and walking through the players' entrance. The players' entrance at Wembley! Imagine! It was such a thrill. And then into the dressing room before walking down the tunnel and out on to the park. So very special.

Being picked to represent England Schoolboys was a real honour and I was a proud young lad. When you think of the sheer number of schoolboys in England, it's quite an achievement. I enjoyed the whole experience of being with the squad, meeting new lads and obviously playing in the games. Guys like Trevor Steven and Paul Rideout played for England Schoolboys at the time, so the standard was exceptional. Mike Hooper, an eventual team-mate at Liverpool, and Andy May, who played for Manchester City, were another couple of guys I remember being involved.

Whenever I played for England Schoolboys, Dave Richardson, the Aston Villa academy chief, would lay on transport for my mum so she could come and watch. It was a great gesture and gave me such a boost. He knew how much I wanted her there. When you're a young lad, and the other kids have the support of their parents, it makes quite a difference. I felt left out if Mum wasn't there, and it also made me feel a bit different from the others. Consequently, if my own children were ever doing anything, I always made the effort to be there. In fact, 40 years on I can still dredge up that sense of loneliness if ever I took part in a big game and none of my family were there.

My mum would often tell me how proud of me she was, and even though she obviously didn't know a lot about football in those early days, and didn't realise that players could make a decent living out of the game, when she watched me at Wembley I think she started to think about just how big a deal it actually was. That was when she started to ease off on the demands that I get some proper qualifications behind me as the day when I would be leaving school and have to get a 'real' job was rapidly approaching. 'Hey mum, football is a real job,' I would often tell her, and I think she was slowly beginning to agree. I reckon Wembley sorted that!

Playing football was my life, but my epiphany came in the shape of the 1974 World Cup. It was the first World Cup I was truly able to take in and enjoy and my eyes were never far from a television screen throughout the four-week tournament. I was ten years old and when I first clapped eyes on Johann Cruyff I realised that here was a guy who played football the way I liked to watch it. Cruyff was a genius, and when he performed that famous double shuffle I was mesmerised. I went straight out after seeing it for the first time and practised it to death. It didn't really suit my style absolutely (how dare you, Johann!) so I adapted it to suit me better and throughout my career it would buy me a yard of space. I worked on it non-stop but luckily I was two-footed so I could go either side, and that gave me a big advantage. Playing wide, obviously you can go inside or outside, so that was probably the main reason my 'adapted version' worked so well for me. If you're trying it going through the middle then you don't know who is on either side of you, but playing on the wing meant there was rarely anyone on my outside. It definitely helped my game, gave me that yard, which is vital, and probably stuck an extra five years on my career.

One moment indelibly etched on my mind is the night I was due to meet Mr Cruyff at Villa Park. He was there to play for Barcelona in a UEFA Cup match and because I was viewed as a promising youngster, I was chosen as part of a small group of Villa youths to meet the great man before the game. While supporters paid £1.30 for the privilege of standing on the Trinity Road terracing, we were preparing for our big moment, autograph books and pens at the ready, outside the dressing room. Just as Cruyff came out to meet us, the former ITV commentator, Gary Newbon physically shoved me out of the way to grab a word with him. I was so upset. I was barely a teenager at the time, and I missed out on getting an autograph because of the awful behaviour of a rude adult. A few years later, when I was in the first team at Villa, I saw Newbon and I didn't miss him. I gave him a piece of my mind and he seemed really embarrassed, and so he should've been. While I was a footballer there would have to be a really good reason for me not to stop and give a kid an autograph, like if I was really late for a game or something. It was part and parcel of the job.

I did obsess about football and I played all the time: at school, during break times, after school, weekends. It didn't leave much time for anything else, and because my mum was working a lot she didn't get a chance to properly implement a bit of discipline and say 'you can only play at certain times' etc. – so my school work did suffer. Because Mum wasn't there, most of the time I didn't bother with homework. I would admit my motivation to study was pretty low, so football always won the day. I think it was just a case of doing what I had to do at school: enough to get by as I didn't really pay that much attention. That said, I enjoyed school and had good fun with my mates but I didn't take it seriously enough. I suppose it worked out alright in the end but I was lucky because one bad tackle could've ended my career and I wouldn't have had an awful lot to fall back on. A few of my mates were in a different boat as they could only play at certain times, as they had to do chores at home or their homework.

Playing for the school team and Newtown Unity was great but it wasn't long before other youth teams in the area started to sit up and take notice, and one of those was Beeches Colts, who were run by the dad of footballer Craig Shakespeare, the future Leicester City manager. I've known Craig since we were eight or nine. He lived not too far from me and he was a decent player. He ended up going to West Brom, and also played for the likes of Grimsby Town and Walsall.

I thoroughly enjoyed playing for the Colts but tragedy was just around the corner when Mr Shakespeare died of a heart attack while he was still in his forties, which was a massive shock to everyone who knew him. Beeches Colts disbanded not long after that, but it was while with them that I attracted the attention of arguably the most successful youth team in the Birmingham area at that time. Dunlop Terriers weren't from Aston, but drew on a wider area for their players.

They were recognised as the team to play for because the manager, Ted Langford, also worked as a scout for Aston Villa, which meant the club offered a pathway to Villa Park for those with the talent and dedication to take their career to the next level. That was an obvious attraction for me, that and the fact that one of my best pals also played for the Terriers, so I had no hesitation in joining when asked. Again, I was playing up front and scoring lots of goals and there was definitely a moment when I felt I might one day achieve my dream of becoming a professional footballer at Villa. At that point I had no interest in playing for any other senior team.

There were a lot of good, young players at the Terriers, and the club seemed to be well run – apart from one major issue, and it was a massive problem, which would ruin many young lives instead of helping catapult kids on to the next rung of the football ladder. For some of my team-mates, the dreams they harboured turned into living nightmares. Ted Langford was married and had kids around the same age as his players. He did have genuine connections with Villa and often spoke of the players he had been able to get to the club for trials. As a 10- or 11-year-old boy with the sole focus of one day playing for Villa, this was music to my ears. It was also exactly what guys like Dean Glover, probably the most high-profile guy who played in the same team as me, wanted to hear. Dean went on to play for Villa, Middlesbrough and Port Vale, while the likes of Bob Hazel (Wolves and QPR) and Brendan Ormsby (Villa and Leeds United) also came through the ranks at the Terriers. We all wanted to be just like Bob and Brendan so we were desperate to be involved. This, in turn, made it easier for Langford to do what he wanted – and that was to abuse young boys. He was a paedophile who preyed on the very kids he was supposedly looking out for. When I eventually discovered what had been going on at the club, many years later, it made me physically sick. I was disgusted by his behaviour and distraught for the lads who had been abused by him.

This might sound a bit far-fetched, but when I joined Dunlop Terriers it was the first time I had really mixed with white kids in such a closed environment. Up until then I mostly knocked about with West Indian kids so when I saw Langford cuddling the other lads and giving them love bites on the neck, I thought it must be normal. It sounds absolutely ridiculous now, but there was even a part of me which felt disappointed that he didn't like me, as he always gave his undivided attention to some of the other lads. Let's be honest, when you're a kid you want to be accepted, to be liked. Looking back, though, there was definitely a 'type of boy' he preferred: the ones with that choirboy look, and sadly he molested quite a few. That was obviously why my friend was molested, as he had that look. On top of that, he had been having a lot of problems at home and Langford pounced on that. He invited my friend to stay at his house 'to get away from his problems' and that is when a lot of the abuse apparently took place. My mate was a really nice lad and we got on really well. He was approachable and sociable, and really just one of the lads. I was quite shy at that time but he was one of the in-crowd, and also one of our better players.

I remember vividly being in the showers after playing a match, and half of us still had our pants on. The showers were really wide and open, and Langford and his sidekick Dave Pitts were walking along the front of the cubicles, Langford with his camera on his chest and clicking away, taking pics of all the kids. We were all shouting at them to get out, but we used to think of it as a joke, and would all just laugh about it and throw things at them.

Langford and Pitts were an odd pair: chalk and cheese, and two guys you would never believe could be friends. Pitts was a really weird-looking guy and I think he might even have worked for the local paper. To be honest, paedophilia is something you didn't hear a lot about in the 1970s. I certainly didn't know what it was. I played with the club between the ages of 10 and 13 and it shows the age group of our squad of players.

When the abuse became public knowledge, and everything was out in the open, the monster was sacked by Villa, but not before he had done some long-term physical and psychological damage to many kids. I was just a kid myself and didn't have a clue that this type of thing was going on. When I went home after a game, or training, I would never have thought to mention anything to my Mum. I had some great pals in that team and I loved playing for them but when I think of what these poor guys were going through it makes me very angry. One aspect of the whole sordid episode that I still struggle to get my head round is that the people who were involved with Villa at that time didn't realise it was going on. How could they not have had at least a suspicion? Even as children, at just ten years of age, we might not have known the extent of the crime, but we did have an inkling that something wasn't right, so as an adult you would definitely have known what was going on. My mate asked if I will speak on his behalf during his court case, as he is taking the club to court. Rightly so as they must take their share of responsibility for the events that took place in the mid-1970s.

My mate wasn't part of the initial court case against Langford in 2007, when the former manager was jailed for three years for 'sexually abusing a string of young hopefuls during the 1970s and 80s'. So it was still going on long after I left the club. It baffles me how someone can get away with such a heinous crime for so long.

At the initial trial, the judge said the abuse, which involved four boys, resulted in them suffering psychological harm. Apparently, Langford, who was 66 at the time, admitted three charges of indecent assault and four of gross indecency. It makes you wonder how many other charges could, and should, have been brought against him.

The monster died in 2012 and it would be nice to think that wherever he is at this precise moment, he is paying for the pain and suffering he caused.

All that aside, I did enjoy playing for the Terriers, and the first time I experienced the thrill of travelling abroad was to play in a prestigious youth tournament in Sweden. As a club with a reputation for producing top talent, Dunlop Terriers were normally one of the first to be invited to the top tournaments abroad. The first I found out about our overseas adventure was when it was announced one night after training. My first feeling was of great disappointment, because I knew Mum wouldn't be able to afford to pay for me to go. Every penny was accounted for in our household and sadly such a trip would've come under the banner of 'unnecessary luxury', and reluctantly I would've had to agree. So you can imagine how elated I was when the next words that came out of the manager's mouth were, 'Aston Villa are sponsoring the trip – so the only thing you will need is spending money!' How to experience both emotional extremes in such a short space of time. We were all jumping around, cheering and already looking forward to visiting Scandinavia – even though we didn't really know where Scandinavia was! It would be a great adventure, and no doubt very different from playing football back home in Birmingham.

The first lad I celebrated with was Fitzroy Latty, and we were both beaming from ear to ear. Fitz would go on to play for Crystal Palace, after being released by Villa, but ended up working as a driving instructor for his dad. One of my room-mates on that trip was Trevor Campbell, who also went down to Palace. But even though there was perhaps only the two of us who played in the top flight, there were still around six or seven, easy, who would go on to play league football. So we had some good players, and we had a great time when we went to Sweden. We stayed with some of the local kids who were taking part in the tournament and we made a real impact. We came home with a collection of trophies and a hatful of great memories.

I played with the Terriers for a few years, and when I was eventually forced to quit the team it was a decision that was made for me. I was playing around five games a week for different teams and, due to overplaying, I developed a condition called Osgood-Schlatter disease, more commonly known as Schlatters Knee, which I discovered during a visit to the doctor. I had been suffering pretty bad knee pain and after the doctor examined me, he sat there shaking his head, and I started to wonder if he was about to tell me I couldn't ever play football again. It was an agonising wait until he spoke, although it was probably only a few seconds, and I was actually relieved when his diagnosis meant I would only have to play LESS football. As a consequence, I told Langford I wouldn't be able to play for the Terriers any more as something had to give. At that time, if you were picked to play for the school team, playing was mandatory. Langford didn't take it well, and I remember at the end of that season, one of my mates telling me he was going around saying, 'We won the league without that so-and-so Walters, who thinks he is too big for us now!' Because of what he'd said I started blanking him, but had I been aware of his paedophile tendencies I would've blanked him far sooner. I had three enjoyable years at Dunlop Terriers but naturally Langford's extra-curricular activities make it a period of my life I'd rather forget. I'm glad he eventually got his comeuppance, although in my opinion it was far too little too late.

When I started out with these youth teams I was always a centre-forward. The reason I morphed into a wide player became apparent when I got into the reserve team at Aston Villa. One thing you always check out is your pathway to the first team. You know you're not ready but it's prudent to look at what's ahead of you – and what I found was guys like Gary Shaw and Peter Withe. Let's be honest, it was going to take something special to dislodge them and I wanted to play football so I thought I might have a better chance out on the wing. I had the speed and was gaining the trickery so it seemed like a good idea. I had also played wide for the England youth team, and England Schoolboys, but whenever I could, or I had the choice, I would grab the number nine jersey. That was my favourite position, and I played there when I was chosen to represent Midland Counties. I was prolific for all my youth teams, and that was in the days when the front players could expect to be smashed regularly from behind, which might also have been one of the reasons I made the switch to the wide position permanent. I was quite small and lightweight and a lot of the big defenders would come right through me, so I ended up getting knocked about a bit. At least it didn't seem so daunting getting kicked by smaller full-backs!

Perhaps another reason for ending up out on the wing was because of how badly I headed the ball. I did receive quite a few lessons on the art of heading, but while I got better, the fact I hadn't headed the ball for so long meant my improvement was minimal. Let's just say I never quite mastered the art properly. Throughout my career I scored five or six goals with my head, probably because it was that close I couldn't miss.

It was mostly grass pitches we played on back in the day but the surfaces were usually horrendous: rock hard, really heavy or icy in the winter. Playing on these dodgy surfaces didn't make it easy if you were the type of player who liked to run with the ball. Many pitches were also constructed on a slope which made it difficult for youngsters, but they were still great days and we just loved playing football. To be honest, we would've played on anything back then, as we weren't aware lush green surfaces even existed!

When I was growing up, Aston Villa were easily the biggest club in Birmingham, and while they might not have been as proactive in the community as they are now, we were all well aware of the club. There were other clubs in the area like Birmingham City, but they weren't as big as Villa. You also had the likes of West Brom, Walsall and Coventry, so there were a number of clubs in the vicinity of the Midlands. In my area of Aston, there could be five or six lads all associated with different senior clubs. It was a big area and there were plenty of options for kids who had a chance of making the grade. I only had eyes for Villa, though, and it wouldn't be long before I got the chance to impress a couple of their top youth coaches.

Chapter Three

Signing on at Villa

I STARTED training with Villa a couple of nights a week when I was about ten. The youth coaches were constantly in touch with the best local under-age teams so there would be around 15 or 16 of the most promising kids invited in and we would be put through our paces on a patch of land just behind the main stand at Villa Park. We had a designated coach and it was such a thrill to be training at a big club. Villa were in the Second Division at the time, but the season I started training there, they finished second in the table AND won the League Cup by beating Norwich City in the final.

It was the first time the final had been contested by two teams from outside the First Division, but there was still a crowd of 100,000 at the Wembley final. I would love to have been there to see the big match but I was content with watching it on television, and I was delighted when Ray Graydon scored the only goal of the game to win us the cup. I'm sure our manager Ron Saunders had a huge smile on his face at the end of the game.

It was a great time to be starting out on my Villa journey and the buzz about the place, thanks to promotion and the

League Cup win – which was only the second time we had ever won that trophy – was palpable. Villa have always had a loyal support, and even when we were in the Second Division we were still getting crowds of 25,000-plus. They are just that kind of club.

I used to love getting into the ground to watch them any time I could, so to be a part, albeit a very small part, of the club was a brilliant feeling. My mind was always focussed on those two nights of training a week and while I was in school all I could think about was one day pulling on the claret and sky-blue top. In the summer we were also invited up to the training ground to watch the first team being put through their drills. That type of experience sowed these little seeds of hope in my mind and I would start to think how wonderful it would be if I could do something I truly loved for a living. Even at such a young age I knew the pathway to making it as a footballer was definitely there, but I also realised it was up to me to knuckle down and achieve my dream as no one would do it for me. It was definitely the first time I realised anything in life is possible.

Throughout my young years, people were always telling me I had the talent to make it as a footballer, but the sad thing was I didn't always share their confidence. I remember the dad of one of my team-mates saying to me – when I was playing for a Sunday youth team – 'you will never be a footballer because you don't pass to anyone'. I still believe it might have been meant as a backhanded compliment, or maybe he was just trying to be funny.

When people are continually telling you that you will make it in the game, you do eventually start to take it on board, but I was such a shy and quiet lad at the time that I didn't take it all in. Ironically, it was football that would bring me out of my shell and give me the confidence that had been lacking for most of my younger years.

Training was going well at Villa and the encouragement we received from the coaching staff was first class. They would organise little areas for different drills and it was hard work, but just to be associated with Villa was a dream come true. Not only that, but they were giving me trainers and kit – not to mention the fact I was getting to work alongside some fantastic players. Mind you, I always had some cracking pairs of trainers when I was growing up, long before I had trained with Villa, and it wasn't until about ten years ago that I discovered how Mum was ever able to 'afford' them. She said that because she worked for the West Midlands transport authority she would get her fair share of lost property. After a certain amount of time had elapsed, and no one had come forward to claim their lost bits and pieces, they were up for grabs! I was flabbergasted, because I always remember how tight money was in our house, but from time to time – not necessarily birthdays or even Christmas – Mum would come out with these stunning trainers or even football boots. I suppose I should be thanking the forgetful folk of Birmingham, and maybe even those who jumped on a bus after they'd had a little too much to drink, for my footwear!

Dunlop Terriers were always represented by around five or six of the players at these early training sessions at Villa, while we also had a few kids from out of town. We always had enough for an eight-a-side match after the training drills.

Dave Richardson was in charge of the Villa youth set-up at the time, while Keith Leonard, who played centre-forward in the League Cup final for Villa, was also doubling up as a youth coach. I used to hang on their every word. Other lads would idolise singers or film stars, but Keith was my Hollywood ace.

However, one night he pulled me aside and uttered the familiar words, 'I know you don't really like passing the ball, Mark, and when you're in the opposition half that's okay, you can do your thing, but when you've got the ball close to your own box you have to keep it simple and always choose the best option. Just slip it to a team-mate. It's a team game, not all about you, and you're all trying to achieve the same goal.' He put it across like a compromise and I started to take it on board.

When I was signed by Villa, and was playing for the reserves, Ron Saunders told me exactly the same thing, so perhaps I hadn't fully taken it on board when I was younger! Mind you, I must have listened when Mr Saunders mentioned it as I recall him staying behind after another training session to have a word, and when he said, 'Glad to see you're listening Mark,' I was well chuffed, especially as the gaffer was a man of very few words, and a highly regarded manager at that.

I had just turned 16 when I left school in the summer of 1980, but even at that age it was a crucial time for me and the club. Villa had just won the First Division for the first time in 71 years, and when I was invited to sign on as an apprentice I was absolutely thrilled. Of course it was something I had been working towards, but just being pulled aside by one of the coaches and told they believed in me was worth its weight in gold. Money didn't come into it. Ron Saunders was manager at the time but Dave was in charge of which youngsters were taken on as apprentices, so he had the final say. I signed at the stadium and it was a big thrill. It was a proud moment for a massive Villa fan and his mum. I now had a real opportunity to make my mark, if you pardon the pun, with my local club.

There were a few of us, probably around eight or nine, taken on as apprentices and we all had high hopes that this was the beginning of something special. We would continue to train under the watchful eyes of the youth coaches and play in youth-team matches, but the next step was the reserves and then, ultimately, the first team.

One of my fellow apprentices was Brian McClair, and if you had said to me back then that one day I would be playing for Rangers and Brian for Celtic, I wouldn't have believed you, but it's funny how football works out. Brian was a bit of a lone wolf and seemed quite aloof. He didn't really mix with the other lads, although I got on fine with him, and we spent time talking about our hopes for the future. He played in midfield then, so I was surprised when he was used as a striker by Celtic and at the start of his time with Manchester United.

As part of our apprenticeship, we had a number of daily tasks to perform at Villa Park. Jim Paul was the kit man and he used to walk around the dressing room wrapped in a towel – like a wee Buddha – telling all the apprentices what to do. It was like a scene from *Goodfellas* with this wee Buddha-like guy dishing out the orders, quite often from the sauna. He would be shouting, 'Come on guys, get those toilets looking spick and span. I want to be able to see my face in that floor, so get the mops working quick-time!' We had a long list of daily tasks to complete, but it was a good grounding and certainly never did us any harm. In fact, it probably instilled a bit of discipline in us, as woe betide anyone who tried to shirk their responsibilities.

A year after I signed for the club, in 1980, we won the FA Youth Cup, and I was a big part of the side that triumphed against Manchester City in the final. We won 3-1 at Villa Park, and while we lost 1-0 at Maine Road, a slender aggregate advantage meant we took the trophy back to Brum. We had a really good side at that time, with the likes of Paul Birch, who played over 200 first-team games for Villa in midfield, and a similar number for Wolves. Central defender David Mail was eight years at Blackburn Rovers and five at Hull City, while Ray Walker made more than 400 appearances for Port Vale, and was named three times in the Professional Footballers' Association (PFA) team of the year.

Another competition we thrived in was the Southern Junior Floodlit Cup. The season we won it I scored a dozen goals. I was playing up front at the time and thoroughly enjoying my football, and it was great to be wearing the Villa shirt in these important competitions. As the name suggests, the Southern Junior Floodlit Cup was evening games only, which takes me back to the days when I would leave the house and see the Villa Park lights illuminating the local area for miles. The only difference was this time when I opened the front door, I wasn't just going to watch the football – I was actually playing. What a buzz that was. On route to winning the Floodlit Cup we beat a very good Chelsea side at Villa Park, and travelled down to Bristol and knocked out Rovers in the semi-finals.

I had made a good start to life at Villa and up to then I had shown a good degree of patience. I realised there was a pathway, and that it took time. I had been happy training with Villa as a kid, and then playing for the youth side after signing an apprentice contract, but with a spot in the reserve team seemingly in touching distance, I started getting itchy feet. I suppose playing at some of the top grounds made me think how it would be when the stadia were full to the rafters for first-team games. 'All in good time,' my mum would remind me.

Noel Blake was a couple of years older than me and joined Villa just before I did. We had played in the FA Youth Cup-winning team together, but he was quite a character and was always up to one dodge or another. I remember on one occasion all the younger players were out helping to collect money for charity and I saw him pocket a couple of quid from one of the buckets. Coming from a religious background, I was pretty shocked and I spoke to him about it, but he told me to mind my own business, so I did!

At Villa, each apprentice was assigned a professional to look after and for me it was Allan Evans, the Scottish centre-half who was a big part of our 1982 European Cup success. I used to clean Allan's boots and make sure his kit was sorted, little things like that. One Christmas he slipped me £20, which was a fortune, and like another week's wages. I was thrilled. Anyway, I stuck the money in my trouser pocket before getting changed to go out for training. After another tough session, I headed back into the changing room, but noticed that my clothes were on the floor, and when I searched the pockets, the money had gone. I was distraught. Looking back, when I opened the changing room door, Noel was standing there looking quite suspicious. I reckon I had just about caught him in the act but I didn't put two and two together at the time. As soon as I noticed it was gone I went straight to the manager. Ron Saunders promised me he would get the money back. Meantime, he opened one of the drawers in his desk and took out a little box. Opening it carefully, he handed me two £10 notes and I was delighted. As you can imagine, £20 was a lot for a 15-year-old to lose so after that the manager could do no wrong in my eyes.

A couple of days later, after we had finished training and were heading home for the day, I noticed a small queue of players standing patiently in line just inside the changing room door, waiting to get out, but first of all everyone was being asked to stick their hands through this funny looking little machine.

Turned out it was an ultra-violet scanner. Anyway, I did it and was told to move on. A couple of my team-mates followed suit and then it was Noel's turn and when he stuck his hand in the contraption it lit up like a disco and he was led off to the manager's office. I quickly realised it was Ron's way of tracking down the dressing-room thief. At the time I'm sure there were a few relieved folk in the changing room, because even though all the lads – including me – knew they were innocent, the finger of suspicion pointed at everyone until someone was caught 'infra'-red-handed!

As far as I'm led to believe, the manager had decided to plant some cash in various places and Noel had obviously taken the bait, not knowing the notes were coated with anti-theft dye. But it wasn't just cash that was going missing. One of the guys had lost a Rolex watch, while others had been relieved of various bits and pieces of jewellery. Even in the 80s, lads were shelling out a right few quid on nice accessories and carrying bundles of notes around with them.

It was then a case of what to do with the perpetrator, and I believe the gaffer left it up to the players to decide his fate. After all, it was the players who'd had their stuff nicked. So the guys held a meeting, and I'm sure there were some who wanted to give Noel a pasting before booting him out of the club. Mind you, he was 6ft 2in and built like a brick shithouse – even as a teenager! But in the end they decided to give him another chance, and I'm sure it helped that Noel – despite his indiscretions – was a popular lad. It was fantastic because he managed to turn his life around and went on to have a really good career with the likes of Portsmouth, Birmingham City and Stoke. I've always been of the opinion that everyone deserves a second chance.

I've had stuff nicked throughout my career. It does happen all over the place. In the early days we didn't have lockers so I started leaving personal belongings or valuables in my car. When I signed for Liverpool, we were assigned a locker which meant I used to keep all my bits and pieces in there. Not everybody used their locker, though, and I remember Glenn Hysen getting a nice watch nicked. I would say it's fairly common in dressing rooms up and down the country.

It was actually Noel Blake who taught me how to head the ball properly. He came up to me one day in training and said, 'Mark, I've noticed you don't head the ball an awful lot in training or in matches. I know you wanna play up front but if you don't head the ball you will miss out on a lot of goals.' The reason I shied away from heading the ball was because I'd been smashed a few years beforehand while playing for the school team and actually knocked out, and for a couple of years after that I didn't put my head anywhere near a ball. So, Noel took me under his wing and helped me learn the noble art of heading.

The first piece of advice was, 'Keep your eyes open, it ain't gonna hurt you. Just head the f****** ball!' Which in itself was probably dodgy advice – unbeknown to Noel – as they are now linking dementia with the constant heading of a football! But I definitely improved. I was never gonna be a Peter Withe or Mark Hateley but I managed a few goals. If it was a school report card it would probably describe my heading ability as 'adequate' – but any improvement at all was down to Noel, and I credited a goal I scored for Southampton to him. It was actually a decent effort and I didn't have an awful lot of net to aim for but I got it on target and that was down to the big man's perseverance with me.

I'm really friendly with Chris Nicholl, a former Villa stalwart. For a while we used to play racketball every Tuesday with Gary Shaw and another couple of the lads. But Chris has been suffering from dementia and it has been difficult to watch him go from a really switched-on guy to someone who latterly couldn't find his way to the gym. In his day, Chris was a cracking centre-half who would head balls for a living. In fact, at training, one of the coaches would stand on the halfway line and smash balls into the box and Chris would stand there all day heading them away. In hindsight, his head must have taken quite a battering and sadly now we could be seeing the results of that.

I progressed to the reserve team quite quickly – thanks to Ron Saunders – and by March of 1982, I had scored eight goals in just ten games for the second string. I was always a decent finisher, and you have to remember I was playing up front then. In hindsight, I really should've been a bit more insistent that I play up front when I moved into the first team, because I felt it was my best position. To be honest, I wasn't mad about playing on the wing then. At that time Villa had won the league and the European Cup with a settled side and I would have been looking to play in the Gary Shaw role, but he was only three years older than me so I felt my best option was to play on the wing. Little did I know Gary would soon become injury prone and that I would definitely have got my chance. Gary was well established in the Villa team at the time and was the PFA Young Player of the Year. He also won the Bravo Award the following year, as the best under-23 player in European competitions, so he was quite a player. If it wasn't for injuries there is no doubt he would've gone on to play for England. Brian Little was also still at the club, even though he was injured. I thought to myself,

'Do I wait for my chance and be dogged about it; do I even go as far as leaving the club, or do I just play where they want me to play?' which was wide left. For whatever reason, Tony Morley – be it because they were fed up with him or he was past his peak as he was ten years older than me – left the club and a 'vacancy' popped up on the left wing, and guess who filled it? I loved scoring goals but I knew the more I played out wide, the less chance I had of scoring goals so I managed to get myself on to penalty-kick duty as often as I could. Did I make the right decision by agreeing to play wide? Probably not. I would like to have played up front more often but I ended up making a good career out of being a wide boy so I suppose it wasn't all that bad a decision.

And when the calendar in my house showed 28 April 1982, all those weeks, months and years of my football apprenticeship suddenly paid off: I made my first-team debut for Aston Villa. Leeds United were the visitors that Wednesday and one of the things I remember about the occasion is being up against Peter Barnes, who I was a big admirer of. I was also in awe of a number of other Leeds players, as I had been watching *Match of the Day* a few days before and all these guys had featured. It was a great experience for me, especially as I was a local lad and had always wanted to play for Villa. It's not often you get to tick something like that off your bucket list at such a young age. It was an evening game and I recall leaving the house that night to walk the short distance to the ground. It was an incredible feeling. In a strange kind of way I had been protected while playing for the youths or reserves. But there was no hiding place playing for the first team. Everything I had worked towards had paid off, but I was in with the big boys now. It was everything I had been building towards. Tonight was the night and I was determined to make the most of it. Sadly, we lost the game 4-1, although it was still an honour to make my debut. Of course, a win would have been perfect, but there would be plenty of them in the coming months and years.

At that time my only goal was to go on and have a long and successful career with Villa, and there's no way I thought I had already made it just because I had played for the first team. It was the first step, but there was still an awful lot of hard work in front of me. All I thought of at that time was how I wanted to play more regularly, try and establish myself as a first-team player and score as many goals as I could.

Mind you, if a week is a long time in politics, then a month is an eternity in football. May was destined to become the most successful in the club's history. The First Division and FA Cup had been won on a number of occasions, but the club had never triumphed in a European final, although that was about to change. Mind you, despite Villa taking part in such a landmark event, the match was perhaps a little bittersweet for me – or so it felt at the time. I had been in and around the first-team squad for a while, and had played my first match, but in my youthful mind I was ready for a prolonged run in the team and also a place on the plane heading to Rotterdam for the final against Bayern Munich. Looking back, of course I wasn't ready, but I was so focussed and driven at the time that part of me was really disappointed I didn't make the squad. Even a seat at the back of the plane, Mr Saunders?

But football can uncover the king of all ironies and so it came to pass that I watched the European Cup Final in a bar in Germany that was packed with Bayern Munich fans. I suppose I wasn't that far from Feyenoord's De Kuip stadium! I was with the Villa youth team to play in a couple of prestigious tournaments, the first of which was the well-known Mannheim Trophy. Once I had given myself a shake and touched back down on planet reality, I enjoyed it in Germany and was voted player of the tournament. As a reward for my efforts, I went home with a snazzy, wee portable television set – black and white of course – and my mum was chuffed to bits when she saw it as it meant I would be able to watch all I wanted in my room and not hog the set downstairs. I remember getting a couple of goals in both the semis and the final, before we moved on to Salem for another international tournament. It was while in Salem that we gathered in a bar to watch the European Cup Final, in the company of dozens of German folk who were cheering on Bayern. There was a great atmosphere in the bar and we were all delighted when Peter Withe scored the only goal of the game to bring the trophy back to England for a sixth successive year.

In fact, I recall speaking to Michael Rummenigge about 15 years after the final and he said it was probably the most one-sided game he had ever been involved in, and he still couldn't believe Bayern had lost. It wasn't too much of a blow for him as he would go on to win the 1987 final with Bayern to make up for the disappointment of 1982. I remember watching intently on TV and worrying, as we'd had our goalkeeper Jimmy Rimmer carried off with a neck injury after just nine minutes. Thankfully Nigel Spink came on as a replacement and played well and made a real name for himself.

I suppose I did suffer from bouts of frustration around that period, probably because when I was out with the England youth team I would be thinking that lots of my team-mates were playing for their respective first teams and it was a source of frustration that I was still in the reserves. I wasn't happy and was getting quite impatient, especially as I was seeing other players who I didn't think were as good as I was playing regularly. In fact, as a measure of how pissed off I was at a lack of first-team action, I recall meeting up with a representative of Birmingham City to see if I could get regular football there. Perhaps that was the reason I eventually got my chance at Villa. If it was, then it did the trick. (And for the record, I'm extremely glad that nothing came of my talks with City!) Anyway, the chairman, Doug Ellis, had decided he wasn't going to renew a lot of the older players' contracts, for whatever reason, be it financial or because the guys were getting into their thirties. He had decided to break up the squad and that meant a lot of the younger guys were given a chance. Admittedly, we did have a lot of excellent young players so it wasn't too much of a gamble, although the flip side was we had just won the European Cup and perhaps the best way forward would have been to capitalise on our great success and introduce a couple of big names into the mix to try and become perennial winners like Liverpool or Arsenal. But Doug was a hands-on chairman who liked to keep his finger on the pulse, and who always got involved in the financial side of the business which, quite frankly, was his prerogative. But breaking up that side did nothing for the continuity of the team and, in my opinion, some of the younger lads, who were good players, weren't yet ready to play in the First Division on a regular basis. Consequently we ended up a mid-table team and within three or four years we had been relegated. It certainly wasn't the best way to take advantage of having just won Europe's premier trophy.

Chapter Four

Proud to be a Villan

I WAS looking forward to season 1982/83, and was desperate to make the switch from fringe player to regular starter in the first team. I suppose, looking back, I managed to achieve something in between. I didn't quite become a fixture in the top team, and despite making my debut the season before, as Tony Barton rested some of his regulars in the run-up to the European Cup Final, when the new campaign kicked off against Sunderland at Villa Park, I was in there on merit – and it felt good. I would go on to play just under 20 league matches as we finished sixth in the table. But while it was good to be involved with the team that season, I was only playing semi-regularly and felt that if anyone was going to get subbed, 11 would be the number to pop up. I was only about 18 or 19 at the time but it was still frustrating. Mind you, we used to have a laugh about it in the dressing room. The story would go that there were certain players that never got subbed even if they were having an absolute nightmare, while others, like myself, were fair game for an early bath. I suppose it's just part of football and growing up but it was tough being in and out of the side and trying to build up a level of consistency.

Before the season had even started, we were dealt a real blow when Gordon Cowans suffered a broken leg during a pre-season friendly in Spain. He ended up missing the entire campaign and any side would've badly missed such a talented player. There wasn't much of Gordon. He was very slight, and also incredibly brave; a bit too brave, perhaps. I remember the match well. Gary Shaw laid the ball off to 'Sid,' as Gordon was known, and you could see this defender steaming in, but Sid got there first and tried to dink the ball over the defender. It was too late, though, and we all heard the crack. Perhaps if he had accepted the pass was short, and tried to protect himself, then it might not have happened, but we're all knowledgeable after the event I suppose. Gordon is definitely one of the best players I ever played with. He was only little but he could tackle, pass with either foot and take a mean penalty. Probably the best I played with at Villa.

We were due to play Manchester United at Old Trafford just before Christmas and I was really looking forward to it. I loved playing in high-profile games, in big stadia, but as I was walking downstairs in my house a couple of days beforehand, I slipped on the staircase and tweaked my hamstring. As soon as it happened I knew I was in trouble. It really was such a freak accident, but to be honest, I think I had played an awful lot of games up to that point and perhaps tiredness played a part in the stumble. My chances of making the game were around 40 to 60 per cent and I probably could have played at a push but I think I would have embarrassed myself, so we thought it better I sit it out. Mind you, it was still a wee bit embarrassing having to go to the gaffer and say I'd got injured at home. I remember picking up a paper the day after the accident and reading of how I would miss the big game after jumping out of my car and slipping on the pavement. I had a chuckle about that one.

Just after the festive season, the players were given an extra incentive to work through a particularly brutal cold snap when UEFA announced the dates of our European Super Cup ties with Barcelona, winners of the previous season's Cup Winners Cup. We were all looking forward to the end of January, and the home and away ties with Barça, who were a massive club even back then. When the games came round, I missed out on the first leg in the Camp Nou, although I was there as part of the squad. It was disappointing not to play, more so because when we arrived at the ground, there was this magnetic attraction to such a great sporting arena that you wanted to be out there performing and not sitting in the stand. But the manager can only pick 11 players and perhaps he decided my time for the big occasion hadn't yet arrived. We lost 1-0 in Barça, which meant it was all to play for in the return leg. I had forgotten all about my disillusionment just seven days later when Tony Barton read out the team for the tie at Villa Park and I was on the bench. I was stripped and part of the 13, which wasn't too bad for an 18-year-old. We all knew the tie was in the balance, and that we only needed a 1-0 win to take our esteemed visitors to extra-time. If that happened, there was an excellent chance the manager would use his substitutes and I might get on for the biggest game of my life.

We were always confident at home and knew we had a great chance of overturning such a slender disadvantage at a packed Villa Park. We received an early boost with the news that Maradona would miss the match through injury. Mind you, it would also have been nice to play against him. That said, if he had played we would've been in trouble and it would have been much tougher as he was easily the best player in the world at the time.

I looked on from the bench as the game started at a frantic pace, and it was soon clear that Barça had come to Birmingham to defend their lead at ALL costs. I don't think I have ever seen a group of players with such determination in their eyes. With around 20 minutes remaining the gaffer told me to go out and loosen up behind the goal. It was a sign that he was thinking of throwing me on.

While I was behind the goal doing some stretches, the buzz among the crowd was electric. The Villa Park faithful were creating an incredible atmosphere. Moments later, the signal came from the dug-out. I was going on. I wasn't just going on in any old match, I was going on to play against Barcelona. From the safety of the touchline, I had looked on as the Spanish side had put in some of the most brutal challenges I had ever witnessed. At times it was as though the Villa Park playing surface had been the scene of a medieval battle re-enactment, such was the ferocity of some of the tackling. But did that give me second thoughts about entering the fray? Not a chance!

I replaced Tony Morley with 76 minutes on the clock, and just four minutes later we were a goal up – and level on aggregate. My instructions were to run directly at the defence and see if I could help create an opening for either Peter Withe or Gary Shaw, and that was exactly what I did. But as the ball went into the box, I saw Peter swing his elbow into the face of one of their guys; he absolutely smashed him, and you could hear the crack in his nose. The incident took place just as Gary scored and I remember their lad getting treatment for ages. Next minute the Barça club doctor – and other officials – were gesticulating wildly at the referee. It was all kicking off. Meanwhile, when play resumed, their players were spitting on us and chopping us down again. It was bonkers.

Gary's goal was the only one of regulation time and just as I'd thought might happen, the tie moved into extra-time. With the first period petering out, I got on the ball and made straight for the box. From the corner of my eye I could see this raging Spaniard coming at me with venom in his eyes so I cut straight across him, went down and we got a penalty. Their players were furious and made straight for the referee. They surrounded him like a pack of hungry wolves but were chased away by goalkeeper, Urruti, who was acting like some sort of UN peacekeeper. Mind you, that would all change moments later. Gordon Cowans grabbed the ball and placed it on the penalty spot, but he had to wait a few minutes for the pantomime to die down before he could take the kick. When he did, he stuck it low to the keeper's left, and Urruti saved it. But Gordon was quickly on to the rebound and fired home to give us a 2-0 lead. But when the keeper got back to his feet he was obviously raging and went for Gordon. He took this massive swipe with his feet and booted him right up in the air. It wasn't just an act of petulance, but all-out assault and left Gordon limping for the rest of the game. Urruti received a yellow card and by the end of the game six of his mates had joined him in the ref's wee black book while Marcos Alonso and Julio Alberto were sent for an early bath. It was fantastic to play against a team like Barça so early in my career but it also taught me how cynical some of the foreign teams could be.

What about the penalty I won? I ain't gonna lie, but I did go down quite easily. Would I do it again? I'm not sure, but the bottom line is that winning the Super Cup was a fantastic achievement considering the team we had and the amount of changes that had been made. Don't get me wrong, we were a good team and we were well organised. We eventually won 3-0, with our captain, Ken McNaught grabbing the decisive third, and we were excellent value for the win. It was a measure of just how good we were at the time that we had what it takes to be undisputed kings of Europe. Looking back, it was quite something.

It was a great time to be at Villa. In my first season we won the league, and even though I didn't play for the first team I was involved with the squad. The second season we won the European Cup and I made my debut for the top side. In my third season at the club I was starting to play regularly and we won the Super Cup so it was quite a start to my professional career. I recall one of the older guys telling me it wasn't always like that!

I like to think I truly established myself as a Villa regular the following season, 1983/84. I played more than 40 times for the first team and also scored a dozen goals, which wasn't too bad for a wide player. Up until I left Liverpool in 1996, my ratio was around one goal in every four games, which I was pleased with. I loved playing football but there was no better feeling in the world than scoring a goal.

We started off the 1983/84 campaign with a home game against rivals West Brom and it was a cracker. I scored in the game and we eventually won 4-3. It could've gone either way so it was pleasing to win such a tight game. Our biggest rivalry was obviously with Birmingham City, but in my time at Villa we had some fierce games against West Brom, as well as the likes of Coventry and Wolves.

And that season we were all in the top league together so we had a derby match to look forward to every couple of weeks. It was great for the Midlands, which was a real hotbed of top-class football in the 1980s.

That season I was also called up to the England under-21 side. We were given a cap every time we played, which is naturally something I look back on fondly and with great pride. I was fortunate enough to represent my country at every level. I absolutely loved pitting my wits against European opposition and scored my first goal against foreign opponents when I netted in our 6-3 aggregate win over Dynamo Bucharest. I had been rested by Tony Barton near the end of the previous season after suffering a loss of form, which I think is quite normal for flair players, as they are expected to entertain and create chances for the strikers week in, week out. At that time, we had just brought in the French international Didier Six, who had played in the 1982 World Cup, so I had competition for the number 11 shirt, and that was something I thrived on.

The next goal I scored in Europe is probably the best I ever managed, or at least it's up there in the top three. We were playing Spartak Moscow away, and they were a top side. I was playing up front and latched on to a hopeful long ball. I brought it down on my chest, did a Cruyff turn and eased past my marker. I was then closed down by another two defenders, and feinted to go right but cut inside. I skipped past another defender and rifled a left-foot shot into the top right-hand corner of the net. It was the first-ever match beamed back live to Villa Park so I can just imagine how our supporters reacted when the ball hit the back of the net. I was in dreamland and I'm sure they weren't far away. It was a great moment.

At that time, we were delighted to have two really good goalkeepers at Villa, which I suppose showed just how big a club we were. Mervyn Day was a bit of a character whereas

Nigel Spink had come to the club as a lad and, like the rest of us kids, was desperate to play for the first team. It's just my opinion but I don't think the club could've been paying Nigel what he was worth. Maybe that's the reason we could afford to have two top keepers at the same time. Two days after making his Villa debut against Stoke, Nigel was injured 'during a crowd incident' at his old club Chelmsford. He had gone back there for a charity match and ended up coming to grief, although I recall details being sketchy at the time. Nigel went on to make over 400 appearances for Villa and was definitely a top keeper.

We had a good youth set-up at Villa and when we were hit by a series of injuries that season, the gaffer, Tony Barton, had no hesitation in throwing in a few of the younger guys. That said, he probably didn't have too many alternatives. And I'm sure the chairman was having a word in his ear, 'encouraging' him to give the younger guys a chance, or else they might just go elsewhere and play.

In my own experience of being blooded into the first team, it definitely helps if you have a few 'older heads' in there to show you the ropes. Sure, in a way they're handing over the baton, but there always needs to be that mix of experience and youth. When I made the breakthrough into the Villa first team, there were a number of younger players given an opportunity, perhaps even too many. Don't get me wrong, most of the players that were thrown in went on to have good careers in the football league but we should still have been capable of challenging for a top-six place despite losing so many of our players to the treatment table. As it transpired, we had to be content with a mid-table finish and our short-lived mantle as the top team in the country was a fading memory. To be fair to everyone at Villa Park, though, there isn't a club in the country who could have coped easily without established players such as Withe, Shaw, Cowans and Colin Gibson. We had some exciting young prospects but they were lacking in top-team experience, and, as we all know, inconsistency and youth go hand in hand.

We had also lost Tony Morley, and that decision might have purely been down to finance. Tony and I were vying for the same position and with him on more money than I was, it was no doubt easier to sell Tony than it was me. I'm sure I was just as inconsistent as some of the other youngsters but because Tony had left the club I was playing regularly, which I'm sure helped my development.

In those days the number on your back meant something, usually relating to a certain position on the pitch, and it was either number 8 or 11 for me. When Gary Shaw was injured, which was becoming more regular, I would fill in for him, or when Tony was out I would be wearing 11. The uncertainty of where I would be playing didn't really bother me too much, although it wasn't long before I was accepted as our regular winger. When both Gary and Peter Withe were stuck on the sidelines, Tony Barton signed a couple of front men to fill in, although he had a ready-made replacement in me. I knew that, but he didn't, and that was down to me not being forceful enough in putting myself forward to play up front. It's something I regret not saying at the time. Paul Rideout was one of the guys brought in to replace our injured front players. He was a good player, but as far as I was concerned, good lad or not, it was another missed opportunity for me.

One guy I would've loved to play alongside regularly was Peter Withe. I considered him the best target man in the business at that time. He worked tirelessly during a game and never stopped running around. I remember sitting on the bench one afternoon and Ron Saunders saying to me, 'Look at Peter, he never stops. Now look at Gary [Shaw], what a contrast!' I always wind Gary up about that, but he would get all the flick-ons and end up scoring more goals than Peter! But they were a great partnership. Peter would chase lost causes all day long and Gary would hang around and stick the ball in the net. Peter was a great team player and could look after himself as well.

And then there was Brian Little: the type of player I had always wanted to be. When I was watching games as a kid I really looked up to him. He was quick, skilful and made some great runs. Gary Shaw was a similar kind of player, and while maybe not as quick, he was a real quick-thinker, very sharp over the first ten yards and could finish with both feet. Gary was a cracking player and but for injuries he could've been up there with the best. He did go on a tour with England but should have been a regular for the national side. I'll never forget the day he picked up the bad injury which all but finished his career. It was against Nottingham Forest and I don't know if Ian Bowyer thought Gary was feigning injury but he dragged him up off the ground and Gary says he heard something click inside his knee. That was that and perhaps the moment a promising career was cut short. I think in the end he probably had too many operations on his knee instead of letting Mother Nature take its course. In fact, he still has issues with his knee to this day.

One stat which pleased me in the early days at Villa was my record of playing in European games. Just two seasons in, I had been involved in all 14 of Villa's matches against continental opposition, including that never-to-be-forgotten Super Cup tie against Barça. There was a different style of football required for European matches compared to the bread and butter of our English league games. There was a slower build-up, it was more technical and depending on what time of year it was the weather obviously had a part to play. I loved playing in Europe. One game that sticks out for me is a European tie against Juventus, when the likes of Michel Platini, Zbigniew Boniek, Dino Zoff and Paolo Rossi all played. Those two games were very special and I felt I had truly arrived as a player after the head to head with Juve. In fact, I remember swapping shirts with Paolo Rossi after the game although to this day I have no idea where that jersey is!

But while we all loved playing in these glamour games, the English First Division was our priority, and it was important to me that I kept up a high standard of performance week in, week out. When you run out on to the park on a Saturday afternoon, you want the team to win, but first and foremost you want to play well yourself. That's the bottom line. If the team have a nightmare, and lose the game, as long as you play well you can just about accept it. On an individual basis, if you're playing for a team that isn't well organised, and doesn't have a proper game plan, everything inevitably goes straight down the middle so the guys who see less of the ball are invariably the wide players and it's easy to feel surplus to requirements out there. Graham Taylor was one of the most organised coaches I played under and he always had a good, solid game plan, where he insisted that his wide players should always be part of the build-up.

Unfortunately, when Tony Barton was in charge there really wasn't much of a game plan, and those who played through the middle would see far more of the ball. With Tony, it was all a bit more off the cuff, and a few of our experienced players also had a big say in how we played. I would rarely get a pass and quite often the only time I would see the ball was if it ricocheted off someone's knee and landed at my feet. It was frustrating, and at times it seemed the only player who would bring me into play was Gordon Cowans, who was comfortable on either foot. It was particularly difficult at first, and it wasn't until I was taught properly how to play in that position that I started to enjoy it. Once I learned all about creating space for myself it definitely became a little bit easier.

I don't think you ever get used to getting kicked but you reluctantly accept it as part of the job: an occupational hazard. You just make sure you're padded up a bit so you can withstand getting smashed a bit better! You also learn when to see it coming and that definitely saves you a bit. But just because you were playing on the wing didn't mean you were going to get injured more often than any other player. I was fortunate that when I played I didn't pick up many injuries, and then you have guys like Tony Daley, who played in my position. Different type of player, admittedly, and he was injured every other week. Quite often it's down to luck, and whether or not you can get back playing to the same standard after an injury.

I was never frightened of being kicked, because I trusted most referees to offer me a certain level of protection. That allowed me to be free to express myself the best way I knew how. I recall playing against Birmingham City at Villa Park and getting smashed from behind, and the referee jumping straight in to protect me. It was a full-blooded derby match and it would have been easy for the match official to get caught up in everything going on around him, but he was fantastic and told the full-back in no uncertain terms what would happen if he continued his relentless one-man assault on me. Meanwhile, I'm lying there on the deck, looking up at the Birmingham fans and they're asking me politely to get back to my feet. Not! But there were other times when referees didn't offer much protection, and that was when I was forced to take matters into my own hands. There were a few times I had to protect myself, and that meant smashing a few opponents myself! I always tried to give as good as I got on the pitch, because if you didn't look after yourself then people would run over the top of you. I wouldn't say I ever left my foot in but I knew how to look after myself.

It's a whole new ball game now as there are so many cameras around and players know that if their offences don't get picked up on the day, the chances are they will have retrospective action taken against them, so there is less chance of anything silly going on, but back in the day it was so different. It wouldn't have been the first time I'd been head-butted by an opponent who had checked quickly to make sure the referee and linesmen were looking the other way. Or defenders trying to pull the hairs out of my legs or saying pretty mean things about my family. Things like that went on quite regularly.

In the 1970s, there were some real tough-guy defenders around, and one of the meanest I ever faced was Mark Dennis of Birmingham City and Southampton. He was crazy and I'm sure he would've taken a gun out on to the field had it been allowed. Don't get me wrong, I wouldn't suddenly develop a fever on the eve of a game against the Blues or Southampton, but I knew I would have to protect myself several times during the game, especially if it came to a 50/50 ball. Playing out wide, you knew that if you were stretching to get a cross in, the full-back was going to smash you whether you got the cross in or not, so in the end I said to myself, 'Hold on a minute, use your brains, just cut back on it so you don't have to follow through,' or you know, little things you start doing so it lessens the chances of getting injured, and while it might annoy the centre-forward who has made a great run to the near post, I was always keen to finish the game with both legs intact. I like to think little things like that, and learning on the job, helped preserve my career. You can just imagine the supporters screaming 'coward' if you pull out of a challenge, but the bigger picture is you want to be around five minutes later for the next challenge. You're no good to anyone lying in a hospital bed. It's not brave to put yourself in that situation, just daft.

I remember having a really bad game for Villa at home and it was the type of afternoon when everything I tried failed to come off. Just one of these games that we all have now and again. The following night I was in the kitchen at home and was preparing some dinner for Mum and myself, and listening to the football phone-in on the radio. The presenter wasn't exactly being kind to me and a couple of callers in succession were giving me pelters. It was tough to listen to but I always tried to take the bad with the good. Next minute, another caller starts sticking up for me and she said, 'Why can't you just leave Mark alone, he's trying his best.' I thought to myself, 'I know that voice,' so I sneaked upstairs and there was Mum in her bedroom, on the phone to the radio show and sticking up for her son. That put a smile on my face and we had a good laugh about it round the dinner table that evening.

We had loads of derby games to look forward to at Villa and in one of these, against West Brom in the Milk Cup, absolutely everything I tried seemed to come off and I ended up winning the bronze boot for being man of the match. It was always great to be recognised individually but I was more interested in trying to ensure the team won: that gave me the greatest pleasure. Remember, I had a great start to my career at Villa and we were winning big prizes in my first three years. The perfect scenario would have been for the team to win handsomely and me to turn in a good performance. But if we ever went through a rough patch, it would really get to me personally and I wouldn't be great company. I didn't ever like taking my 'work' home with me, but I took great pride in my performances so inevitably you get upset when you've had a bad game.

Chapter Five

Time's Up at Villa

ONE GUY who didn't have any confidence issues was my cousin, Robert. He could do just about anything with a ball, but sadly he wasn't able to follow in my footsteps and take up the game professionally because of just one small problem: he couldn't run! We played against each other in schools football and he was very talented. And every Friday we played in these massive 20-a-side games in Aston Park and they were so much fun. The games would go on for hours and players would go in for their tea, and when they came back out the game would still be in progress. In fact I remember getting injured on one occasion and having to miss a school game the following day, which my teacher wasn't too happy about. Our school took football very seriously in those days and I was warned about my future participation in these 'illegal' matches. Did I listen? What do you think? Robert always took part in these games but as there is quite a bit of running involved in football he would get the ball at his feet, do a little trick, and then pass it to a team-mate. He was definitely one of those kids who made the ball do the work. He looked great when he had the ball but he couldn't get past anyone. Mind you, he did get into the Guinness Book of Records for his ball-juggling skills. If memory serves me right he kept the ball in the air for almost 17 hours – minus a couple of toilet breaks of course. I remember watching part of his attempt at the record in 1987 and, because he was heading it quite a bit, I noticed how flat his Afro was getting, and apparently by the end it was completely gone! In fact, I'm going to be honest and say I don't even know if we were genuine cousins. We came from the same part of Jamaica and had the same surname, but as everyone is related to everyone else in Jamaica then there had to be a bit of dubiety. We got on really well, though, and I suppose we were cousins in the sense that your mum would say all those years ago, 'This is your Auntie Mildred,' when in fact it was just a lady that mum had known for many years!

When Sky Sports started their live Monday night football coverage, they often featured Robert performing tricks in front of the cameras. I must admit, some of the things he could do with a ball were just crazy. He was super talented.

Another discipline which involved a certain degree of skill, and which became quite popular in the 70s and 80s, was the indoor soccer sixes, which quite often took place at Birmingham's National Exhibition Centre. It was a good competition to play in as it was pretty intense and there was always a good standard of player involved. However, the surface was hard and unforgiving and in 1984 I fell heavily on my shoulder and did a bit of damage. Sadly that was the start of many problems for me and the moment I fell I knew it wasn't good. I dislocated the clavicle, which left it susceptible to popping out now and then. It was never the same again and at the start of the following season I was playing in a pre-season game and a former team-mate of mine, Ray Walker, tripped me up as I was flying past him and

I hit the ground with a thump. On impact, the shoulder popped out again and I ended up missing the first couple of months of the season. It was my final season at Villa Park and we were relegated, and I missed an awful lot of games so I wasn't best pleased with Ray, especially as it was only a pre-season friendly.

I'm not saying it was the case with Ray Walker, but when I was playing football a lot of defenders thought it perfectly acceptable to stick the boot in – and leave it in, probably because they would get away with it more often than not. Nowadays it's so different, in fact it's perfect. I would love to be playing in a front three now because the referees are right on the case if anyone starts dishing out helpings of brutality. And it's about time too because flair players should be allowed to get on with their job of trying to entertain the paying public. The pitches are better and I'd like to think I would have been able to produce better football on today's surfaces. At the beginning of each season, Villa Park was a dream to play on, but the moment winter crept in, the pitch would deteriorate and by Christmas – when, ironically, we had our busiest spell of matches – it was usually horrendous. It's no surprise I produced my best football at the start of each season. My game started to suffer when the pitches became muddy and it was difficult to run with the ball. The middle of our pitch would become a quagmire in the winter – and Villa Park was one of the better ones. I reckon Gordon Cowans was only about 11 stone but he would plough through the mud all day long while others around him were floundering. How he did it I will never know.

And when the pitches were wet, in would come the sliding tackles, with defenders citing poor playing conditions when a ref dared give them a row for catching an opponent somewhere up around the midriff!

One criticism supporters have these days is that players are over-coached by their clubs. I don't think it's something that ever applied to me. When I was at Villa we were never given any in-depth tactical instructions before getting out on to the pitch. I do remember Andy Gray getting smashed in the middle of the park during a game and Ron Saunders being furious because of where it happened, not because it had happened. He said, 'I don't mind you getting smashed in the opposition box, but what's the point of risking injury in the middle of the field where we gain absolutely no advantage?' And it was the same with me to a certain extent. He didn't want me messing around with the ball in my own box. It was okay for me to get whacked in and around the opposition box, and then we might get a free kick or even a penalty! I suppose it was also more about self-preservation, and burning up needless amounts of energy, than coaching. Our team talks were never over-technical.

I would agree that footballers need to be told what's expected of them when they're playing in a certain position, and if everyone knows their job then it's often possible to create something out of nothing. Whereas if you are constantly just doing things off the cuff then, as a team, you will never really get anywhere. In the main, attacking players should be left to attack or do what they think is right in the last third. You know more or less where your fellow strikers are going to be so the end game is always the same. Get the ball in the middle, or play someone in or try and get to the byline. There aren't too many options open to you. Part of the problem nowadays is that we analyse all the big games to death. Football genuinely is a simple game but we do tend to over-complicate it at times, and all that does is make it more confusing for those who might be starting out.

That's what I enjoyed most about my era. It was a simple game, and the coaching I received from Villa's youth coaches was fantastic. They taught you the basics of the game – the stuff you needed to know in order to progress – and didn't fill your head with nonsense. Villa was a fantastic place to learn and I made many friends for life through my association with the club. I think it's just the way life is that you are never going to get on with everybody but by and large I got on well with my team-mates. Mind you, it was so much easier when the team was doing well; there was a great camaraderie about the place, but when things were going badly, and we were down there fighting relegation, little cliques started to form and the mood in the camp wasn't great, but that wasn't unique to Villa. To be fair, I can't really think of too many bad apples at all the clubs I've been at.

I got on particularly well with Neale Cooper when I was at Villa. He is one of the funniest men I've ever met – and a really nice fellow. When I was at Rangers, Graeme Souness asked me about him and I told him that while he'd had a bit of bad luck with injuries, he was a top lad so I was delighted when he signed for us. I also got on really well with Gary Shaw and still do. Paul Birch, who sadly passed away about ten years ago was also a good friend. There was a group of lads who progressed from the Aston Villa youth team up to the top squad and we all got on well, including guys like Dean Glover and Ray Walker.

Two or three years before making my debut with Villa I was watching the likes of Peter Withe, Gary Shaw and Tony Morley on the TV, so to get the chance to play regularly alongside these guys was fantastic, and I certainly made the most of it. It was also great to be associated with the team that won the league, as it was the first time in 71 years we had achieved such a feat.

Guys like Gordon Cowans, Des Bremner and Dennis Mortimer welcomed me into the dressing room when I made the step up from the youth side. Here I was, a supporter, now sharing a dressing room with these guys so you can imagine how I felt. I was very respectful of the top pros, the folk I had admired from afar for so long. I was cleaning their boots at first and even that was an honour!

And anyway, there is no way you can be cleaning someone's boots one minute, and then be giving it the big 'I am' in the dressing room the next, so respect it was! I had no problem integrating into my new environment. I think had I been the arrogant or aggressive type then I may have had a few problems, so in that respect I think my personality helped a lot, because although the Villa dressing room was a friendly place, there were a lot of big characters in there who wouldn't have stood for any nonsense and would have been quick to put you in your place.

Andy Gray was a huge voice in our dressing room. Probably the best way to describe him would be 'effervescent'. I remember one time when we were heading off early for an away match and all the players were reporting to Villa Park to get the coach, Andy turned up wearing a suit that was way too big for him and we were all falling about laughing. It turned out he'd fallen out with his partner and she had decided to cut up all his clothes, so he'd made a quick detour over to Neale Cooper's place to borrow some clobber. It didn't help that Neale was about twice Andy's size!

We always had a laugh at Villa and would regularly take the piss out of one another. Let's be honest, if you can't have a laugh then you don't last long in that sort of environment. Fortunately I was up for a bit of fun.

Mind you, my final season at Villa was anything but a hoot. We had been relegated to the Second Division, and it was a demotion that should never have been allowed to happen. Just a few years before we had been champions of England and Europe, but instead of building on such rock-solid foundations, the club was allowed to slip into mediocrity due to a succession of bad management appointments and prudent contracts being offered to top players. I was saddened by our demise, and equally gutted that I had been injured for large chunks of the campaign.

Just before the start of the 1987/88 season – the final one of my contract – I was surprised when I was asked to take a wage cut. That more or less told me it was time to move on. It hadn't been the greatest of seasons for me, as the injured shoulder meant I was in and out of the team, but it's also something that seems to happen to the local lads: they never get treated the same as the players that are bought in. There was a feeling that I was getting used so I decided I would knock back the salary decrease and refuse to re-sign. I went to see Doug Ellis and he said to me, 'Mark, you haven't played a lot this season and when you have, you didn't play well and we got relegated, so I'm afraid there is no alternative but for you to take a pay cut.' I reminded him that I had been at the club since I was ten years old, and that everyone was on more money than me, but I was more or less told it was tough at the top and I'd just have to accept it. I asked for time to think about my situation and that was when I started on the month-to-month contracts.

I was 23 years old when the season started with a match at Ipswich Town's Portman Road. I was up front alongside Simon Stainrod and we managed a 1-1 draw. Martin Keown was at the heart of our defence after being released by Arsenal, the club he would eventually return to and make his name at. We then suffered back-to-back defeats against our rivals, Birmingham City, at Villa Park – which didn't go down too well with the faithful – and Hull City. But we soon picked up and Graham Taylor had us motoring after a month or so. We embarked on a 15-game unbeaten run, which included an impressive League Cup win over Tottenham Hotspur at Villa Park, in which Warren Aspinall and Alan McInally were on target.

I then played in my final second-city derby match, at St Andrew's, and we won 2-1, with Garry Thompson scoring twice. The games were coming thick and fast and we drew with both Sheffield United and West Brom, before I made my last appearance in a Villa shirt. Three days after Christmas, we fought out a tough 1-1 draw with Huddersfield Town at Villa Park, and the next morning I was heading north to speak to potential suitors. I truly had mixed feelings.

Obviously I had known for a few months that I would be leaving the club as soon as something juicy came up, but nothing prepared me for the day I actually left Villa. It was tough. They were my hometown club and my family were all around me. I was the supporter who made it to the first team, but I also knew that if I wanted to progress and win things – like I had done in the first three years of my professional career – then I would have to leave, because the team we had at Villa wasn't ready to win trophies. And after being the local lad more or less taken for granted in many respects at Villa, I quite fancied the idea of being the guy who was brought in for a few quid and who would be treated well. That sounded good. I recall as I was walking out of the front door for the final time, the Villa secretary saying to me, 'To be honest, Mark, we never thought you would leave. We thought we would get you to change your mind. You are a part of the furniture here.' And therein lay the 'local lad' problem. Don't get me wrong, I was overjoyed to play for my local club, but when you see the way outsiders are treated when they sign for the club, it does leave you hankering even for parity.

I made a point of never falling out with Doug Ellis, even though I didn't always agree with some of the decisions he made. We spoke often, and when I returned to Villa as a coach, he said to me, tongue in cheek, 'Oh Mark, I see you've re-educated yourself now,' and we had a laugh. He then added, 'Are we paying you for being a coach, because I know you're a millionaire now, and we shouldn't really be paying you.' I've always admired Doug and at the end of the day he is a businessman, and it's alright people saying spend millions on this player or that one, but we've seen so many clubs overspend and end up bankrupt. To be fair to Doug, during his time in charge, the club never owed a penny to anyone, so he did a good job. He's a good age now but still comes to the games, and because he isn't involved in an official capacity any more it probably means he can enjoy his day a bit more. His heart has always been at Villa so I have a lot of respect for him. Don't get me wrong, there were times when he frustrated the life out of me. He would let a player go, seemingly because of a few hundred quid, or refuse to buy a player because he was just a wee bit too expensive and you would be willing him to improve the team, so that could be frustrating. But when you're able to take a step back and realise that throwing money around could bankrupt your club, that's when you see the true value of men like Doug.

Mind you, after I left Villa, Graham Taylor brought in David Platt from Crewe Alexandra for £200,000 and sold him a couple of years later to Italian side Bari for £5.5m. I bet you Doug was beaming from ear to ear that day!

But I now realise why, for instance, Doug let the likes of Tony Morley leave the club. At the time I was thinking, 'It would be great to have both Tony and I competing for the number 11 jersey. Surely competition for places can only benefit the team.' But then you look at it from a chairman's point of view and you see someone paying two wages when only one can play. From my point of view, the best incentive for me to play well was when I would see a guy who played in the same position as me sitting in the stand with his suit on, because I knew if I allowed my standards to drop I would be out the following week. Having competition for places is a powerful motivation. Let's be honest, if there is no one challenging me for my position, then human nature dictates complacency may set in, and that isn't what I wanted as an ambitious young player.

Of course, some of the managers I played under at Villa wouldn't have been slow in telling me when I was underperforming, or letting my standards drop. That was, if they had stuck around long enough to get to know me!

Chapter Six

One Gaffer Per Season!

I MIGHT have played for the first team at Villa for just over six seasons but I certainly didn't expect to average around one manager per campaign! Sadly that's the way it turned out, although rumours that Doug Ellis was considering having a revolving door fitted in the reception area at Villa Park are, I believe, without foundation.

My first manager at Villa, Ron Saunders, was something of an iconic figure at the club. He was your old-style gaffer who went by the name of Mr Saunders to the younger lads trying to make the breakthrough under him, and probably many of the more experienced guys too. He wasn't one of those folk who went around shouting his mouth off and making you feel terrified to come into your work. He was quite measured and while he never shied away from dishing out a row or two, he certainly used his words sparingly. Why slag someone off when an icy cold stare would do an equally effective job? That was Ron. Sorry, Mr Saunders.

In my opinion, he was an excellent manager. Take one look at his CV and I don't think that can be questioned. As a man, he was unpopular with a lot of people due to his dour, uncompromising approach and he certainly didn't suffer fools gladly. But he led Villa to their first league championship triumph in more than 70 years when they won the title in 1980/81 and no one can ever take that away from him. No Villa gaffer has managed it since, so it was quite an achievement.

On a personal level, I found him fair and he always had a word of encouragement for me. His teams were well organised and disciplined but he never discouraged players like myself from using individual flair in games. In fact, he actively encouraged it.

But I didn't play under Ron for that long. I was in the reserves at the time – which was still his domain – but he more or less spent the bulk of his time with the first team. That said, he would, from time to time, still take second-team training sessions and keep a close eye on what was going on. He was an old-fashioned manager in that he liked to run the club, not just the first team. Mind you, it was still something of a shock when he left. I couldn't believe it when I heard the news. Not quite a JFK moment, but still a real shock. Everything seemed to be going well at the time. We had won the league the season before and were in the quarter-finals of the European Cup. Next minute, Ron simply upped sticks and left. As timing goes it was pretty rank, but it must've taken something awfully serious to have him leave a team he was moulding into such a force. It genuinely was a real head-scratching moment for the players and I wonder if he ever regretted leaving. From time to time I wonder just how far he could've taken Villa. Could he have been the man to have the club challenging for honours year in, year out?

But if his timing was questionable, what happened next was almost unthinkable. The talk at the time was that Ron had been unable to negotiate a decent contract with the chairman, something befitting of his achievements. I've spoken of how Doug would dig in and refuse to give an inch, and with Ron knowing him better than most, perhaps he felt his contractual situation was never going to end in anything other than defeat. But then came the bombshell. Not long after he left Villa Park, he was unveiled as the new manager of ... Birmingham City! That's right, our arch-rivals. Who saw that one coming? It was unprecedented as far as I was concerned. And there probably weren't many people who could've got away with that. And not content with managing the two biggest clubs in Britain's second city, Ron's next job was at The Hawthorns, as manager of West Brom, so he had succeeded in managing the three biggest clubs in the Midlands, without so much as a break in between. Not even a temporary manager's job in Scandinavia, or somewhere else that might have allowed the situation to cool a little. I don't think anyone has achieved that feat since, and probably won't in the future either, but Ron was a one-off.

Tony Barton was Ron's assistant – a task he performed admirably – but probably wasn't anyone's idea of the perfect replacement. At the time, we were a big club; in fact, you might say we were punching above our weight with the trophies we had won. We were where we were on merit, that's for sure. And there is no doubt Tony had played his part in that success, but his appointment still surprised a lot of football people. He had been chief scout when I signed for the club as a kid and he knew the players well, but would he be manager material?

Tony was only in charge for two years, and while he oversaw the winning of both the European Cup and Super Cup, he was unable to prevent the start of our decline, and descent down the league. I think he eventually left because he was getting a bit of stick from the supporters. Normally if it's not the manager's head they're shouting for, it's the chairman's, although Doug Ellis had thick skin and was going nowhere. I had a good relationship with Tony; he definitely brought the best out in me, and it was under his management that I became a first-team regular. The only criticism I have is that I felt he allowed many of the older players to run the team, and more or less pick who was in and who was out. Tony was either a little bit weak or perhaps too easily influenced, but when you've been an assistant for six or seven years and are suddenly handed the top job, then it's very difficult, especially when you have the man above, in my opinion, telling you what to do. I'd like to think Doug never had a hand in picking the team but he was definitely influential. If he walked in here today and told me he had picked the team on a number of occasions, I wouldn't be too surprised.

One thing Tony did say to me was that I had to get more aggressive. It was a fair assumption by the gaffer because I was playing in the type of position – and era – when full-backs were used to smashing wingers and I'm sure he just wanted me to stand up for myself more. When someone has six studs up and you just want to get on the ball, it's a different kind of aggression. I'm a great believer that anyone can go over the top in a tackle, that's not a hard man, but can you receive the ball when studs are flying around and you know you're going to get whacked, particularly in the 1970s and 80s when you knew that the first tackle against you wasn't going to be particularly pleasant. It was good advice by Tony and was definitely something I took on board.

When Tony left the club I was sorry to see him go, because he was the guy who had faith in me and he was always very encouraging. I had nothing but respect for him, but I also thought he wasn't treated as well as he could have been. Everyone knows that football management is a precarious business, and unfortunately Tony found that out the hard way. After leaving Villa Park, he had a short stint as manager of Northampton Town.

Graham Turner was next in and joined Villa from Shrewsbury Town, where he had been player/manager. Graham had guided the Shrews to the Third Division title and was just 36 when he took over the Villa hot seat. I knew a little about him when he joined us, but one thing in particular, which happened quite early on, told me a fair bit more about his character. We were playing against one of the top teams in the league one afternoon and Graham looked more like a supporter than our manager. He was walking across the pitch, looking completely in awe of some of the opposition players, and taking photographs of a few of their better-known guys. We all thought to ourselves, 'Jeezo, they've appointed a supporter as our new manager!' He hadn't played at a decent level either and I just had the feeling there and then that it wasn't going to work out for him because, once again, Doug was always going to be there in the background offering his opinion. Sadly it worked out the way I predicted. Graham was only a young man in his thirties and getting one of the top jobs wasn't something which happened a lot in those days. Most of the managers were much older than the players and that helped with the whole issue of respect. Don't get me wrong, I don't think you have to be a good player to be a successful manager but part of the problem was that most of the lads hadn't heard of him. I had because I was local, and he'd managed not too far away at Shrewsbury, but most of the others were in the dark. Perhaps he just needed to have a better pedigree, because Villa were a big club at the time and had won the European Cup and the league, and we now had this manager that most of the lads hadn't heard of, so right away that kind of undermines him, which wasn't a good thing. The dressing room can be such a tough environment, and if the manager is only a year or so older than a couple of the players then it can be a recipe for disaster. As it turned out Graham went on to have a really good managerial career, but maybe the Villa job came along just a bit too soon for him. I personally thought he was a good man and potentially a good manager for the club – but in the end his inexperience cost him dear. When Graham left Villa he managed Wolves before starting a 14-year stint at Hereford United.

And then there was Billy McNeill. We got along to a certain degree but I ain't gonna lie and say I had a lot of respect for him, because I didn't. How could I, when we would be in the middle of a tough training session and we'd look over and see his car heading out the main gate and off into the distance. That didn't exactly endear him to the players who were covered in mud, sweat and tears, and the manager is halfway home in his fancy big car, so I'm not sure he was ever there for the right reasons. When I eventually moved up to Scotland, he did thank me for not divulging certain things about his time at Villa, because the club really was shambolic during his tenure. Whenever I was interviewed at the start of my Rangers career, I would almost certainly be asked about Billy's time at Villa and I would always just say that Moses would've struggled to turn us around at that time. In fairness, miracles were expected from him but he couldn't stop the rot.

His time in charge of the club was a disaster, there is no getting away from that, and he was the manager who presided over our relegation to the Second Division. In fact, if memory serves me right I think he was also largely responsible for taking Manchester City down in the same season, which must be some kind of (unwanted) record. We were all gutted when we went down and McNeill must take his fair share of the blame. I think what we needed at the time was a Sam Allardyce-type who could've ground out some results and helped us stay up, but it wasn't to be. To be honest, that's probably the only way we would've stayed up. McNeill was in charge for around eight months and the moment we were relegated, he was sacked and headed back up to Scotland to manage Celtic again. It's probably a period best forgotten by Villa fans.

As McNeill was driving out of the gates at Villa Park for the final time, that seat marked 'manager' in the home dug-out was fast becoming the hottest potato in English football, but by the time his successor had been appointed, I had more or less made up my mind to leave the club. And then Doug Ellis appointed Graham Taylor, and that was almost enough to make me change my mind. Graham, who sadly passed away in January of 2017, arrived after a largely successful ten-year spell at Watford, and was a fantastic choice to take the club forward. He grabbed Villa by the scruff of the neck, implemented a proper game plan, a set pattern of play and the players bought into it. Oh, and he stood up to Doug as well. He must have accepted the job on the condition that he would be allowed to do things his way, because he was certainly making changes and doing things the way he wanted, which hadn't happened at Villa since Ron had been in charge. He wasn't frightened to get rid of some players who were perhaps at the club for the wrong reasons, which earned him a lot of respect from the majority of the lads. Results also turned for him and we were soon heading in the right direction. We also took a few impressive scalps in the cup competitions during our season in the Second Division.

The more I saw of Graham, the more I respected what he was doing and everything he was trying to achieve. It got to the stage where I had second thoughts about leaving because, even though I played out wide, I was a big part of his game plan and I was enjoying my football again. Things were starting to go well but I wasn't too happy playing in the Second Division and there were no guarantees that we would be able to bounce straight back up to the top flight, so I had a decision to make. I only played under Graham for about six months but it was an experience I thoroughly enjoyed. He was a terrific manager with great ideas about how the game should be played. He had an attacking philosophy and it was one which I believed would eventually bring success to the club.

But being on short-term contracts was more or less a player's way of saying, 'I'm not fully committed to this club, come and get me.' And even though I was starting to enjoy life under Graham, I did quite a bit of soul searching and decided it was still best if I left the club. Graham tried very hard to get me to stay, and offered me another contract, but I had made my mind up. To be honest, I was impressed by the manner in which he had tried to talk me out of moving to Rangers, but nothing was going to stop me emptying my locker. If Villa had been in the First Division at the time it might have been different, but the bottom line was I needed a change as much as anything else. It was all far too cosy at Villa, with my Mum living virtually across the road from the stadium, while I was based in Sutton Coldfield, which is eight or nine miles from the ground. My car drove itself to work and things were just far too stale.

Several English teams had shown an interest in signing me, although none of them seriously floated my boat. When Everton came on to the scene, followed quickly by Glasgow Rangers, that was different. My interest was well and truly piqued and I knew then that I had played my last game for Villa. We were heading towards the end of 1987, and the new year seemed the perfect time for a new adventure. It was time to spread my wings and fly the nest. As they say when the President of the United States leaves the White House, 'Phoenix has left the nest!'

We'd had so many managers at Villa in such a short space of time and that itself is normally a recipe for disaster. There is no way you can build any continuity with so many managers, because they all have their own ideas, and just as you're buying into the new guy's philosophies, in walks another new guy. They all have their opinions on the type of players they want, and even how training should be undertaken, so each time a manager left or was sacked, it was a case of the players once again having to get used to a new regime. The turnover in managers we had at that time certainly wasn't good for the players or the club.

When I left, though, I made sure there were no hard feelings with either the chairman or the manager. Villa was still my club. I had supported them all my life and my love for them would never diminish, even though it was definitely the right time to move on.

Chapter Seven

Heading North

MENTALLY, I had decided to leave Villa long before I actually did, but when I made it official, I had this sudden bout of fear. What if no one wants me? Thankfully that wasn't the case and within 24 hours of publicly stating that I was leaving, I had offers from the likes of Leeds United, Derby County and Watford. But while I was flattered by their attention, I wasn't really interested in any of them. At the time, Watford were heading for the Second Division, while Leeds seemed no nearer to getting out of it. Derby were in the top flight but fighting relegation. I wanted to play at the top level, for a top team, so it was a firm 'No' to all three. Otherwise, what was the point of leaving Villa?

As Christmas 1987 approached, Everton threw their hat in the ring and that did interest me. And then Italian club Pisa registered an interest. When I sized up the options my favoured destination was Goodison Park. Colin Harvey was the manager of Everton at the time and he sold the club really well. It was a good option as Everton were one of the top teams in the country and had won the First Division title the season before. They had some big names, like Peter Reid, Trevor Steven and Neville

Southall, and played good football, so I felt we were a good fit. But the night before I was due to head up to Goodison to meet Colin, the phone rang. I didn't have a mobile at the time so the call was made to my house, and I was quickly trying to work out who owned the Scottish accent. When the caller said it was Graeme Souness I thought it was one of my mates pulling my leg with a dodgy accent, and I'm like, 'Yeah yeah, mate!' Graeme eventually convinced me it was actually him and we started to have a proper chat. He obviously had his finger on the pulse as he knew I was due at Goodison the next day. He asked if I would do him the courtesy of coming to Ibrox the day after so we could have a chat. I am a great believer in keeping my options open, and as a big admirer of Souey from his time at Liverpool, I agreed. To be honest, I didn't know an awful lot about Rangers at that time but I had seen one of their European games on television a couple of months before and had been completely blown away by the atmosphere. They were playing Dynamo Kiev, who were a real top team, and the crowd sounded so loud. Souey had taken in the dimensions of the pitch that evening to counter Kiev's love of playing wide, and he struck me as a guy who was fully invested in what he was doing at Ibrox. That incredible atmosphere had remained with me, and with English teams banned from Europe for five years, and the European arena one that I loved, Rangers were a definite attraction. A late attraction, but a genuine one; like the horse no one has backed in the Grand National timing its run to perfection and roaring up on the rails to pip the favourite on the line.

There was a slight stumbling block, though, as Villa had already agreed a fee with Everton, and then we had Souey chucking his curveball into the equation. Had he not called when he did, I would've agreed to join Everton. But he did call, so I flew up to Goodison as planned and met with Colin, had a look round their facilities and told him I would make a decision after I had been to Ibrox. He was very understanding. The next morning I flew from Liverpool Airport to Glasgow and was picked up at the airport by Rangers coach Phil Boersma in Graeme Souness's Daimler, and whisked off to the south side of the city. Souey did things in style.

It was only a 20-minute drive from the airport to Ibrox, but one look at the stadium and I was smitten. Goodison quickly became a fading memory. I'm sure Souey knew exactly what he was doing by meeting me at Ibrox. That incredible façade, those huge blue gates, and then there was the front entrance which leads through to the marble staircase, which tops everything off nicely. The stadium oozed class. I was sold. I remember Andy Gray saying a lot of folk in English football had been shocked to see me choose Rangers over Everton, the English champions, but quite frankly I didn't think there was anything to be shocked about. And I know Andy was delighted.

I signed for Rangers – for a fee of £500,000 – and while that meant letting Everton down, I was convinced I had made the right decision. One thing that many people have assumed over the years is that Rangers must have offered me a king's ransom to sign on, to trump the English champions, but that wasn't the case at all. The main reasons for choosing Rangers were my admiration for Souey, and the great job he was doing at Rangers, the fact Ibrox looked an incredible place to play your football, and the opportunity to play in Europe. Those were genuinely more important than the money. If Souey had turned round and offered me three or four thousand pounds a week more than Everton then it would definitely have been about the money, but the difference was a couple of hundred quid. Don't get me wrong, it was a lot of money, but it wasn't the deciding factor.

Playing European football excited me. The highlight of my career at Villa was the win over Barcelona in the European Super Cup, but the challenge of playing in the Scottish Premier League – at new stadia and against new players – also appealed. Anyway, it had been three years since I last played in the UEFA Cup with Aston Villa and the experience had been an enjoyable one.

The idea of performing in front of 40,000-plus crowds also excited me. At Villa the usual audience was around 25,000 at that time, so it was a big leap. Of course it helped that Rangers had players on their books such as Terry Butcher and Chris Woods, both established England internationals. Rangers really were bucking the trend of the best Scottish players heading south by bringing these guys up from England. The likes of Terry and Chris had gone to Scotland and carved out a really good career for themselves. I was also a big admirer of Trevor Francis from his days at Birmingham City, and then you had the late Ray Wilkins, who was also doing well at Rangers. These guys were all big names and it helped make the club a more attractive proposition. I had played against all four before and was well aware of their quality.

I was only 23 when I signed for Rangers, which was quite young, but I knew even back then that a footballer's career can be a short one so I was keen not to waste any time. I wanted to get into a position where I could pique the interest of England manager, Bobby Robson. There was no doubt I had become stale at Villa, and although I admired what Graham Taylor was doing at my club, the time was right to leave. Lots of folk in England had been talking about Souey and his Rangers revolution, and while the Scottish Premier League had once been regarded as a joke by many down south, it was a league they were coming to respect. It was the place to be and as soon as I walked into Ibrox, I knew I would become a Rangers player. To be honest, it didn't take Souey long to talk me round, and once the formalities had been completed, I had an interesting chat with Walter Smith. He said he was present the day I played for England Schoolboys against Scotland, the first time I had played north of the border, but a match I had almost forgotten all about. I was delighted Walter had remembered me, so I guess I must have made quite an impression.

But while I didn't know a lot about the Scottish game in general, the changes made by the new management team were big news all over the UK so I had a good idea of what had been going on at the club. Anything I knew about the Scottish game had come from Neale Cooper, who had spoken a lot about playing at Ibrox when he was with Aberdeen. And when I told him I was signing for Rangers, he filled me in about the Rangers-Celtic matches and the atmosphere I could expect. I had obviously played in a few Birmingham derbies in my time, but I was prepared for something quite different at Parkhead. I must admit I was surprised to see Rangers sitting fourth in the table – behind Celtic, Aberdeen and Hearts – although the manager convinced me it wouldn't be that way for too long.

As for Glasgow, the perception down south was that everyone liked a good drink, which was soon knocked on the head when I discovered that half the first team didn't touch a drop! I grew to really love Glasgow although at first I was advised on which areas of the city I should avoid, and which were safe to visit. In that respect it was just like Birmingham, which is another city with its good and bad parts. I suppose if you want trouble in any big metropolis you will find it easily enough. It's more about being sensible than anything else.

So, how about a nice quiet match for starters? Perhaps a mid-table team in a league fixture, or one of the lower league clubs in the cup? Nope. The fates decided I should make my debut in an Old Firm game – away from home, and at the new year! There were mixed views on whether or not it was the best fixture in which to play my first game for Rangers. The arguments were sink or swim, or ease him in. Celtic were playing well at the time and then there was all the carry-on that we knew would happen with the racism. Looking back, it was probably a good start for me personally because I had a fair idea of what to expect, and I think Souey was smart enough to say, 'Let's not put him on the bench. Let's throw him in at the deep end and see how he handles it.'

Let's just say I will never forget that game, for a number of reasons, but mainly the atmosphere, which was unbelievable. Oh, and also because of some of the outrageous objects that were thrown at me. I expected the bananas, but there was also a pig's foot, darts and golf balls. They absolutely crossed the line when they started throwing objects like that.

Throughout my career I didn't read an awful lot of newspapers, but on the morning of the game I picked up a paper and was mulling over a preview of the game. Jim Craig, one of Celtic's Lisbon Lions, winners of the 1967 European Cup in Portugal, had been asked to rate that afternoon's combatants. On yours truly, he said, 'I haven't seen him play but from all accounts he is a winger in the same class as Davie Cooper. Celtic will have to watch this new boy very carefully.' No pressure then. He had only gone and compared me to arguably one of the most skilful players ever to pull on the Rangers jersey!

So what kind of game did I have? Well, not the greatest, but I did give it my best shot although I suppose the occasion got to me. Perhaps the 60,000 crowd, and most of them giving me a hard time as it was an away game, was all a bit too much and I know I didn't perform to anywhere near my capabilities. That alone disappointed me. I think the four out of ten I received in one of the Sunday newspapers was about right. We lost 2-0 and as far as the team were concerned, we slipped seven points behind Celtic and they had a game in hand. This was in the days of two points for a win, so while we were never going to throw in the towel, we knew we had the proverbial mountain to climb. We didn't play well collectively, and it was well into the second half before we had our first shot at goal. And then we lost Chris Woods to injury with around 20 minutes remaining which meant Graham Roberts had to go in goal.

If I was to take anything positive from the game it would be that I was sitting in our dressing room and looking around at guys like Wilkins, Gough and McCoist, these fantastic players, and I realised it was a great opportunity to play in a great team, despite losing that game. I remember going back down to Birmingham that night and telling my mates, including guys that had played for Villa, all about the game and the atmosphere and they were all keen to know as much about the afternoon as possible. I was explaining to them how I had literally blinked and the game was over. It absolutely flew by. I remember at one point getting the ball and just wellying it. I can't recall where it ended up, but Ian Durrant came running over to me and said, 'For f***'s sake Mark, just calm down.'

That first season was all a bit hit and miss but it would soon herald the beginning of our dominance over Celtic and I was glad to be a part of it. Mind you it has all changed now and

Celtic are going for eight league titles in a row, so we need to get a good team together, one that can challenge them. The fact that Steven Gerrard has been appointed as manager will give the team a real boost and hopefully the gap between Rangers and Celtic will close as a result.

But it didn't take me long to discover just how much Old Firm matches meant to Rangers supporters. In fact, it took a lot less than 90 minutes. In that respect, my debut had set me up for life. The atmosphere was electric and no matter how close you were to someone on the park you could hardly hear a word they were saying. I had never experienced anything like it in my life. I've spoken to guys who played in the Milan or Madrid derbies – and many others around the world – and nothing sounds quite the same as an Old Firm match. At times, though, the atmosphere was bordering on the poisonous. I'll be honest, I used to leave town and head straight back to Birmingham after the game had finished; I always made plans to come back home after an Old Firm match, and even if we didn't have the Monday off I'd drive back up the road on the Sunday night. It was all a precaution because you would read the papers on the Monday and there would be assaults and lots of trouble, and maybe even an attempted murder, so I always felt it was better to get out of the way. But it was still an extra-special fixture and I loved playing in them. When I played in the Merseyside derby you would hear of Liverpool and Everton fans heading off to the game together, going for a pre-match pint and even sitting together. That would never happen at Ibrox or Parkhead!

Anyway, I was feeling a bit down the day after my debut, but when I read some of the comments about me in particular, rather than my performance, I was given a lift. Souey said, 'Mark is a player I've admired for a while and he will be a big asset to Rangers. He has a lot of passion and enthusiasm for his football and in the Premier League he will need it. He's an entertaining player and on his day a devastating one.'

Graham Roberts, our stand-in skipper at Parkhead, added, 'I thought Mark had an especially good first 45 minutes and he will be a big player for Rangers. I've played against him a lot of times in England. He's flown past me on many an occasion, although I did stop him in his tracks a few times! He is very quick, has good close control, and knows the way to goal. I was pleased with the reception he got from our fans and I know it meant a lot to him. Mind you, I was disappointed to see bananas thrown on to the pitch, but Mark is bigger than that and has made it clear that racist taunts won't worry him. Having played with so many great coloured players at Spurs, I still find it sad that some spectators in different parts of Britain find it necessary to abuse them. Mark had as tough a debut as he could have possibly got and he will have another hectic 90 minutes when we play Hearts at Tynecastle.'

Graham was spot on. Well, almost, because it was actually a whole lot worse at Tynecastle, but before that I had my home debut to think about – and it was against the team at the bottom of the league. We thumped Morton 5-0 and after the game I walked into the dressing room and realised I had made the right decision to stay on at Ibrox after all the nonsense of the Old Firm match. Don't get me wrong, the first hour of the match against Morton had been pretty dismal, until we shook off the lethargy and clicked into gear. Morton, despite being bottom markers, were a plucky lot, and we had struggled to break them down. But when we did, we did so with devastating effect. Ally McCoist scored three times, and as home debuts go, I was delighted with the way the game eventually panned out. It was afterwards I realised I was part of something special at Rangers. We had some cracking players, and Souey was building something lasting.

I reckon that night was the first time the Rangers fans got a glimpse of the real Mark Walters. I was pleased to be involved in the goals, but what pleased me most after two difficult games was the way the fans got behind me – and began chanting my name. It was all a bit different from what I had experienced at Celtic Park, and it was very welcome.

But I felt sorry for Terry Butcher, who was still recovering from his broken leg, because he was quite clearly missing his football. As a result of his frustration, he banned himself from watching the team. He had given himself a target of being back for the second leg of our European Cup quarter-final tie against Steaua Bucharest, ironically a match I would be watching from the stand as I hadn't signed in time to be eligible to take part. It was certainly a big miss not having Terry around the dressing room before games.

Next up was a trip to Edinburgh to play Hearts. I was pre-warned about the Tynecastle atmosphere, the close proximity of the fans to the pitch, and the rivalry between Glasgow and Edinburgh. But nothing could have prepared me for that match, absolutely nothing, and it will remain, for the rest of my life, the worst abuse I ever experienced on a football field – but more about that later on. During the match I went to take a corner and I was getting hit with coins and all sorts of things from the terracing. It was an absolute nightmare, but I remember getting back into the dressing room at half-time and the lads ripping the piss out of me because I had slipped just as I was about to take the corner and had made a complete mess of it. One of the guys shouted, 'Oi Mark, half-a-million quid and you can't even take a corner properly? It's not as if you were getting stick or anything!' Without doubt the boys taking the piss definitely helped me get over the nonsense that had been going on with many of the Hearts supporters.

The game itself was incredibly tough. There were boots flying in and quite a few players were booked. In fact, when I looked at the stats after the game, and noticed we had four players booked to Hearts's one, I couldn't help but think the figures were disproportionate, as Hearts had committed the greater number of fouls. Please explain that one Mr Referee! I'd had a number of bad fouls committed against me and yet they'd only had one player booked, Hugh Burns, who at times looked as if he might want to see what I looked like sliced in two! Rather inevitably, he later fouled me inside the box and we were awarded a penalty from which Ian Durrant scored to level it at one apiece, so we didn't leave Edinburgh empty-handed. When I signed for Rangers it was the perfect move for me at that stage of my career, but after the match at Tynecastle I would be lying if I said I didn't have second thoughts. Rangers are a massive institution but were they worth losing an eye for? When I look back and recall seeing darts lying at the side of the park, it still scares me.

At the time I was thinking, 'Will it be like this every week?' but then I read in one of the papers that it would soon be illegal to throw objects and I felt mighty relieved. Let's be honest, should it ever have been legal? At that point I was able to knuckle down and get on with concentrating on the football. Graham Roberts had taken over as captain from Terry, and just like he had done at White Hart Lane, when I was with Villa, he came out and condemned the thugs who had thrown objects at me and hurled racist abuse, which was a big comfort.

One guy with blue blood coursing through his veins was John 'Bomber' Brown. He signed midway through January from Dundee and was a great addition to the squad. Bomber was a guy I took to right away and we remain friends to this day. We also brought in a Danish lad, Jan Bartram, but he wouldn't be around too long after crossing Souey via the Danish press.

As you will already have gathered, Souey set incredibly high standards for everyone at the club – but those high standards also included him, as we witnessed when he criticised himself publicly for a sub-standard performance in the 1-1 draw at Hearts. He admitted he had underperformed in his last couple of matches, and said he wouldn't hesitate to drop himself if those standards continued to decline. That was the type of thing players liked to hear. The last thing you want is to be working under a player-manager who thinks he's beyond reproach because he has the stripes. Thankfully Souey was never like that.

There was a lot of frustration around in my first season at Rangers. We were always playing catch up with Celtic, and it was difficult as they had a good squad. We had a lot of injuries and new players but I think Celtic deserved to win the league. I don't think our strength in depth was as good, but when you get injuries to key players it definitely affects you. So we didn't have a lot of luck but it was never going to continue like that because luck has to change at some point, and thankfully it did.

When we played Steaua in the European Cup, naturally I was hoping we would get through, but of course there was an ulterior motive. I wasn't eligible to play in the quarter-finals but if we progressed I would be available to play in the semis. We lost 2-0 in Bucharest and I knew it would be an uphill struggle in the return leg. I didn't travel over to Bucharest, but apparently there was a bust-up between Souey and a journalist on the return flight, which was quite embarrassing to say the least. Apparently this guy – and most of his colleagues – had been under the impression that Ally McCoist wouldn't play in Romania, while Souey is supposed to have told just a single journalist that he would play. I don't know if that's an accurate assessment or not but it all kicked off on the plane and it even looked as though Souey was going to flatten the guy at one point. It was one of the main topics of conversation the following week at training, although we did all have sympathy with the gaffer as the pressure he was under from certain journalists was horrendous.

The second leg was eventful, to say the least. We knew we had a mountain to climb as Steaua were well organised, but it was up to us to open them up. Sadly, we lost an early goal and while we ended up winning 2-1, we were out of the competition on the finest of margins. My chances of playing in Europe that season were over. That said, we were more or less guaranteed a spot in Europe every season so it wasn't as if they had gone for ever. Oh, and who could forget Souey making 'that' challenge? The gaffer is lucky video assistant referees, or VAR, weren't around at the time or he might've been facing a hefty ban. But I could see from watching that game that we were geared towards playing regularly in Europe.

The following day, Souey challenged us to mount a Custer-style last stand in a desperate bid to hold on to our league title. He asked for the same determination we had shown against Steaua, saying that it was an injustice we were out of Europe, but we had eight games left in the title race and he wanted everyone to give it their best shot. He also said that with myself and Terry Butcher in the team, we could've won the European Cup. It was quite a comment, and one I appreciated.

I had only been at Ibrox a short time when the club decided to 'throw a protective shield around me', and told me not to speak to the press from either side of the border. No interviews. That was fine by me. I had been under a fair bit of pressure and the last thing I needed was putting my foot in it or being misquoted, probably more by the English press. It had been a stressful period and no matter how brave a face you try to put on things, I knew I didn't need any more emotional turmoil in my life. I'm sure Souey was just trying to protect me and allow me to concentrate solely on my football and I agreed.

Near the end of my first full month at Rangers, we welcomed Falkirk to Ibrox and I was astonished to see more than 41,000 inside Ibrox for a game against one of the league's smaller clubs. We moved up to second in the table after winning the game, and once again Ian Durrant converted a penalty after I had been pulled down in the box. I remember Souey bringing on Davie Cooper as a sub and asking me to switch to the right wing to accommodate Coop on the left. Anything for Coop!

A few days later, Rangers were making a different type of headline when Souey refused to allow Ally McCoist to join up with the Scotland party at Gleneagles after he had turned up late for training with Rangers. Ally was a notoriously bad timekeeper but the manager had decided enough was enough and slated him in the press. It was the main topic of conversation in the dressing room for a while as Souey had spoken about there being so much unemployment in Scotland, and here we had a young man doing a highly paid job and he couldn't be bothered turning up for training which didn't start until 10am. The manager's words, not mine! It was quite a verbal attack, but perhaps he was just frustrated at Coisty's timekeeping, and with the benefit of hindsight it must have been frustrating for the management team. But everyone at the club got a huge boost when Ally's mate, Durranty signed a new four-year contract. Durranty was a great lad and a top player.

We were a few points behind Celtic in the league but I still felt we were capable of winning it. There had been a lot of doom and gloom around when we lost at Parkhead but we soon picked up and started winning matches again. Despite being a little inconsistent, it was still a good title race. But it wasn't just us and Celtic vying for the title. Aberdeen and Hearts were also involved. After losing to Celtic on my debut, we went nine league games unbeaten, which put us back in the frame. At the time I believed any club from the top four was capable of becoming champions and I was enjoying being with a side who were involved at the right end of the table for a change. Certain elements of the Premier League might have had their problems with this black player, but I loved being a part of it.

When we went up to Pittodrie and beat Aberdeen for the first time in six years, positive vibes returned to the dressing room. Ally McCoist was back in the gaffer's good books and scored his first-ever goal at Aberdeen's ground, a goal that came hot on the heels of the Italian club Pisa reportedly showing an interest in signing Coisty.

The spirit in our dressing room was a real eye opener for me, and my team-mates made me feel like I had been a Rangers player for years, which I really appreciated. I was thrilled to get my first Rangers goal when we hosted Raith Rovers in a midweek Scottish Cup replay. It was another one of those games where we didn't really come alive until late on but scored three times in the last 12 minutes to book our place in the next round; and the icing on the cake for me was a neat chip from just inside the box when I spotted the keeper off his line, a goal which Graham Roberts called 'extra special'.

In fact, the next morning I was reading one of the papers at breakfast and a journalist described my goal against Raith as 'the type to light up Scotland's TV screens'. That pleased me because throughout my career I was aware that I was part of the entertainment industry. Supporters worked hard all week and wanted to relax at the weekend. They wanted to be entertained, whether that was by going to the cinema, the football or whatever, so I always had that in mind. Souey said I was one of the most exciting players not just in Scotland, but in Britain, and that was also nice, but I knew I was being well paid for doing something I loved. The goal against Raith was obviously special because I laughed when I read that the Rovers boss said, 'I'm never too happy at losing a goal, but I just felt like standing up and applauding with the rest of the crowd.' That was a great quote.

But it was only my first goal for Rangers and I was aiming to score as many as possible before the season was out. I had only managed four for Villa the season previous, although I had spent a large part of that season – three months, to be exact – on the sidelines with a pretty nasty shoulder injury. Just before the game against Raith, assistant manager Walter Smith spoke to me about my lack of goals. Not that he was worried, but because he could see it was bothering me. Not once did Rangers ever put pressure on me to score, and for that I was grateful. I always liked to score around ten a season, anything less and I was disappointed, but when I got my first one I could say I had scored for Rangers and that was important to me.

Another reason it was important to get off the mark was because with Ally McCoist injured, we needed the others chipping in with goals, and I wanted to do my bit. And we did that against St Mirren by scoring four times. The goals were shared between Davie Cooper, who was celebrating his 600th appearance for the club, Ray Wilkins, Richard Gough and me. You know what they say about waiting ages for a bus, and then two come along at the same time. But the goal against St Mirren is one I'll never forget, because I don't know how I managed it. I remember jinking along the byline – virtually running parallel with the white line – and it looked as though the only avenue open was the cut-back, but I went for goal and somehow it squeezed past the goalkeeper and his near post.

A few days after the win over St Mirren, Souey dipped into the transfer market again and paid around £1m for Saints midfielder Ian Ferguson. It was yet another statement of intent by the club and gave the midfield an injection of steel. But Fergie could also play, and his forward raiding and passing were second to none. Oh, and he didn't drink either!

When we faced Dunfermline Athletic in March, I scored for the third game in a row, but while the home side's Dutch keeper, Guido van de Kamp, praised me after the game, saying that whenever he had played against me when I was at Villa, I was devastating on the ball, he also had a pop at the team, which I felt was completely wrong. He reportedly said, 'For a team with so many star names they really disappointed me.' I don't know what more we could have done. We won the match very comfortably, 3-0, and I thought we played well.

One of the Sunday papers opened a can of worms when they looked into what the top players in Scotland were supposedly earning at the time, and their exposé claimed Rangers had the five top earners in the country, with Souey heading the list allegedly on £2,500 a week. Terry Butcher,

Graham Roberts, Chris Woods and Richard Gough made up the quintet. I don't know if an article like this was in the public interest, or if they just wanted to stir things up in the dressing room, but it had no effect on the other players and we just got on with our jobs.

One team we always seemed to struggle against was Motherwell, especially at Ibrox, where it seemed like they had sneaked into the ground the night before and built a brick wall in front of their goal – and this was long before the term 'parking the bus' became trendy. Late on in the season, they arrived at our place and it took an Ian Durrant goal to finally break their resistance. That game has stuck in my memory for one particular reason, and that was the moment Souey played the ball back to our goalkeeper from the halfway line and was roundly booed by our own fans!

The final Old Firm game of the season was upon us and this time it was John Colquhoun giving his opinion on the Rangers team. About me, he said, 'Most exciting player in the Scottish game, and Rangers's best buy. Great entertainer and never scores ordinary goals – they are all exceptional. 10 out of 10!' Wow, great words, but nigh on impossible to live up to. I did manage to play well enough in the game but it was Celtic who left with a 2-1 win. I'm sure we all thought that was that, but there was further bad news after the game when Trevor Francis announced he was leaving to sign for QPR. To be fair to Trev, he was being used more and more sparingly by Souey and I think frustration was getting the better of him. I was really sorry to see him go as we had struck up quite a bond.

But I received the perfect pick-me-up in the shape of the Scottish Brewers Player of the Month award, and the accompanying cheque for £250 and a trophy, which I received from the ex-Scotland rugby star John Rutherford, who was apparently a big Rangers fan.

And then the shit really hit the fan.

At the end of March, Souey was savaged by Jan Bartram in a Danish newspaper. Under the headline of, 'My boss is a bastard', the biggest selling Copenhagen daily – *Ekstra Bladet* – quoted Bartram's explosive outburst extensively. Jan allegedly told the newspaper that he had been instructed to kick opponents, and that Souey should have been red-carded for a vicious tackle in the game against Steaua. The report also claimed Bartram once saw Souness kick a TV set after a game. Big deal!

At the time, the player was in Italy with the Danish Olympic team preparing to face West Germany in a Seoul Olympics qualifying match. Bartram was quoted as saying, 'I didn't go to Scotland to risk breaking other players' legs. I'm very much against this style. Souness wants us to be hard when we're in trouble. He is a bastard. I will not follow orders and deliberately kick people. He should have been shown the red card against Steaua. He likes to get the ball and slaughter other players and I don't think I can learn this type of play. I like to see the beautiful things in the game so I am prepared to be fired. There will always be another club for me, and at the moment I am glad to be back among my Danish countrymen so that I can play real football again.'

You can imagine this was the main topic of conversation in the Ibrox dressing room before, during and after training. Of course, we were all used to being misquoted but this was pretty explosive stuff and, if the truth be told, I'm not sure we were looking forward to Jan returning from international duty. You must also be thinking by now that we were a bunch of gossips in that dressing room!

Anyway, more of the Jan Bartram gossip later!

Meanwhile, we had a match to win at Dens Park in Dundee, a ground we never had it easy at, and this occasion was no different. Perhaps the frenzied nature of the contest – and five goals in a match that had everything – took a little of the heat off Bartram. That particular game was played at 90 miles per hour and it eventually took Ray Wilkins to calm things down by putting his foot on the ball and slowing down the tempo. Ray was great at having a look around him and picking out a pass. He really stamped his authority on the game that day and we were soon playing on his terms. Oh, and normality was restored late on when I was brought down in the box and Durranty slammed home the penalty. There was a pattern emerging. For a little while at least, Bartram wasn't centre of attention.

Mind you, a spotlight was quite rightly shone in our faces when we lost to Morton at their place. It was a huge embarrassment for everyone, especially as the papers put it, 'the millionaires of Rangers were humbled by the team at the bottom of the league, and with the worst scoring record in the country'. Freak results happen in football but for them to get their first win in 31 games, and against us, was awful. After the match, we were quite rightly booed all the way back to the dressing room by our supporters.

The following midweek, the focus shifted from a pretty awful performance on the park, to an even worse one off it. Terry Butcher, Chris Woods and Graham Roberts had been involved in a fracas during an Old Firm game before I had arrived at the club. They were due at court for sentencing and I thought it was a wind-up when Terry and Chris ended up with a criminal record because of a handbags incident during a match. What were the Scottish authorities thinking about?

Our lads were accused of conducting themselves in a disorderly manner and committing a breach of the peace for a 30-second nothing-incident in a red-hot Old Firm match. Big deal. Sadly, Terry and Chris were found guilty, and fined £250 and £500 respectively, while Robbo's case was deemed not proven. The Celtic player involved, Frank McAvennie, was found not guilty. I had witnessed far worse in games where players hadn't even been booked. Honestly. I wouldn't say it was a laughing matter but the mentality around the dressing room was to treat it as a joke. I think the lads knew nothing terrible was going to happen to them, like being thrown in jail, so they were relatively comfortable about it, but I can't believe they ended up with a criminal record.

Terry Butcher had fully recovered from his broken leg, but had been out of the side for five months and had been a big miss. Who wouldn't miss a guy with his pedigree? During his absence, Robbo had been a superb deputy, but he then picked up a knee injury and was ruled out for the remainder of the season. I had only arrived halfway through the campaign, but as title defences went, it had been a bit of a damp squib.

We had just three league games left and, as if to prove the Jekyll & Hyde mantle we had acquired, easily won the first 3-0 at St Mirren. I was pleased to score again, but there was a pre-match shock in store when Souey announced he was dropping Ian Durrant due to a 'lack of professionalism'. He told the media, 'If a footballer chooses to do things away from training in his social life which prevent him from giving 100 per cent on a Saturday then he is in the wrong business.'

Our final home game was against Aberdeen, and we lost. Everyone was as flat as a pancake. In his programme notes, Souey said, 'Frankly, I hope I never have to go through another season like it.' It certainly wasn't what the gaffer had been used to during his playing career, and I had a feeling he wouldn't have to suffer another like it while at Ibrox.

With the season fizzling out, and Souey no doubt already preparing for the new campaign, there was one final bombshell for Rangers supporters (and players). Sadly, Graham Roberts's time at Rangers came to an abrupt halt when he fell foul of Souey and left the club. It all happened so quickly. Just a few weeks before the incident that led to his departure, we were all out for a meal, Graham included, and he had just signed a new five-year contract. It looked to all intents and purposes that he would finish his career at Ibrox, but something was said between Graham and the gaffer and I literally never saw my team-mate again. He was banished to the Highlands with the reserves and that was that. End of story. What was said sounded pretty trivial to me but if it had disrespected the gaffer then it wouldn't end well for Graham. To go from the highs of signing a five-year deal to leaving the club under a cloud literally a few weeks later ... It makes me wonder if there was something else to it, and perhaps something was said behind the scenes which we weren't party to. Without doubt, that decision sent out a big message to the rest of the players. I remember thinking that if any of the others had a gripe they would be keeping it to themselves, unless of course they wanted to leave. If Souey had been looking to enhance his reputation as a disciplinarian he definitely went about it the right way. As for Graham, the gaffer obviously felt he was replaceable, and that proved the case as Richard Gough was settling in very quickly. There's no question it was Souey's way or the highway and he had stamped his authority on the dressing room. I'm not sure he would get away with it nowadays as players have so much more power than we ever did. There were a lot of big personalities in that Rangers dressing room, but Souey was the boss. The lads also loved playing for Rangers so much they weren't going to risk their future. The likes of Ian Durrant were Rangers through and through and would've pulled on that jersey for nothing.

Meanwhile, Robbo was put up for sale. The guy who had been interim club captain was out, and wouldn't be given an opportunity to say goodbye to supporters in our final match of the season at Falkirk. It was a tough one for me to take, because he always had my back. I was sad to see him go.

From the moment we ran out on to the park at Falkirk, all we could hear was the massive Rangers support chanting for Robbo. It was as though the game itself was a sideshow. We won 5-0 and I was delighted to score twice – as did Coisty – but the game was played out to a backdrop of 'Robbo must stay' chants and banners being unfurled in support of the popular defender. The supporters were trying to send a message to Souey, but we all knew he wasn't the sort to back down. I recall scoring our opening goal after just a couple of minutes, and as I made my way back to our own half, all I could hear was 'Robbo, Robbo give us a wave.' I thought it was brilliant of the fans to show their support for him in this way. Rangers fans have always been loyal and passionate, and that is two qualities you like to see your supporters show.

After the game, I believe Souey only wanted to answer questions about the game to waiting reporters, but even they only had one name on their lips, and the gaffer eventually decided he would try and put the subject to bed by saying, 'Due to the reaction of the supporters, it is necessary for me to make the situation clear. After a game it is every manager's right to express his opinion and every player's duty to accept what the manager has to say. Graham Roberts took exception to the remarks I made after the recent 1-0 defeat by Aberdeen at Ibrox. His response to my remarks was, among other things, that he asked for a transfer. This took place in front of all the players, Walter Smith and Phil Boersma. When done in this way, there is no alternative for me but to put the player on the transfer list. In the end, I'm not doing what's best for Graeme Souness but what I believe to be best for Rangers. That's why Graham Roberts has played his last game for us.'

That certainly put the matter to rest for the majority of us, especially when the news came through that Davie Cooper had been offered – and accepted – a new one-year contract. As the guy that was allegedly brought in to replace Coop, I couldn't have been happier. When Souey handed out the extension, he reckoned Coop could play in the top league for at least another three years and I was inclined to agree.

And the final word went to the gaffer. He decided he would play fewer games the following season and distance himself more from the players. Souey would leave training to Walter Smith and Phil Boersma. He was willing to do anything to ensure Rangers would be back at the top of the league.

Chapter Eight

Racism Rears its Ugly Head

T HE song 'Nice One Cyril' was penned in honour of one-time Tottenham player, Cyril Knowles, but with a couple of added letters, it could well have been written to pay tribute to Cyrille Regis, a fantastic footballer and a very good friend of mine, whose life was tragically cut short due to a heart attack in January of this year.

When he first made the grade for West Brom in the late 1970s, Cyrille was a pioneer for black footballers. I was about 13 years old and, to be honest, racism hadn't been an issue for me. At that time I was playing with a local youth team and training with other kids at Villa, and making sure I had somewhere to play and learning my 'trade' were my biggest concerns.

Racism didn't become black and white for me until I signed my first senior contract, and it was something which was more or less exclusive to away games, where opposition fans would taunt you with monkey chants and you'd get the odd earful whenever you ventured anywhere near them. Most of the time it was isolated abuse by little pockets of tanked-up supporters, but in the 80s there were a few grounds where you were almost guaranteed to get slaughtered. These were West Ham, Newcastle, Leeds United and Millwall, where everyone seemed to be a skinhead and decked out in Doc Martens. Those four grounds were definitely the worst. I did suffer racial abuse from certain players now and again but it was mostly fans that dished it out.

I didn't score with many headers in my career but I remember getting one against Spurs, although the main reason I recall that game is due to the racial abuse I suffered at the hands of one of their players – and it really got to me that day. I genuinely can't remember his name, but I do remember Spurs's defender Graham Roberts intervening and telling his team-mate in no uncertain terms to calm down and shut up. Just before Graham became involved, he was walking towards me menacingly and I thought he was about to join in with the abuse but thankfully I was wrong, and of course Graham and I would later become friends and team-mates at Rangers.

But if I thought the abuse I had suffered in England was bad, it was about to fly off the scale when I joined Rangers. Somehow it was as though certain groups of supporters up there had never seen a black man before. I was just 23 years old and the first black guy to play in the Premier League, and boy how I would soon know it. I arrived in Scotland to sign for Rangers on New Year's Eve 1987. A couple of days later I made my debut at Celtic Park, home to our greatest rivals. Souey spoke to me beforehand and warned me what to expect, before joking, 'Frankly, Mark, you would have a bigger problem if you were Catholic!' I could laugh about it later but I wasn't in the mood for chuckling before the game, as I was a bag of nerves.

I remember reading one of the papers on the morning of the game and there was this lad who had bought boxes of fruit and was standing there proudly, telling all the readers what he was going to do with it. 'This is for Mark,' he said. We had a good laugh about it at the back of the bus on route to Celtic Park, but the reality was this clown had just spent 30 quid on fruit just to throw at me. Instead of feeding his family, he'd spent all that money on boxes of bananas to throw at a black guy! It was pathetic.

The abuse started the moment we got off the team bus, and continued when we walked out on to the park for the warm-up. My team-mates were brilliant and tried to start some banter in an effort to deflect the chants and monkey noises coming from many of the Celtic fans. Our own supporters were very much in the minority but they gave me a great reception and that perked me up.

We ended up losing the game 2-0 but I was singled out for the type of stick I had never experienced before. It had nothing to do with football, and it made me think whether or not I could handle it every week. We're talking 60,000 people in a stadium and 55,000 of them are caning you. I'm not exaggerating when I say that, and if I'm wide of the mark it certainly didn't feel like it. Previously I had played in front of 25,000 fans, 30,000 maximum, so I'd gone from being just another player to being singled out by more than 50,000 people which, at the time, was really hard for me to comprehend. Remember, I was only a young man.

Souey had said to me before I signed that due to a lack of black players I might take some stick but I'd never imagined how bad it would be. After my debut I thought to myself, 'What kind of place have I come to? What type of people populate this country?' I tried hard to shrug it off but it was an awful experience and I considered my future after that game. I did a lot of soul searching but one of the things I took into consideration was the support I had received from the Rangers fans. They got me through it. Maybe they gave me more support because of the abuse but, for whatever reason, they were brilliant and that was why I decided to make a go of it. It wasn't a case of I was going to leave if they weren't cheering for me because you have to earn those cheers and prove yourself as a player, but they made me feel so welcome and I really did appreciate that. I struck up an instant rapport with our fans and that had a huge bearing on me staying at Ibrox.

During the game at Celtic Park I started to think, 'Hang on a second, I've just run a metre inside that line and there is a scary array of missiles that have been thrown at me.' I didn't hear any of them hit the ground, and I didn't notice them flying through the air, so I'm wondering whether or not I had been the intended target in the first place, but deep down I knew I was. Probably the scariest items there were darts, as they could've taken my eye out. My first thought was who on earth would be crazy enough to take darts to a football match just to throw at a player. It wasn't normal behaviour. Obviously there was all the verbal abuse as well, but that wasn't uncommon in England so it wasn't as though I hadn't heard it all before. But there were also a number of other black players down south, whereas in Scotland I was firmly on my own.

Maybe if I hadn't been playing so wide I wouldn't even have noticed it, but because I was out there on the wing, and taking corners, then I was bound to notice all these objects lying on the running track. Usually I don't hear much during a game, as I'm so focussed on what I'm doing on the park, but you couldn't help but hear some of the insults when you were only a few feet away from the baying mob.

From the moment I started out on my journey to become a professional footballer I knew racism was something I would eventually have to deal with if I wanted to go all the way. It's really different nowadays because you can walk off the pitch or do other things, but your options back then were zero. Racism within football was 'just one of those things' but I know lads who couldn't take it and walked away from the game. Their attitude was 'Why should I have to put up with this rubbish?' And who could blame them, because they were getting into trouble sticking up for themselves and it was giving them a lot of added grief. Thankfully I've always been pretty level-headed and tried my best not to bite, and more often than not it worked. Occasionally I got the referee involved, but it wasn't very often. Having the type of personality that helped me handle it was without doubt another reason I was able to carry on. I think it shows far more weakness in the person dishing out the abuse than the guy on the receiving end. A couple of times I did get angry, but managed to calm myself down pretty quickly. The thing is, if you're playing well there isn't an awful lot that is going to get to you. It's when you're having a nightmare that it's more likely to affect you and get inside your head.

One thing that shocked me in the aftermath of the Old Firm match was the police reaction to the behaviour of the crowd. They 'praised' fans for their behaviour, and part of a report read, 'Fears of scenes of abuse when Mark Walters – the Premier League's first black player – made his Rangers debut proved unfounded. Only a few stupid fans greeted him with chants and fruit throwing. But Walters coolly lobbed a piece of fruit back over the touchline.'

The author of that report was obviously at a different match to me, as I can assure him those fears of abuse were not unfounded, and that more than just 'a few' opposition fans had racially abused me. There were 'only' 25 arrests made, and all for minor offences. I wonder if racial abuse was considered a minor offence, or perhaps no one was arrested for it at all.

When I arrived for 'work' on the Monday morning, my team-mates were fantastic, and wanted to make sure I hadn't suffered too much over the weekend. It was appreciated, but at that moment I believed the racist issues wouldn't be going away any time soon. All I could really do was get the head down and prepare for the next game, which was away to Dundee. I worried about what lay in store for me at Dens Park, as it was a place I knew little about. Thankfully the answer was very little. There was no repetition of the banana-baiting I had received at Celtic Park, and probably the only issues were random shouts from supporters no doubt curious about watching the league's first black player. There wasn't an awful lot for me to get upset about.

After that, I had my first home match to look forward to and I received a warm welcome when I ran out of the tunnel to face Morton. We won 5-0, and everything in the garden seemed rosy – that was until we visited Tynecastle, which is in Edinburgh and the home of Heart of Midlothian, or Hearts for short. A majority of the home support certainly didn't live up to their name that afternoon as there was very little love inside their packed stadium. Once again, though, the Rangers fans were 100 per cent behind me, and all I can say is thank god for that.

But if I thought the scenes at Celtic Park were bad, then what I endured at Tynecastle – both on and off the park – was ten times worse.

Somehow, though, I was able to turn in a good performance and we managed a draw, but sadly the result didn't make many headlines in the papers 24 hours later. Reports spoke of how I had managed to silence the mindless racists by turning in a dazzling display to help us secure a point. If only it had been that simple. For some reason, the moment I stepped on to the turf at Tynecastle for the pre-match warm-up, I had a feeling I wouldn't be in for an easy ride. For starters, the crowd were almost on top of you. In the past, I had bemoaned stadia with a running track between the pitch and supporters, due to their lack of atmosphere, but that afternoon I would've loved some extra space between us.

I got stick during the pre-match warm-up and it continued when I went to retrieve the ball to take a corner in the first half at the Hearts end. I placed the ball on the little arc, took a couple of steps back, and the first bunch of bananas landed just a foot or so away from me. The next one hit me on the shoulder, though, and many others landed close by. I took the corner quickly and got the hell out of there. Of course, there were other instances when I had to go grab the ball for a throw-in or corner and inevitably the objects would come flying through the air in my direction. It was awful and it seemed never ending.

I was also having a torrid time of it on the park too, especially from the Hearts right-back, a former Rangers player called Hugh Burns. He would come thundering into challenges and I had to have my wits about me as I quite fancied leaving Edinburgh that night with my legs intact.

And then came the moment I won my team a penalty. I picked up the ball inside the Hearts half and made straight for the box, twisting and turning. I saw Burns coming in to tackle me, and I managed to wriggle past him. Next thing I knew I was on the ground, the referee had pointed to the spot, Ian Durrant had grabbed the ball and Burns was screaming abuse at me – and it was less than complimentary. The referee booked him for his tirade and Durranty fired home from the spot.

The fall-out from that game brought the subject of racism in football – a problem Scotland apparently didn't know it had – to a head and the following day the papers went to town on the subject. One paper in particular made the topic their main back-page lead, as well as a comment piece, which I thought was incredibly hard-hitting. It read:

Rangers' signing of Mark Walters marked a football milestone and a challenge to Scotland. Our reputation for racial fairness and decency was on the line the moment Mark signed his contract. In England, black players endure barrages of abuse and taunts from racist thugs masquerading as supporters. Now, fans of Hearts have let their side down, just like Celtic supporters did at Parkhead a fortnight ago, by hurling fruit on the pitch. Can Scottish football fans still live up to their boast that they're better behaved than their counterparts down south? That particular battle is now on.

And the theme continued in the comment piece:

I never thought I'd live to see the day I would admit to being ashamed to be a Scot – but it happened at Tynecastle yesterday. It happened because a young and brilliantly talented player called Mark Walters was showered with bananas when he took a corner kick. His only offence? He happens to be black. We've got our own problems in this little country of ours, but blatant, fascist racism has never been one of them. English stars Terry Butcher, Graham Roberts and Chris Woods have all told me they have been overwhelmed by the warmth of the Scottish welcome. Does Mark Walters deserve anything less? I trust the REAL football fan at every club makes sure the lunatics are well and truly sorted out.

It was really bad at Hearts. So bad, in fact, that it's the closest I have ever come to walking away from football – just a couple of weeks after I had decided to stay. Suddenly, everything Cyrille Regis taught me I had forgotten. But the main problem, and what made me think 'Can I take any more of this?' was the objects being hurled in my direction. I could just about handle the verbal abuse. I'm the kind of person that when I'm playing, even if opposition players are fouling me, I still try to concentrate on the football, but when objects are flying all around you, you would have to be pretty tough not to fear for your safety. It was downright dangerous and that was the bottom line.

When I signed for Rangers, being the first black player in the Premier League didn't worry me. I had always found Scots to be fair. I had played against Scotland at schoolboy, youth and under-21 levels and never failed to enjoy it, but this was different, something far more sinister.

Of all the players I came up against in Scotland, the one that really stands out as the worst is Hugh Burns of Hearts. When we were awarded the penalty, the abuse he gave me was unbelievable. Did he use racist language while lambasting me?

That's a question I can't answer with hand on heart, because the noise from the crowd behind the goal, and elsewhere in the stadium, was deafening and I don't know what words he used, but I remember lying on the ground, staring up at a face wracked with hatred and him mouthing off at me. He absolutely slaughtered me, and as the team bus left Edinburgh after the game, I wondered just what the hell I had got myself into.

After the games against Celtic and Hearts, I received lots of letters of support from fans all over Scotland, not just Rangers supporters. They told me to keep my chin up and reminded me that not everyone in the country was a racist. I'd experienced racism in England, so it hadn't come as a complete shock, but it had been on a different scale to the problem down south. My Mum used to always say that if I was getting abuse, I had to play ten times better just to shut them up. Sadly, she was right, but I think it gave me an inbuilt resilience and taught me that if I was just another average player, being black I would get a lot of stick. But if I was better than them then I had a chance.

I remember saying in an interview after that first Hearts match that I would just ignore the morons, but that was just a front. I can assure you it wasn't as easy as just ignoring them. If the abuse had been coming only from the terraces it might have been achievable, or certainly a bit easier, but when you're also getting it from some opponents then there is no escape. It doesn't matter who you are, or if you have the thickest skin on the planet, but when a large group of people are slaughtering you it's very hard to take. Everyone has a threshold.

It wasn't all doom and gloom, though, as one of the letters I received was from a Hearts supporter apologising for throwing fruit at me. He said he had gone home and thought long and hard about his actions and was thoroughly embarrassed with himself. So much so, in fact, he had decided to ban himself from attending football. When I read that, I realised there was hope.

There was also the story of the Hearts fan who turned up at Tynecastle a couple of days after the game with a letter of abject apology for being involved in the banana-throwing incident. To prove he was genuine, he handed back his season ticket. I remember getting to read the letter and part of it said, 'I am writing to apologise for the treatment of Mark Walters. I now feel absolutely disgusted and embarrassed about my behaviour. A combination of a few drinks and the atmosphere made me act like an animal. I have never behaved in this way before and will never do so again. I am aware of the trouble this has caused Hearts FC and I am full of remorse. I have let the club down badly so I will not be at Tynecastle for the remainder of the season as my punishment.'

Another Hearts man wrote a letter to the Rangers News saying he had been a Tynecastle regular since 1968, but that he wouldn't be going back. He said, 'I am ashamed to say I am a Hearts supporter after last week's game against Rangers. Besides the banana throwing, I was appalled and disgusted by the jeering. I can only assume these so-called supporters don't wish to see top British players at Tynecastle.'

And far more recently, I got a message from a Celtic fan on Twitter, apologising for his actions back then and saying he was ashamed even now, 30 years on. The way I was brought up was that everyone deserves a second chance. Invariably it is down to education, or a lack of it. Perhaps they've seen their father or friends acting like that, and they don't understand how hurtful it can be to people. When they become adults, and if they still act like that, then that's different as they are probably never going to change.

It did get pretty nasty for a spell, and it was usually when there was a big crowd, and perhaps many people felt braver being part of a large group. If it had happened to me walking down the street, and I had been abused by an individual, that would've been different. But, for me, the hope was that those individuals who were making up the crowd would sit down and think about what they had done when they got home, once they weren't surrounded by their friends.

Thankfully it did all eventually die down and it was fantastic not to have to put up with people throwing objects at me just because the colour of my skin was different to theirs. All I had to worry about then was having a bad game or getting kicked: normal things.

I recall Hearts chairman Wallace Mercer going out on a limb to slam the racists within his own support, and threatening to ban anyone who was found to have chucked fruit at me or made monkey noises. That was a great comfort; especially as someone in such a lofty position had taken an interest in trying to stamp out the racist behaviour, and taken it seriously. It was also a great comfort to me knowing that, hopefully, the black kids who were following me might not have to put up with the same nonsense I had been subjected to. Cyrille Regis was a real pioneer for me, and the hope was that a young kid following on could say, 'Mark has managed to put up with it so whatever happens in my career, I'm going to make sure that if I fail it won't be down to racism.'

As a club, Rangers also dealt with the problem very well. I remember being shocked to read about a RANGERS fan being banned from Ibrox for life for shouting racist abuse at me during my home debut against Morton. Rangers were right to make a stance. Not just because it was the right thing to do, but because they would hardly be in a position to dish out moral advice if they had problems in-house and weren't dealing with them. The fan was told not to come back and had his £110 season ticket ripped up. Our security guy, Alistair Hood said the seat would lie empty for the rest of the season as a warning to others. What pleased me was that the incident had been reported to police by this guy's fellow Rangers fans. It proved they were willing to stand up for me and what was right.

Alistair Hood also spoke to me about the carry-on at the time and told me he was going to speak to the SFA about the problems I had been encountering at grounds with objects being thrown at me.

The matter even reached the House of Commons, where Scots Liberal MP Menzies Campbell tabled a motion condemning sections of the Tynecastle crowd for racism and wishing me a long and successful career in Scottish football. I thought it a fine gesture.

After the Tynecastle match, Graham Roberts said, 'Mark was tremendous against Hearts. He isn't just a big asset to Rangers, but also to Scottish football. It was justice when he won us the penalty. Asides from that, his piece of skill in bringing down Nicky Walker's kick out was as good as anything I've ever seen and only a fine save from Henry Smith prevented us getting a second goal. What a shame about the abuse he takes though. It's sickening.'

At the time, I recall John Barnes going through a similar situation when he played for Liverpool against Everton in the big Merseyside derby. And as the clubs prepared to do battle again, there was a warning from the Everton chairman that a repeat of the banana-baiting could threaten a return to Europe for English clubs. Philip Carter was also President of the

English league, and he warned, 'This match is going out on TV worldwide and UEFA officials will be watching. It would be an absolute disaster if there was any racial abuse, because no one is prepared to tolerate that.'

I'm sure he was also concerned that the taunts could affect John, even if he didn't say as much.

But fast-forward 30 years from the racist behaviour of Hearts fans in my day and you can imagine how dismayed I was to read that a problem may still exist at Tynecastle. Esmaël Gonçalves, the black Portuguese player, claimed that being subjected to racist abuse from a minority of Hearts fans had played a big part in his decision to quit the club. He said his family could no longer watch him play because of the racist comments made towards him. To think some supporters still believe behaviour like this is acceptable saddens me. A lot of pioneering black players put their necks on the line to eradicate this disease from the game and it seems that three decades on we still have work to do.

Chapter Nine

Who's Up for the Title Then?

NEW season, new team-mates, and the first to arrive, Gary Stevens, was such a good addition to the squad. He was your modern-day full-back who could bomb up and down the park from the first minute to the last. On top of that he was also a really good lad. It's not until you're a manager or coach that you realise the importance of having players with the right personality and attitude. While you're playing it's not something you give much thought to, but having players with the right attitude and make-up is vital to achieving success. Gary was all of that and more. In fact, if there was a better right-back in Europe at the time I'm not sure I'd seen him.

Souey laid down a marker by paying Everton £1m for Gary. We'd just endured a disappointing campaign but by shelling out that type of money during the close season, he was saying, 'We're determined to go one better this season.' Or how about, 'We WILL go one better this season!' It was a wake-up call to our rivals and let them know that Rangers would never settle for second best. We already knew that nothing other than first would do, but the gaffer wanted the best and Gary slipped effortlessly into that category.

We also brought in Kevin Drinkell and he was another guy who provided exactly what we were looking for. Kevin was a fantastic link-up player, gave us something different from what we already had in the squad and he worked incredibly hard. He was also a great finisher and a really top bloke off the pitch, although he could smoke for England. In fact, if memory serves me right, I'm sure he might have enjoyed the occasional fag at half-time, although I'm not sure Souey ever knew about it. Sorry mate! I roomed with Kevin for a while and we got on so well. We would chat about anything and everything but inevitably the topic of conversation would swing back towards football.

Bringing Gary and Kevin in made the squad even more competitive. We were getting stronger and had top players battling for just about every position. Even the guys on the periphery of the squad could come in and do a number. Souey was on top of it. You don't assemble good squads overnight; they take time and the gaffer was doing things right. We were beginning to look pretty formidable and off we went to the Il Ciocco training camp in Tuscany for pre-season in fine fettle.

Personally, Il Ciocco must rank as the toughest pre-season I've ever known. Davie Cooper had been with the club for years, and would talk about running up and down the sand dunes of Gullane, in East Lothian, under legendary Rangers boss Jock Wallace, and how it used to kill the players, but even Coop reckoned Il Ciocco was the hardest of the lot. In fact, I think Ian McCall might even have collapsed during one of our visits there. I think he had asthma, and I'm not sure if that had a bearing, but it was certainly hard work. It was a means to an end, though, and I had the (slight) advantage of having worked under Graham Taylor the previous pre-season at Villa – and he was renowned for working his players hard.

On the way home from Tuscany, we stopped off at the Lilleshall rehabilitation centre in England, where we were put through a number of tests in order to gauge the fitness of the squad. It was another mark of the thoroughness and professionalism which the gaffer had introduced to the club. He wasn't leaving anything to chance. Footballers are generally one-sided, so we were hooked up to a machine which would show if any specific limbs needed building up or strengthening. We also took part in the bleep test, which involves running from one marker to another and having to reach your destination before a bleep sounds. It's a tough one but shows up a combination of fitness and sharpness. Going back to Gary Stevens, I think he was by far and away the top Ranger that year with a score of about 22. Now, Sebastian Coe, the Olympic champion runner, was the only guy I'd heard of who had a higher bleep-test rating, which shows just how fit Gary was. The average score was around 15 or 16. I think I scored 14 and anything under 11 was considered an abject failure.

The worst I witnessed in my time in football was while I was at Liverpool, and Jan Molby scored eight. It was a mental thing as much as anything and if you didn't think you could achieve a good score, you probably wouldn't, it was as simple as that. In Jan's defence, he was technically one of the best players I ever played alongside. If he could have run as well as he picked out a pass he wouldn't have been at Anfield, he would've been a feature at Barça or Real Madrid. His technique and range of passing was scary.

The start of the season was overshadowed slightly by the incident involving Jan Bartram. I knew Jan relatively well as we'd signed at roughly the same time and were living in the same hotel. We got on well enough but mentally he was a very strong character. He knew exactly what he wanted but I'm not sure he signed for Rangers for the proper reasons. I remember hearing he had insisted on getting all his money paid up front, which was very unusual at that time. Obviously your wages were paid over the period of your contract, but as far as I'm led to believe he got the lot up front. I presume that was the only way he would put pen to paper. For me, though, that was a bad sign, because if you're thinking that way then you're not going to be here long term. As a player, though, he was physically strong and got up and down the wing well. We played on the same side of the park so we would link up a lot. We also had Stuart Munro in the squad at the time and I reckon Stuart was more consistent than Jan, and less maintenance, if you like.

Jan had apparently called Souness a bastard in a Danish newspaper, which I couldn't quite believe at the time. I'm not sure if he had or hadn't but the boys were a bit shocked at it, and even though I tended not to get involved in other people's business, it was impossible to ignore the fall-out, so it came as no surprise when he left Rangers and headed back to Denmark. He was such an opinionated guy but when it came down to it, there was only ever going to be one winner.

Not long after we came back from Il Ciocco, both Derek Ferguson and Ally McCoist signed new long-term deals. Along with the new players who were arriving, it was more good news and you got the feeling we were gearing up to have an excellent campaign. Of course, a football season is a long one but certainly the signs at the start were very optimistic.

Every team needs a goal-scorer, and we had that in McCoist, while Drinkell was almost certain to be chipping in with double figures, so I was looking forward to playing with these guys and I felt there weren't many games in which we wouldn't score, certainly not with the firepower we had.

We started the season with a match against Bordeaux for Davie Cooper's testimonial. It was a full house – which we all expected – but there were thousands locked out as the game was pay at the gate. The game itself was a fantastic way to start off as we were up against guys like Jean Tigana, Clive Allen and Enzo Scifo, who were all top players.

I was also delighted that Davie had such a successful testimonial because he was so deserving of it. In fact, he was one of my favourite players long before I ever made it anywhere near Ibrox. When we were team-mates at Rangers he probably got sick of me asking questions, but I knew I could learn so much from him. The main reason for this was not because I was supposed to replace him – as everyone has a shelf life – but because I had been desperate to play alongside him. And let's be honest, Davie Cooper was irreplaceable. His style was so different to most other wide players anyway, so I was never going to replace him like-for-like. I loved playing in the same team as him. It was the perfect scenario as there weren't many around who could lace Davie's boots.

Souey had announced he was to take a back seat from playing and that meant Ray Wilkins would be used more in the central midfield role – and that was right up his street. Ray was a great player with a fantastic range of passing, but he could also get stuck in when the need arose. He was an intelligent player, and I was surprised when Ron Atkinson labelled him 'The Crab', as if the only passes he could make were across the park, but Ray's recycling of the ball was first class. He could break up play well in the midfield and start moves off with 30- and 40-yard passes. His pass-completion rate, as they call it now, must have been in the high 90s because he was so accurate. I don't remember him giving the ball away too often. He was definitely one of my favourite players.

Souey introduced Sunday training sessions that season and quite a lot of the old-school players weren't too happy about it, but it was just something we had to accept. If you crossed Souey in those days you knew it wasn't going to end well so there was nothing to do bar get on with it. It certainly didn't bother me that much and while it's fairly common nowadays, it was like a bolt from the blue for some of the older guys. Sports science was in its formative days in the late-1980s and the guys practising it were of the opinion it was better to come in the day after a match for a light session rather than wait till the Monday.

But I'm sure we weren't too bothered about coming in for extra training on Sunday, 28 August – the day after we hammered Celtic 5-1 at Ibrox. Funnily enough, I actually remember quite a lot about that game. Apparently it is still Rangers's biggest win over Celtic in the modern era, and it's certainly a game I will never forget. The atmosphere that afternoon was something special, arguably the best I've ever played in. Before the game, Souey had given us our team talk, and then Walter went round a few players individually to offer some last-minute advice or instructions. Most of the planning took place on the training ground in the week leading up to the match, so everyone knew their jobs well in advance.

Running out of the tunnel at Ibrox that day was incredible: the noise was deafening. In fact, midway through the first half, Ally McCoist shouted something to me. He was less than ten metres away and I couldn't hear a word he was saying. He came closer and we still struggled to connect. It was mental. It was a beautiful afternoon and with the majority of the crowd on our side, we were right up for it. The pitch was in great condition and we couldn't wait to get started.

Celtic scored first, but we absolutely slaughtered them after that and were 5-1 up after an hour. But here's the thing, I've spoken to many, many Rangers supporters over the years and often they bring up that game, but usually the first questions are, 'Did the players take the foot off the gas after the fifth goal? Why didn't we keep going at them and rack up a record Old Firm score? We wanted you guys to score six, seven!' First and foremost the manager is only interested in winning the game. He wants to keep a bit of distance between the sides so that the points are safe, but I'm sure the last thing he wants is the players going gung-ho in search of loads of goals and leaving big gaps all over the pitch. It's all about being professional. As far as I'm concerned, getting ten goals would've been lovely, but more importantly we won the game with a bit to spare AND laid down a marker for the rest of the season. Even 30-odd years later I still get goosebumps when I recall the atmosphere at that game. It will stay with me forever.

It was a double triumph for me that day as I had been asked to keep tabs on the Celtic right-back, Chris Morris, who liked to get up and down the wing. I often read the Rangers News and in the following week's edition big Terry Butcher praised me for keeping Morris quiet for the majority of the game, while creating a few chances at the opposite end – and scoring the final goal – so I was chuffed to get the job done, not once but twice! Defending was never my forte but I always tried to cover that side of the game as well as I could.

One guy I really enjoyed playing on the same side of the park with was Stuart Munro; he was the perfect foil for me. We worked well together and if I needed a ball played long he would know that; his distribution was excellent. He was a cracking professional and a great team player. Quite often in the last third of the pitch, you don't need the full-back overlapping, as they tend to just bring more opponents with them, and Stuart was very good at knowing which situation called for which action. I preferred playing with Stuart as opposed to Jan Bartram. Particularly when games were tight, and I was looking for a bit of space, Bartram would be sprinting past and alongside him would be a couple of defenders. Stuart, on the other hand, was capable of cutting infield and taking defenders away.

It was probably my best-ever start to a season, but there was a problem brewing, because amidst the goals and skills out on the wing, I had picked up three bookings – and it was still only September. It wasn't like me to get involved in petty confrontations with opposing defenders, but I was letting myself get too upset by some of the challenges on me. It was difficult not to retaliate at times but I had to control myself better as I was no use to Rangers sitting in the stand and the last thing I wanted was to lose my place in the team through suspension. I never asked referees for special protection, but some of the challenges I had to put up with were way over the top.

My first European outing for Rangers was against Katowice at Ibrox. We were looking for a good lead to take to Poland for the second leg but we managed just a single goal – scored by yours truly, although that match is memorable for one of the most bizarre things I ever saw on a football pitch. The fact that the Poles were indulging in a little time-wasting wasn't a shock, but the way Bomber Brown dealt with it was. Not for the first time an opposing player went down clutching his leg when he had hardly been touched, and once again the referee waved the trainer on to the pitch. By all accounts it looked as though there wasn't much up with the lad, but the trainer was treating him as though he had been shot by a sniper. By this point Bomber had clearly had enough and he ran towards the player being treated and with one swing of the left boot (no, it's fine, he didn't kick the 'injured' player), the trainer's medical bag was heading for the running track. Picture it in slow motion. Bomber kicks the bag and all these medical implements and bandages are flying through the air. It was as comical as it was outrageous. The contents were scattered all over the track and the trainer was furious. Mind you, so was Bomber, and you didn't mess with him when his valve was overheating. The referee flashed the yellow card and Bomber was later suspended for two European matches by UEFA. Rangers were also fined for the incident. As it transpired, we won 4-2 in the away leg and eased through to the next round.

Sandwiched between the ties against Katowice was a trip to Edinburgh to play Hearts. We managed to win a tight game 2-1, but on a personal level, playing at Tynecastle was just something I never enjoyed. I really didn't like the place and I used to take a shedload of stick every time I went there. Thankfully, the hatred failed to reach the heights of my first visit, but when I eventually moved back down south that was one ground I was glad to see the back of. The terracing was so close to the pitch that you could almost hear every word, and thugs throwing objects didn't exactly have to be champion darts player Phil Taylor to be in with a good chance of hitting you.

It didn't help that I was often in direct opposition to a guy called Walter Kidd, who was uncompromising to say the least, so I would have this guy clattering me regularly and objects and abuse being hurled from the home support – so you can see why it wasn't exactly my favourite ground. When there are coins whizzing past your eyes it does get inside your head a bit. It crossed my mind a few times that I could be blinded by one of these thugs, but I always tried my best to push it to the back of my mind and try to get on with the game, although it wasn't easy.

Just a couple of months into the season, I was walking along a corridor at Ibrox when Walter Smith told me the gaffer wanted to see me. As you do, I instinctively started to wonder what I had done wrong, but when I walked into his office, he said, 'I think we need a wee bit of extra firepower up front and I have a guy in mind. What's your thoughts on Andy Gray? You played with him at Villa, do you think he could do a job for us?' My answer was 'Absolutely'. All Andy ever talked about when we were at Villa was Glasgow Rangers. He was a massive Rangers fan and I knew he would jump at the chance to move to Ibrox, but I was also sure he would prove a good signing. It was important not to base my answer purely on sentimentality. Souey said it would be a short-term move and thanked me for my input. A few days later, Andy signed for Rangers and when he walked into the dressing room for the first time he was like the cat who got the cream. Talk about broad smiles. I was delighted for him. We had a warm embrace and I welcomed him to Ibrox! Andy was a top professional and he knuckled down and worked extremely hard. And it paid off as he scored a few vital goals for us that season. While we were at Villa together, he was the first person to talk to me about moving to Glasgow and tell me just how big Rangers were. The man was my hero as a kid and it's ironic that we ended up at Rangers together.

I could finally understand why he had kept banging on about the club all the time!

Andy had an instant impact when we played Hearts in the Skol Cup semi-finals at Hampden and he made one of my two goals. He didn't give defenders a moment's peace and created mayhem in the opposition box that invariably led to chances for our strikers. That was one game I thoroughly enjoyed and we fully deserved our 3-0 victory. I've always been quite level-headed as a player and believe that if you take the plaudits thrown your way after a successful performance, then you have to suck up the criticism if you've had a stinker. Mind you, I wasn't prepared for a comment attributed to Terry Butcher in one of the papers after the Hearts game. 'Is there anything Mark Walters can't do? After his part in our two wins in five days against Hearts, it wouldn't surprise me if he sprouted wings and started flying.' Terry definitely had a way with words.

But everything wasn't a bed of roses. I missed an absolute sitter in a match against Dundee and paid a heavy price the following week in training. It also meant I had to wear the dreaded yellow T-shirt, the domain of that week's worst trainer – or for someone who might have committed the sin of missing an 'unmissable' sitter. If memory serves me right, I think I wore it quite a lot!

In October that season, I was enjoying the freer role given to me by the gaffer and I was top scorer in the Premier League and the Skol Cup. I thought, 'Who needs to play through the middle?' I felt as though everything was coming together nicely – and it was great not to be stuck out on the wing all the time, as you rely heavily on others bringing you into play when you're out there.

One option I'd always had in front of goal was the lob. It was a kind of go-to option when I had the ball at my feet and the goalkeeper was off his line. In fairness to the keeper, he would be coming out to narrow the angles, but I knew that if I could catch it right I had a good chance of getting it on target, and if he was far enough off his line. If I'm honest, I probably did it a bit too much, but what the heck, we were there to entertain. Whenever I scored from one, the media always heaped praise on me, but the gaffer kept on at us not to listen to praise via the media, as we had to remain focussed and not become complacent. And he was 100 per cent right because once you start to believe the hype it's so easy to take your eye off the ball. At the time we were beating a lot of teams with ease and it would've been easy for the guys to get a little too relaxed, but Souey and Walter always ensured our feet were firmly planted on the ground.

Sadly, one match I will never forget was a 2-1 defeat at Pittodrie. More significantly, it was the game in which Ian Durrant suffered a sickening injury due to a horrendous challenge by Neil Simpson. It was one of the dirtiest matches I had ever played in. Durranty aside, I recall Ally McCoist having stitches inserted in a head wound, and Bomber suffering a pretty bad leg injury, which also required stitches. I was also injured in that game and failed to make it out after the break, but that paled into insignificance as far as Durranty was concerned. And here's the thing; a few weeks after the game, I was told Simpson indirectly blamed ME for the incident! He blamed me for him losing his cool and challenging Durranty the way he did. Unbelievable. I think it was the late Neale Cooper who had the misfortune to impart that ridiculous information. In Simpson's mind, I had challenged him clumsily in the lead-up to Durranty receiving the injury that almost ended his career. I couldn't believe it when I was told that. I know I couldn't tackle to save my life, but surely it's stretching it a bit to lay the blame for the challenge at someone else's door. As far as I'm concerned it was a disgraceful tackle and perhaps he was just trying to find any excuse to avoid blaming himself.

After that game, the whole dynamics of the Rangers v Aberdeen fixture seemed to change. There was a hell of a lot of hostility on the pitch and in the stands. As far as I'm led to believe, the matches weren't ever like that prior to that day in 1988, but they were certainly like that afterwards, and beating them became just as important to a lot of Rangers folk as beating Celtic. It was a pity because our matches against the Dons had always been tough, and most players enjoy that. Stewart McKimmie was one of the hardest full-backs I came up against in the Premier League, and they also had the likes of Willie Miller and Alex McLeish in their side at that time, so it was sad to see so much nastiness creep into the fixture.

When we played Katowice away in the second leg, and lost a goal in the first few minutes, I thought we were in for a tough evening, but that was the night I realised the level of character that the Rangers team possessed. When you have guys like Terry Butcher alongside you, you are never beaten. He didn't know the meaning of the word defeat. And the likes of Bomber would put his head where you wouldn't dare put your feet. There were many more. Most of the credit for that has to go to the manager, because not only did he assemble a squad full of very good players but he also ensured the players he brought in were made of the right stuff.

I was thoroughly enjoying my football in Scotland, although that didn't stop a seemingly never-ending line of high-profile pundits south of the border queuing up to have a pop at the

English players at Ibrox. I remember the former Spurs and England international Jimmy Greaves having a real go at me in *Shoot*, which was a popular UK-wide football magazine in those days. He reckoned I had done my chances of playing for England more harm than good by signing for Rangers, adding that Terry Butcher, Chris Woods and Gary Stevens had all been well established in the England squad before heading north.

To be honest, I didn't see an awful lot of logic in his remarks as I had left a team in the English Second Division to come to one of the biggest clubs in the world, and I was playing at the highest level of European football and in front of almost 50,000 every other week. Surely that was enough to give me the type of profile that Jimmy felt I needed to attract the attention of the England manager Bobby Robson. If it wasn't, then I didn't know what would. At the time, Jimmy was good value as a TV presenter but he was no authority on Scottish football. Perhaps if he had bothered to come up and watch a few games at Ibrox he might have changed his views.

We also had the likes of Gordon Banks, Malcolm Macdonald and Malcolm Allison having a go at our English lads, despite having limited knowledge of the Scottish game, so when Souey advised Banks to shut his mouth I admit I did have a laugh about it.

Just days after Greaves had offered his unwanted opinion, I was reminded of exactly why I had come to Scotland in the first place. We were playing Aberdeen at Hampden in the Skol Cup Final and the place was packed to the rafters. The atmosphere was electric and it was a great game to play in. It reminded me of everything I stood to lose if I headed back to England to take my chances of chasing an England shirt. That was never going to happen.

While at school you dream of playing in cup finals at a national stadium and this one didn't disappoint. It was a tense match but we deserved to win and had a great time celebrating our victory that night. The camaraderie we had at Rangers was second to none and it was almost worth a goal of a start every time we walked out on to the pitch. It was so different to the situation I was in when my days at Villa were drawing to a close. Then, things weren't going so well for us on the pitch and little cliques were starting to form in the dressing room. I tended not to get involved in any of them but it wasn't great listening to all the bickering and dressing-room politics which inevitably rear their ugly head as a result. You knew that if anyone played badly they would be getting slaughtered behind their back, which was horrible. Team spirit comes initially from winning games, and that is transferred into the dressing room and everything is rosy. It definitely helps if you can get on with your team-mates because you each share a common goal.

That was certainly the way it was in the Skol Cup Final, as it was our collective strength which helped us prevail. Oh, and there was the individual prize awaiting me after the match. Because I had scored five goals in that year's competition – the same number as Hearts striker Iain Ferguson – I received vouchers to the tune of £1,000 and put them towards a fantastic holiday in the United States at the end of the season. The Skol Cup was a competition I always seemed to do particularly well in, and in my first full season I scored in every round bar the final.

The week after the cup final I was lucky enough to pick up another award, this time as winner of the B&Q-sponsored Skills Award competition for October. My reward was £1,000 worth of vouchers for the DIY store. I had shelves and garden furniture coming out of my ears!

Something I struggled to understand was having to play that cup final just three days after a tough European match against Cologne, away from home. Don't get me wrong, on the day we probably deserved to lose to the Germans, but the 2-0 deficit left us with a mountain to climb, and we had three tough league matches to play prior to the second leg. It might have been nice for the Scottish league fixture schedulers to give us a little break and actually help us in our quest to go as far in the competition as possible, perhaps by moving games a few days here or there, but to my knowledge Rangers have seldom had any help from the powers-that-be, unlike in other countries where the football authorities seem only too pleased to help out their European representatives. Surely a good run in Europe reflects well on that particular association, but it was as if the authorities didn't care how far Rangers got in the competition. A case in point was 2008, when Rangers were asked to play a stupid amount of games on route to the UEFA Cup Final in Manchester. Did they get any help in shifting fixtures? No, as the authorities apparently didn't want to set a precedent. Why not? Surely the best time to set a precedent is when you're trying to help out a member club.

Anyway, that first leg in Cologne in the Müngersdorf was one of my toughest ever matches. I was up against Jürgen Kohler and, boy, was that guy a player. He was a tough defender, had great pace and stamina and everywhere I went he was my shadow. I don't think I got a kick of the ball that night. When I nipped into the loo at half-time, I half expected him to be standing next to me!

We then lost at Celtic Park before drawing 1-1 with Cologne at Ibrox, which meant we exited Europe, and when I heard Bobby Robson had watched the Euro tie, that was it for me.

We also lost at Tynecastle, and I was sent off, and I remember Walter Smith saying to me after the game, 'Mark, why do you try and tackle folk? You're no good at it. Just leave the tackling to the others.' And he was right, I was terrible at it. But I still maintain that both the challenge I was booked for and the one that brought the red card did not deserve the punishment given out. I learned more from that one game than any other during my time in Scottish football. I knew that if I got stick from any defender, I simply couldn't afford to retaliate in any way and would have to hope that I would be protected by the officials. There were certain places where you could do certain things and I reckon had that game been played at Ibrox, I would not have been sent off.

So, it was a miserable spell after the Skol Cup Final but the gaffer responded by giving us all a fortnight off in the lead-up to Christmas, which meant I could head back down to Birmingham to recharge the batteries, which was sorely needed. Souey was a fair manager, and if you did the business for him he stayed off your back. Getting a fortnight off at that stage of the season was virtually unheard of but he no doubt realised we'd had a lot of matches and decided a wee break would help in the long run.

During the break, I got a call from a journalist to say I'd made it into *World Soccer* magazine's top 20 players in the globe. I was fair chuffed as the only other Englishman in there was John Barnes. I was number 19 and when you consider the top three consisted of Marco van Basten, Ruud Gullit and Frank Rijkaard, with Maradona sixth, I was in exalted company. It was a nice way to end the year.

I enjoyed the time off and reported back from the break fit and well and ready for the second half of the season. First up was a home match against Celtic and, while it would've been nice to emulate our incredible 5-1 success from earlier in the campaign, we weren't in the slightest bit bothered that we came up just a little bit short.

Once again, Celtic were ahead in the first couple of minutes, but we didn't panic and won the game with relative ease. I'm convinced the fortnight off meant our legs were fresher. I was delighted to score twice in a 4-1 win and it put us seven points clear of Celtic. It was an emphatic victory. The two goals put me on to 13 for the season and I was relishing being one of the main guys up front, along with Kevin Drinkell. Ally McCoist was still injured so it was ideal that a couple of us were able to chip in with goals. It also said a lot for our strength in depth that we had come through a spate of injuries and emerged the other side still well clear at the top of the league.

We continued our great start to 1989 by winning at Pittodrie, with Derek Ferguson getting both our goals. Derek was an excellent player but his situation wasn't helped by the fact that he didn't appear to get on with Souey. They seemed to clash an awful lot, and he didn't help himself by getting into a bit of trouble off the park as well. When you're at a club the size of Rangers you can't be bringing that kind of unwanted attention upon yourself or the club. I loved the other side of Derek, though, as he had the ability to make you laugh in an instant, and even when we go away with the Rangers Legends nowadays he still has that infectious, bubbly personality that I love. The good thing was that Derek's young brother Barry seemed to learn from his mistakes.

During one of the first pre-season training camps in Tuscany, Trevor Francis was lying back reading a copy of the newspaper *La Gazzetta dello Sport* when Derek asked if he could read it after him. Trevor was multi-lingual, and said to Derek that it was in Italian and, jokingly added, 'You can hardly read English.' So we had a bit of banter about it and were lazing around the pool when this smell of smoke started to waft up my nose. I looked up and Derek had set Trevor's paper on fire with a cigarette lighter! Trevor wasn't best pleased.

Following the win over Aberdeen – even though it was only January – we felt we were good enough to win the league. The confidence you take from beating your main rivals is immense. After that we went down to play Gretna in a charity match for the victims of the Lockerbie disaster, which was something that touched everyone in the country; it was good to be able to help out in a small way.

I loved my football and the only thing that came close was sleeping, so it was no surprise that I would miss the alarm going off now and again. I lived in Bothwell close to Richard Gough and Ray Wilkins and we would take turns at picking each other up. When it was my turn with the car they would remind me about being on time, because if we were late for training we used to get fined. I did get a ticking off from Walter on the odd occasion but by and large my timekeeping was pretty good. I can understand why it would be frustrating for the management if players were walking in late, and at different times, so Souey and Walter were pretty strict about things like timekeeping.

I did a photoshoot at Ibrox that season which took me straight back to my childhood. A couple of guys who represented Scotland, and were champions at Subbuteo, the table football game, popped in to publicise an international match they were taking part in. Subbuteo was a game I loved when I was a kid and I remember heading out on to the track at Ibrox for the shoot and a pitch being set up. The moment we started playing all the memories came flooding back. Naturally, I always preferred the real thing, but during the dark nights, or when the weather outside wasn't conducive to playing football in the street, my mates and I would set up the Subbuteo and play for hours. We used to have competitions – like the World Cup and European Cup – and it was great fun. That day at Ibrox was brilliant and brought back lots of great memories for me.

Near the end of the season, I was thrilled when Nigel Benn visited Ibrox while he was in town for a big fight. I've always been a massive boxing fan so I was delighted to meet him. While I was at Liverpool I went to Nigel Benn's fight against Chris Eubank and it was a great night. A half-brother on my father's side, Pele Reid, was a professional boxer so I've always had a big interest in the sport. In fact, he was no ordinary boxer and is one of only two fighters to have knocked out the great Ukrainian Vitali Klitschko in a kick-boxing match, before both guys switched to conventional boxing. Obviously my father got his way when naming my half-brother, a battle he had lost to my mother when attempting to call me Santos! When Pele KO'd Klitschko – who is now the Mayor of Kiev – he wasn't supposed to. They met in the European Championships in Bulgaria in 1992, but it was all about points-scoring and not being hit. When he knocked Klitschko out, they were going to disqualify Pele, but in the end they gave him a break because the move had been so clean. When he moved into boxing, he had a succession of quick knockouts, and the world was at his feet. But a loss to Julius Francis, in a British and Commonwealth title fight, set him back. We are all still very proud of what he achieved, though.

Not long after that, Rangers signed Mel Sterland, who was a bit of a character. I had played against Mel a few times in

England but when he came up to Ibrox – even though he wasn't with us that long – he did us a turn. He had a good sense of humour, although he didn't see the funny side of things at training one day. We were in the middle of a session when Souey called a halt. Everyone was wondering what was wrong, when the gaffer turned and said to Mel, 'I didn't pay £800,000 for you and expect to have to teach you how to trap a ball.' I did laugh but it must have been awful for Mel, and he didn't take it at all well, which is completely understandable.

On April Fools' Day 1989, the joke certainly wasn't on us when we went to Celtic Park for what was to all intents and purposes a league decider, perhaps not in mathematical terms but certainly psychologically. We knew that if we pulled off our first win in nine years at the home of our rivals then not a lot could stop us. There were 60,000 in attendance and we went there with confidence. By then, I was enjoying Old Firm games because you knew you would get a bit of space to play as Celtic were one of the few teams in the league that wouldn't just sit in and defend against us. That game in particular was one of my favourites at Parkhead, not just because we won 2-1, but because I turned in a top performance, which wasn't always the case in games like that. Sure, you always tried to make an impact, and stamp your authority on the game, but there were so many top players on show that it wasn't always possible.

At that point, Ally McCoist was back playing and we were tied on 16 league goals apiece, just one behind Celtic striker Frank McAvennie. I was delighted with the number I had scored, but it was nothing compared to the feeling I had a few weeks later when we clinched the league title with a superb 4-0 win over Hearts. Mel Sterland and Kevin Drinkell scored two apiece, while our old pals Celtic and Aberdeen fought out a goalless draw up at Pittodrie. To win the league at Ibrox was extra special. It was my first league title and at that moment I realised I had been right to move on from Villa, despite many at the club thinking it was a mistake. In those days it was also financially beneficial to win things. The basic wages weren't anywhere near the salaries of today and it was through win bonuses and winning trophies that you were able to make some extra cash.

That afternoon, we knew a win against Hearts, and the right result at Pittodrie, would see us crowned champions. But at Rangers there is a mindset that means you go into every single game thinking you can win. And when we did it was just the beginning of a fantastic night as we partied into the early hours. I was a league champion and it felt just as special as I had always imagined it would. In fact, after we had been presented with the league trophy on the pitch, and completed an incredible lap of honour to share the moment with our great supporters, I just flopped on to the bench when we got back into the dressing room. I was mentally drained. I sat there, with my head in my hands, and thought about what I had just achieved. It was a powerful moment. Winning the championship was the greatest thing that had ever happened to me, and after getting a taste of it, I wanted more. I was convinced it would be ten times harder to defend it the following season, but that was already the goal. I was like a junkie, and winning the next one became my *raison d'être*.

We thoroughly deserved to be champions and in the end we had won it by a comfortable margin. Some of the results we got at crucial stages of the season knocked the stuffing out of our opponents, and we were able to go to difficult grounds and win when it mattered most – and that was the mark of true champions.

Sadly the season would end on a low note as we lost the Scottish Cup Final to Celtic. There was just a single goal in it but I'll never forget the feeling. It was painful. In fact, after the presentation, I think Souey was so disappointed he tossed his medal away. We were sitting in the dressing room after the game and everyone was so downhearted. Souey stood up and said, 'Just remember this feeling. It's the worst in the world and I want you all to dredge it back up when the new season starts.' He also announced he had something special in store for us, but that we would have to wait a little longer to find out what it was. We were curious.

To miss out on the treble was a terrible feeling. It's something which isn't done too often, and I think Souey felt it more than most as he would have gone down in history as one of the very few managers to have achieved such a feat. I know I was gutted as were the rest of the players. That said, winning a title is always more satisfying than winning a cup.

But on a personal level, the season ended well for me as I won a whole raft of supporters' clubs player of the year awards, which was something I always took seriously, as it was like confirmation from the most important people that you had played consistently well over the whole season. It is lovely to be appreciated by the guys who watch you week in, week out and I ended up with loads of trophies. Of course you are never going to please all the supporters but knowing the vast majority were behind me was a great feeling. Let's be honest, we all prefer to be liked.

I was presented with a clock in the shape of the African continent by the Johannesburg Rangers Supporters Club and I loved it. In fact, I used it right up until it finally conked out, and I thought it might be a wee bit cheeky to send it back to get it repaired. Seriously, though, it proved the appeal of Rangers was truly worldwide. It's incredible to think Rangers supporters' clubs exist in every corner of the globe.

The way I was treated during my time at Ibrox is one of the reasons I still look out for the Rangers score every weekend. It might be three decades since I last played for the Gers but the affinity I have with the club will be there till the day I die. Everyone knows I grew up a Villa fan, but that doesn't stop me loving Rangers. I love everything about the club. When I played for Villa, and things weren't going well, we used to get slaughtered by the crowd, especially the season we got relegated. In fact, I remember playing in one game at Villa Park where we were 4-0 up and the crowd were still getting on our backs; it was ridiculous. There seemed to be a big difference between home and away games, as we didn't receive as much stick on our travels. Perhaps I played for Villa at the wrong time, as the start of the 1980s was littered with unprecedented success, winning the league, European Cup and Super Cup – and it was always going to be downhill from there.

I ended up with 17 goals from competitive fixtures in my first full season at Rangers, which I was happy with. I had been handed a free role for much of the season, which helped, although I can be quite hard on myself and it would've been nice to get 20. My best ever total for Villa in a season was 14, so to better that was pleasing. Something else I enjoyed was scoring four goals against Celtic in four league games. I think that proved I was a big-game player, and it's no secret I enjoyed Old Firm games the most. For some reason, they always seemed to bring out the best in me. If scoring goals gave me a big thrill, it was ten times better to see the ball hit the back of the Celtic net.

When the season finished the club paid for us to go on a short break to Israel. We were based in Tel Aviv, which is a beautiful city. It was my first time in Israel and I thoroughly enjoyed it. We had a couple of great nights out, although it usually ended up in us watching a match or two. While there, we watched the English First Division decider between Liverpool and Arsenal. The match had been put back a month to after the FA Cup Final out of respect for those who had tragically lost their lives in the Hillsborough disaster. The Gunners had to win by two clear goals to win the championship and they did just that, with Michael Thomas scoring the vital goal with just seconds left. We were all on the edge of our seats watching the match in Israel, while back in the UK I believe a record TV audience tuned in. I remember John Barnes getting the ball out on the wing in the dying moments, and instead of hanging on to it and wasting precious seconds, he lost it to Kevin Richardson and Arsenal mounted their final – but ultimately successful – attack, and Michael scored one of the most dramatic goals ever seen. Ironically, he would become a team-mate of mine at Anfield a couple of years later.

On returning to the UK, we learned that Souey had again been busy in the transfer market, and that Trevor Steven would be joining us from Everton. He was a fantastic player who would make us even stronger. Our rivals must've shaken their collective heads in dismay at the quality of player we were attracting to Ibrox – and Trevor was in the top bracket. He had a great engine and scored goals, and his range of passing was first class. It was the perfect news to end the season.

Chapter Ten

A Few Ibrox Icons

WHEN I signed for Rangers I didn't just join an incredibly successful club, I was also fortunate enough to become part of a very special dressing room. It's a well-known fact in football that a happy dressing room tends to be a successful one. I've been part of both, and I know which one I prefer. At every club in the UK you will encounter many different types of characters. We had that at Rangers, and some amazing characters too. Each region of the country has its own accent, sense of humour and character traits, but I doubt there is a double act anything like the one I met in the home dressing room at Ibrox. Two guys who would keep everyone going with their impersonations and gags; but while they were comedians off the park, they were deadly serious on it. I had never known a duo like Ally McCoist and Ian Durrant.

Durranty was a couple of years younger than me, probably about 20 or 21 when I arrived at Ibrox, but he was already a permanent fixture in the first-team squad. He loved a joke or two and was always quick with a gag, but what a player he was. From what I witnessed of Ian, I reckon he could have been world class. He was one of the finest box-to-box players around, and he had a real eye for a goal as well. He was the complete player. The injury (in the match against Aberdeen) came at the wrong time for him (not that there is ever a right time for that type of injury!) as he was surely destined for great things. Rangers were a massive club, but if he'd wanted, he could've played for any of the richest teams in Europe, in my opinion. I'd played alongside, and against, players who were real box-to-box guys, but Ian had a couple of the most vital components most of them lacked, and that was his ability to remain composed in the most difficult of situations – and then stick the ball in the back of the net. His ability to chip in with 10 or 15 goals a season made him invaluable. And he also had the knack of scoring in big games. He was, in my eyes, a David Platt type of player, although I reckon he was much better than David, and you see what he achieved in the game. Coincidentally, Platt's old club Sampdoria were reportedly interested in signing Durranty, and the fee quoted was around £1m. A new rule had just been introduced in Italy which allowed clubs to sign three foreigners from the beginning of season 1989/90, but thankfully Graeme Souness was having none of it. I had a lot of time for Durranty and I was delighted when he eventually made a full comeback from that horrific injury and went on to enjoy many more years doing the thing he loved most, because he really had been to hell and back.

The other half of the double act was the man supporters dubbed Super Ally, although we had our own nickname for him in the dressing room. Ally was something else. If ever a moniker represented someone perfectly then Golden Bollocks was made for Ally McCoist. While we would all be working hard to make something happen, or trying to make intelligent runs to shake off markers, the ball would simply fall at Ally's feet six yards from goal with the keeper lying on his backside. He just had that unbelievable knack of being in the right place at the right time. In all seriousness, though, there was a hell of a lot more to his game. For starters, it doesn't surprise me one bit that he is Rangers's all-time top goal-scorer, because as well as having the gift of knowing the penalty box like the back of his hand, he was one of the best finishers I ever played alongside, and he was an absolute pleasure to play with. He was also a very loyal servant to Rangers. Oh, and he took the penalties, which no doubt helped the Ally tally!

Mind you, I don't care what level you're playing at or what league you play in, to score a goal is one of the hardest things in football, and for Ally to score the number he did for Rangers – which I believe is around the 400 mark – is an incredible feat. There might have been a degree of luck attached to a few of his strikes but he was a gifted player and knew exactly where the goal was. I remember Souey brought in Mo Johnston and that saw Coisty spend quite a bit of time on the bench, but if one of them was going to tough it out and remain at Rangers for many more years it was always going to be Coisty, so it meant he had to be patient, await his chance and that's exactly how it all played out, because Ally was a Rangers man through and through. If you were to ask me who was the better footballer between the pair then I would probably have to agree with Graeme Souness and say Mo, but it's mighty close. They were different types of players but Mo scored a lot of goals as well and was perhaps a better all-round footballer, so I think he just edges it. That said, they were both valuable footballers. It's probably a bit like asking a parent to name their favourite child. There was an edge to

Mo's game, and he probably had more about him than Ally, but Ally's goals tell their own story.

Ally was linked with Pisa during my first season at Rangers and I'm sure that had he gone to Italy he would have been a big success and scored goals as he was a natural in the penalty box. He would've performed well anywhere, but I'm sure he did the best thing by staying at Ibrox because Pisa – who I almost joined myself – weren't a club who were regularly up there challenging for honours and Ally was a guy who thrived on winning trophies.

I got to know Ally really well while I was at Rangers and he was a really funny lad. You couldn't help but be attracted to his infectious personality. Let's be honest, you aren't loved by everyone, as Ally was, if you're a fake, but he had a heart of gold and did a lot of things for people that others didn't see. I read somewhere that he regularly visited a former employee of Rangers who was in a care home; that's him all over. He is a lovely guy who does things for people as a matter of course, not for personal reward.

His sense of humour was something else and when he and Durranty were on form there was no better duo in the country. But Ally the footballer was a different guy altogether. He was channelled and focussed and mentally very strong. He was also physically a very tough guy. Let's be honest, there are some uncompromising defenders around and Ally would never have survived, let alone thrived, if he hadn't been up to the task. He was able to look after himself. Rangers and Ally were a marriage made in heaven.

During a 23-year career in the seniors I played alongside some very talented guys, but one of the best has to be Davie Cooper, he was such an incredible talent. I was sort of disappointed that I was supposedly brought to the club as his replacement, as Coop was irreplaceable. Of the few players I knew about in Scotland before I arrived, he was the one I admired most. I had seen the goal he scored against Celtic in the Drybrough Cup Final when he played keepy-uppy in the opposition box, knocking it over a few defenders before scoring. It was a sensational goal, and the first time I saw it on YouTube I just sat there staring in admiration at the screen. Coop was definitely my type of player.

Before training every morning we used to play head tennis in the warm-up area under the enclosure and because I was two-footed I was always quite confident of winning, but I don't think I ever got the better of Coop. Because he was predominantly left-footed, I would stick everything to his right side but he was so good at angling his body in an instant that he would inevitably return everything with his left peg. He used to beat me easily. He was a genius with the ball, and at times you would think it was tied to his feet with a piece of string. His close control was something to behold, and what made it so difficult for defenders to get the ball off him was a combination of skill, strength and balance.

His nickname was Albert Tatlock (the grumpy character from Coronation Street), because if you didn't know him well you would've thought he was a miserable bugger, but he had this incredibly dry sense of humour and he was a really funny guy at times. If the truth be told, I was in awe of Davie Cooper. I used to study the way he trained and played, because he could do things with the ball that others could only dream of. He was definitely one of my all-time favourite players.

I wasn't surprised to see him enjoy further success when he left Rangers. It wasn't all about speed with Coop, he had such a deft touch and could place the ball on a sixpence, plus he could score the odd goal or two, so he was always going to play on. I would have been surprised if he hadn't. I think he was about 38 when he eventually quit. When he passed away I was in tears; it was so sad and a terrible shock. He was a great player but I also really liked him as a person. He was a very good human being.

Coop was definitely in his twilight years when he left Ibrox, but one player who should have been in his prime when he moved on was Graham Roberts. When Graham had his well-publicised fall-out with Graeme Souness I was really sorry to see him go, but he got a decent move to Chelsea in a deal worth £475,000 and he was a big loss for us. Graham was a tough, uncompromising defender and he certainly left an impression on the Rangers supporters, who absolutely loved him. I'll never forget the closing stages of my Old Firm debut, when he absolutely smashed a Celtic player and I was thinking, 'Jesus Christ, that was some challenge!' When the referee produced the yellow card I was relieved, as I was convinced he was off the park, but I suppose it was back in the days when that sort of challenge was pretty much acceptable. Heaven knows I was on the receiving end of quite a few. But Graham was an intelligent defender. He knew when to smash people, and when not to. He wasn't stupid. When he was walking a red-card tightrope he would dumb down his challenges.

As a person, though, he had some great morals, and stuck up for me many times when we were at Rangers. As I've previously said, I had come in for a fair bit of stick when I first arrived in Scotland and Graham was always the first to defend me. I loved having him in my corner, but far from being my guardian angel, I also really liked him as a person; that's why I was sad to see him leave, prematurely in my opinion, because he still had so much to offer the club.

Another guy I got on really well with at Rangers was Stuart Munro. I hadn't known Stuart before I went to Ibrox but we hit it off almost instantly. We socialised a lot together and our wives became good friends. We would go out for dinner quite often and Stuart was a good guy to sit and chat to – and it wasn't always about football. He had many worthwhile views on a whole range of subjects.

We had such a good relationship off the park, and no doubt that helped on it as well. Wherever I played, I always tried to get on with everyone around me. Life is far too short to make enemies.

Chapter 11

Watch Out, Mo's About!

REMEMBER the 'something special' that Souey had in store for us? Well, it turned out to be one of the most controversial signings in the history of Rangers Football Club, although in a strange sort of way it relieved the pressure on me. No one will ever forget that press conference, when the door between the Blue Room and the manager's office opened and in walked a sheepish-looking Mo (the only time I ever saw him look sheepish!) and Souey. The press sat there open-mouthed ... and so it began.

I was delighted with the signing because I remembered him from his days with Watford and he was an excellent player. He caused English defences a whole raft of problems with his busy style and eye for goal and I was looking forward to teaming up with him. I know the signing caused problems with some of our supporters because of his religion, but that was something which had never been an issue with me.

Mo was a bubbly guy and he was sure to improve our squad and that was the only way I looked at it. That said, I understood how some people felt about the signing, because the club was apparently breaking with years of tradition. I used to laugh when guys like Ian Ferguson were talking about Mo, because Ian was obviously a traditional Rangers man, but while Mo's personality could be called into question, as he did some silly things off the field, he couldn't be questioned for his abilities as a player. I remember Ian slaughtering him on a number of occasions at training. Was it banter? I would like to think so but only Ian would be able to answer that.

Even though Johnston and McCoist were more often than not vying for the one position, I didn't notice any nastiness creeping in on behalf of the one who might find himself benched. If Ally had to move over a little, he was fantastic about it. No backstabbing or anything as a result. In many respects I think it improved Ally as a player because when he did get the nod, he usually responded by scoring a goal or two. Competition for places is easily the best motivator for any footballer. Very few can play well week in, week out when they have no one else vying for their jersey.

The signing of Mo was massive for a few reasons. First of all, it came hot on the heels of Trevor Steven moving to the club and once again Souey had made a quality addition to the squad. It made us a lot stronger. And not long before he put pen to paper for Rangers, I saw him paraded in a Celtic top – so to usurp our biggest rivals in the signing of a talented player was massive in terms of putting one over on Celtic before a ball had even been kicked.

But let's say Mo had signed at the same time as me, back in December 1987, then I would have been none the wiser about the wider implications of Rangers signing a high-profile Catholic. It was only because I had been up in Scotland for a year and a half that I realised the full implications of the signing. Rangers are traditionally a Protestant club and these values were still particularly strong in the 1980s. Added to that, Johnston had been public enemy number one for Rangers fans on many occasions and I could see how it might turn out to be a really contentious signing. A lot of our supporters weren't happy but I'm sure Souey's only interest was in making sure we were as strong as possible, and Mo was a smashing player as well as a proven goalscorer.

Thankfully we did manage to lighten it up a little in the dressing room and one of the first times I spoke to him I thanked him very much for taking the pressure off the black guy, which we had a good laugh about. I was taking the piss but it was ironic that his signing meant the main focus was no longer on the first black player to play in the Premier League. Mo was a friend for life for cutting me a bit of slack!

When I spoke to Graham Taylor about Mo, he insisted we were getting one of the best finishers in the game. Graham had Mo at Watford for just over a season and told me he would let him do his own thing in training as he was such a fit guy. Graham spoke really highly of him and I know he would like to have had him at Vicarage Road a lot longer than he did.

Mo had his problems off the field but he did the business where it mattered most, and that was on the park for Rangers. I remember one year we went out for our Christmas party but we had to be in at 10am next morning for training. We all chucked it in the early hours, but not Mo. He went on a wee bit longer and was still the best of the bunch during the shuttle runs the next morning – or the same morning. We were all dying of alcohol poisoning and Mo was way out in front. He was super fit.

Whatever our supporters thought of him as a person, you couldn't deny that his work ethic on the pitch was phenomenal.

He would run all day for the team. Mind you, he probably had to work that bit harder than the rest if he was to be accepted by some folk. Anyway, we had our training camp in Italy to 'look forward to' and while it was a hard slog, it was a necessary evil and something we needed to help get us up to an acceptable level of fitness, as we had a long season ahead. We also had a bit of free time, which was usually spent relaxing as there weren't an awful lot of 'sightseeing' opportunities in the Tuscan mountains! Personally, I loved being fit. For me, there is no better feeling in the world than when you've just finished a hard training session. Whether that's the release of endorphins or not, I don't know, but you feel fantastic. It's such a buzz.

Going to Il Ciocco was probably the best thing for Mo, as it got him away from the spotlight of Glasgow, the press scrutiny and everything else that goes with living in a goldfish bowl. There were a few guys in the squad he didn't know, like myself, so it was a good time to bond. I didn't really socialise with him so something like the trip to Italy was the best way to get to know him. He seemed to have a good way about him and certainly wasn't aloof or anything.

The biggest problem I reckon he had was the two burly minders looking after him 24/7. I understand why he had them, but if someone is giving you a bit of stick then you just have to walk away from it, and having a couple of muscular guys by your side is only going to bring more unwanted attention. There always seemed to be a circus surrounding Mo but he had a good relationship with the other players and I suppose if he was doing the business on the park there wasn't an awful lot anyone could complain about.

One of his first outings on home soil was a friendly match at Airdrie's Broomfield Park, and as usual it was packed out with Rangers fans – despite it being just a pre-season challenge match. Inevitably there were sections of the crowd giving him a bit of stick, but I don't remember him reacting to it. He probably knew what was coming. I think it was inevitable that the first high-profile Catholic to join the club would provoke this type of reaction as people don't normally react well to change. But we got through it okay and knuckled down to begin the defence of our championship.

But given that our preparations were spot on, and the quality signings we had made, I was astounded at the poor start we had to the season. We only managed two wins from our first eight league games and at one point we were second bottom of the table. Great credit must go to Souey because he refused to panic. Don't get me wrong, he was far from delighted, and while not many teams could've recovered from such a terrible start, we were one that could. It's a long season and we had far too much quality to be languishing in the relegation zone for too long, and just to show how crazy Scottish football could be, when we beat Celtic 1-0 at Ibrox in the November – with Mo scoring the only goal – we went top of the league! That is another afternoon I will never forget.

Afterwards, Mo said it was the best he had ever felt after scoring any goal, and I bet that ruffled a few feathers on the other side of the city. Mind you, it looked like the game would end goalless that day. We only had two minutes left to play when Gary Stevens swept a ball into the box that was only half cleared. Mo was lurking on the edge of the area, took one touch and fired it low past Pat Bonner in the Celtic goal. I wasn't too far away from Mo when he scored the goal but I had to move quickly to join in the celebrations as he was off like a shot over to the corner of the Copland Road Stand and enclosure. An abiding memory is of Mo being booked for his celebration, but still flashing the biggest smile I had seen in a long time. I tell you something, it was a while before that smile was removed.

After the game a few of us went up to the players' lounge to relax and have a drink or two. Imagine my surprise when I was asked to pop along to the McPhail Suite to receive the man of the match award. Getting an award like that in an Old Firm game was special, and when I realised the award was to be presented by the chart-topping group Wet Wet Wet I was made up. I had a good chat with the guys and was astounded when Marti Pellow told me they always tried to schedule tours around the dates of our big matches. There is no truth in the rumour that I asked for a job in the band. I loved Wet Wet Wet but was more than happy with my job at Ibrox – especially after having just won an Old Firm game; singing in the shower was about as far as I went!

In the September, we were up against Bayern Munich in a European tie, but it didn't go too well. The first match was at Ibrox, and I scored from the penalty spot to put us ahead. But we then somehow contrived to concede three goals, and while we managed a 0-0 in Munich in the return leg, we had given ourselves Mount Everest to climb. They had some great players in their team, and took their chances clinically in the first leg, and that proved the difference between the sides.

We also lost the Skol Cup Final to Aberdeen at Hampden Park, and I was substituted in the second half with a suspected cartilage injury. I hadn't trained fully for a fortnight so it was a difficult time. Thankfully there was no lasting damage and it turned out it was only severe bruising to the knee.

Ray Wilkins had also decided to move on just before Christmas and that was a big blow not only to the team but to me personally. I had become good friends with Ray and we also lived close to one another. He was such a nice guy and we got on really well, but I think he felt the time was right to move into the coaching side of the game and he went down to Queens Park Rangers as a player/coach. He was also from London so I can understand why he left. I will always be indebted to Ray and his wife, as well as Trevor Francis and his wife, as they all looked after my fiancée and I when we first arrived in Glasgow. I couldn't have had two better guys looking out for me.

Souey moved swiftly to bring in Nigel Spackman, not as a direct replacement for Ray, but more to bolster the squad, and Nigel moved into a house not too far from me in Bothwell. Nigel had a dream start to his Ibrox career by scoring the only goal in a 1-0 win at Celtic Park just after the new year. What a way to endear yourself to your new supporters. I was delighted for him.

Just before that, we won 2-1 at Tynecastle, and it was yet another bruising encounter. I equalised but was then sent off – and received a three-match ban for my troubles. That really angered me as the shit I took at Tynecastle, and other grounds, was relentless at times. I always tried to behave in the correct manner by not complaining too much, as it's a tough game, but there had to be a balance between getting kicked and sometimes taking exception to it. And despite the way some things were painted, I honestly believe I never once committed a bad foul, yet that was my second red card at Tynecastle. I was only sent off a further three times in 19 years, which says it all.

I hated missing any game, such was my love of football, so I was pleased that I was never sent off for something stupid like dissent. It was bad enough getting my marching orders for a clumsy or mistimed challenge, but I didn't miss many games in my career through either suspension or injury. I think I ended up playing about 615 league games over a 21-year period and I'm proud of that stat more than anything else. When I look at the injuries suffered by team-mates like Gary Shaw and Ian Durrant, I realise how fortunate I was.

But I was still gutted at having to sit out three matches, even though I was back in time to play my part in a 2-0 win over Aberdeen, which meant we were four points clear of the chasing pack. The match against Aberdeen was a frustrating one, as we tried all we could to break them down but with no luck in front of goal. Thankfully I managed to break the deadlock that day by holding off a really strong challenge from Alex McLeish before shooting into the far corner of the net. Coisty relieved the pressure by bagging the clincher in the dying moments. It was always fantastic to beat Aberdeen but that one was even more significant because we'd beaten our three biggest rivals for the title within the space of a few weeks. That was massive. At the time, it looked as though Aberdeen were emerging as our main challengers. Celtic were going through a transitional period, I believe due to a lack of real investment, and so it was left to the Dons to try and keep up with us.

It was testimony to Souey and the players that we were able to keep our noses in front as we had also suffered quite a bit from injuries in the first half of the season. Because of that, I'd found myself moving around the park a little, and even ended up on the RIGHT wing at times. Playing wide on the left had definitely become my favourite position, but while we were carrying a few injuries I didn't mind filling in elsewhere. Luckily, I was also able to use my right foot to good effect, so it wasn't really a problem. The most important thing from my point of view was to play regularly and put a run together after having a spell on the sidelines through injury and suspension.

Part of the problem I could see was that the tackle from behind was legal in Scotland. Once outlawed, it would make my life a hell of a lot easier.

One visitor to Ibrox in March, of 1990 caused more than a little controversy and split the players down the middle – or maybe more like 70-30. The Conservative leader Margaret Thatcher arrived at the stadium – the first serving Prime Minister to visit Ibrox – and we were all wheeled out in our finest clothes to meet her. I remember quite a few of the players weren't that keen on her – me included – but the most vocal against the visit was Stuart Munro. He was furious to see her at Ibrox, and insisted politics shouldn't be mixed with sport. I've still got a photograph of Stuart looking the other way while she's talking to a couple of the dignitaries at the stadium. A lot of my team-mates used to call me the 'left-wing left-winger', as my roots were steeped in Labour. It would be easier to tell you who liked Thatcher in the Rangers team at that time. I know Souey and Terry were fans, but there weren't many more. Mind you, Bomber and Scott Nisbet seemed to also enjoy chatting to her. I wasn't massively into politics but I was brought up a Labour voter. In fact, the first time I went to vote, I remember my Mum coming into the polling booth and instructing me to put the X next to the Labour candidate. I said to her, 'Mum, I don't think you're supposed to be in here with me,' but I reckon she was just making sure I didn't vote Conservative!

But I was happy to once again be sporting blue when Celtic visited our place for a crucial league match in March. I managed another goal and we won 3-0, which meant it was the first time since the Premier League began that Celtic had failed to register at least one league win over us. More importantly, it moved us six points clear of Aberdeen with five games remaining. We were unstoppable that afternoon. We played some fantastic football and Celtic didn't have the answers. I scored first from the spot before Mo and Ally completed a miserable afternoon for Celtic. A second successive title was now ours to throw away.

That victory also meant that our next game, against Aberdeen, was a must-win for the Dons, and boy how it felt like it as we had both Gary Stevens and Ian Ferguson carried off in the first 20 minutes. There were tackles flying in everywhere, but the match ended goalless, which suited us far more than it did them. After the game, Souey took a pop at those who were stifling the flair players with their tough tackling, saying, 'We soon won't be able to attract quality players to Scotland if they continue to be physically abused in the Premier League.'

There is no doubt Rangers players were targeted more than the guys from other teams because we were by far and away the best side in Scotland and therefore saw more of the ball than the opposition. When that happens there is an increased chance that defenders will be lining up to leave the foot in and stop the crosses getting into the box. As a wide man you know that and the more you have the ball, naturally the more chance there is of you getting hurt. It was definitely a problem back in the day, but I felt Souey was bang on with what he said.

And if we needed a reminder of what can go wrong when some players are sticking the boot in, we were told that Ian Durrant was heading off to America in a bid to save his career. Durranty had already taken part in a few reserve games but the club doctor suggested he undertake revolutionary surgery in California to ensure that if and when he did make it back to the Premier League, he would be properly prepared. I remember reading, around that time, of how the Rangers doctor hadn't seen an injury like it in over 20 years in the profession, and how he reckoned it was more like the type you would see in a road traffic accident. All our thoughts were with Ian as he battled to save his career.

With three matches remaining we travelled up to Tannadice to face Dundee United, knowing that a win would give us the championship – and I ended up with quite an unusual assist that day. I took a very quick throw-in to Stuart Munro, and he wasted no time at all in getting it into the box, where Trevor Steven arrived bang on cue to bullet home a header. The support we had that day – just like every other away game we played – was phenomenal, and the victory was as much for them as it was for anyone at the club. It was fantastic to win a second title and it might just have been even sweeter than the first. Many folk reckon retaining your title is often more difficult than winning it the first time. That was especially so for us after such a bad start to the season. It meant another night of celebration, and we were able to let our hair down knowing the job was done. In the end we won the league by seven points, which I reckon was a fair reflection of the season. We had been through the mill but the club's 40th title was well deserved.

Personal recognition arrived when I won another raft of supporters' clubs player of the year trophies. Among these was an award by the Melbourne Rangers Supporters Club. I was a very proud recipient. I was also chosen by the Western Australia RSC as their top player and was given a diamond, which was the perfect way to end another fantastic season.

We might have been finished with football for a while, but Souey was still hard at work, was keen to let folk know we wouldn't be standing still and made another marquee signing. This time it was former AC Milan and Monaco striker Mark Hateley. Mark had built up a reputation as a good player, target man and goalscorer, so this was Souey sending out another message to the rest of Scottish football. As far as I was concerned, Mark Hateley was great for me because he had the ability to make an ordinary cross look special and he liked to attack everything that was put into the box. We now had McCoist, Johnston and Hateley ready to battle for the forward places, and also a couple of players vying for each position throughout the team. Souey was creating a really competitive squad, one that he hoped would be able to show its true value on the European front.

But football was put to the back of my mind as I had my own personal match of the day to look forward to. My fiancée Tracey Henry and I were set to tie the knot in her home town of Coventry. We were 15 when we first met and I was close to leaving school and joining Villa. My mate and I used to go ice skating in Birmingham city centre but, funnily enough, the night my mate met Tracey and her twin sister, I couldn't make it as I was training. The following night he told me he'd met these amazing girls and we arranged to go out on a double date the following week, so Tracey and her sister came up from Coventry and we went to the ice skating. I thoroughly enjoyed her company and we started going out regularly. When she left Stoke Park Comprehensive School, she got a job in a shoe shop and our relationship blossomed. Birmingham is just half an hour from Coventry so it was quite easy to maintain the relationship.

Our ceremony was beautiful and then we flew out to Florida on our honeymoon, where we were given the use of a villa in Boca Raton by Jack Moncrieff, a Rangers supporter I had met during my time at Ibrox. It was a fantastic gesture by Jack and we had a lovely time in Boca Raton, which is just an hour north of Miami, and surrounded by a wealth of beautiful beaches. It was bliss.

Chapter 12

Title Number Three: Don and Dusted!

A S HAD become the norm, we spent pre-season at Il Ciocco to get our fitness up to speed and shed a few excess pounds (if any needed shedding). Everything was going well until Mo Johnston had words with Souey and was sent home for 'acting in an unprofessional manner'. It's very difficult for something like that not to impact on the rest of the squad as one minute he's there, and the next he's on a plane home. Apparently he had spoken in an inappropriate way to the gaffer and in that situation, as I've said previously, there can only be one winner. When we arrived back from Italy I believe Mo apologised unreservedly to Souey and that was the end of the matter. If he hadn't, he would've been gone.

When I was at Villa, and Ron Saunders was the manager, nobody crossed him, and disciplinary matters were few and far between. Contrast that with Graham Turner's time in charge when things couldn't have been more different. Training wasn't great and the players perhaps weren't as fit as they could have been, and the knock-on effect was that performances and results suffered. That's probably when I realised just how important it is to have the right manager in charge. Because of dressing-room dynamics, and a couple of dozen players vying for air time, it requires a strong guy at the helm. There are lots of different personalities in a dressing room: egos, loud guys, quiet guys, and the gaffer has to be able to show his authority, which isn't easy, but once the manager has control of the dressing room – and the players know exactly who's in charge – the easier it is for him to get on with the task of blending these players into a winning team. There is always an internal battle to win before a manager tackles anything else.

Souey was in charge at Ibrox and we all knew that. Sure, there would be a dissenting voice every now and again, but it wouldn't take him long to douse the flames of an over-exuberant individual. That said, it's not as if we all had to keep our mouths shut; far from it. We had some massive personalities and characters in the Ibrox dressing room and to keep them silent would've been counterproductive, so the manager had a balancing act to perform: keeping his authority while allowing his players to express themselves. It can't have been easy.

But I had a personal investment in Souey's next signing. In came winger Pieter Huistra – the first Dutchman to sign for Rangers, I believe – and there was now competition for the number 11 shirt. First and foremost, I got on incredibly well with Pieter; he was such a nice fellow. In fact, my daughter, Mischa, was only three weeks old when Pieter got married and I took her to the wedding. But Pieter was at Ibrox to do a job and I knew that were my game to drop off, he would be handed the jersey and there would be no hard feelings. As much as I loved playing, I believed that competition for places was healthy and that had to include my own position. Every jersey in the team was up for grabs and the gaffer wouldn't have been slow in dropping you if you weren't doing the business. Pieter was a great player so I knew I had to get my finger out.

I was also starting the final year of my contract so I'm sure Souey had that in mind when he signed Pieter. It's only when you get into coaching that you start to think as a manager, so at the time I would just have seen Pieter as a team-mate and competition for my place. As a manager, though, you have to always be one step ahead.

We started off the season with a couple of high-profile friendlies against Dynamo Kiev and Manchester United and, believe me, we weren't happy at losing both. Many supporters might think the results of these matches don't really matter, but they did to me. I had an absolute stinker against United and I remember going home that night feeling really disappointed in myself.

I also felt sorry for Mark Hateley who, for some reason, had become a target of the boo boys. In all my time in football, there were sections of just about every club's support that seemed to require a scapegoat, someone they could shout at when things weren't going particularly well for the team. It's not right because it can make or break that individual and seriously impact their career or, in extreme cases, their life. There is often a lot more to a player's loss of form than people might think. They could be experiencing any number of personal problems in their lives – just like supporters – so it's really unfair to target individuals because of a loss of form.

I was still surprised at Mark getting all that flak. He had been a big success at clubs like AC Milan and Monaco and we all knew he wasn't 100 per cent fit as he'd had a couple of bad injuries. We also knew that once he was fully over the knocks and up to a really good standard of fitness he would be a sensation at Ibrox. It was the job of his team-mates to help him through a difficult time, because you never knew when it might be your turn for the stick. I've always maintained that if your manager is picking you for the first team, that's the only vote of confidence you need. It's the biggest boost you can get, and as history shows, Mark did turn it round and become a big favourite at Ibrox.

We then signed another Englishman, Terry Hurlock, and he shocked me with his level of technical ability. Let's be honest, Terry was known as a tough-guy midfielder who would add a bit of steel to the side. At least that was my view when he was with the likes of Brentford and Millwall. In fact, I remember reading a newspaper poll in which he had been voted the 23rd hardest player in football. I thought he would have been higher up than that! Seriously, though, the first time I trained with him it really opened my eyes. Terry was a fantastic player and could receive the ball and make great passes, which was probably the reason he had played for the England B team a few times. Of course, he also had the hard-man reputation, so in effect he perhaps had the best of both worlds. He was a really nice guy and we would sit for ages talking about all manner of things. Terry and Mo actually got on like a house on fire.

Sadly, I heard he had fallen on hard times. It seems some folk had taken advantage of him and left him with almost nothing. It's something that happens quite often to footballers. Part of the problem is that, while you're playing and you're, say, 25 years old, you don't tend to think about life afterwards because in your mind you're going to be young and kicking a ball around forever; you can't picture the moment you have to give it all up. And many footballers don't have the know-how to look ahead in a financial sense and make the proper decisions to protect their future. Every player is a commodity and once the appeal has gone, or you're unable to play anymore, you're offloaded and they move on to the next guy. That's the way it is. At many clubs, once you're gone, you're gone.

For some reason I was called on a few times to help make cup draws. The TV stations, or SFA, would request a player and up would go the cry, 'Mark!' To be honest, I didn't mind. It was usually the Skol Cup. I quite enjoyed it, although it was around this time I first heard about square balls and those heated to a certain temperature. Of course, nothing like this ever happened to me but it was part of the banter about whether or not Rangers or Celtic were getting easy draws.

For the first Old Firm game of the season I found myself on the bench. A few weeks beforehand, I had been on the receiving end of some tough treatment against Dunfermline, and had limped off with an ankle injury. But I was desperate to play against Celtic and, even though I always tried to make myself available, even if I wasn't 100 per cent fit, the gaffer thought it best I start on the bench. But you sit there and wonder if you could make a difference, perhaps score or even create something for a team-mate. Feeling helpless is the hardest thing in the world for a footballer. I eventually came on for Mark Hateley that day and we drew the match so at least we got something from it.

Next up was a European Cup trip to Malta, to play Valetta, and I remember getting booked for taking a free kick. Apparently the ref had said not to take the kick until he had blown his whistle, but I hadn't heard him and went ahead and passed to a team-mate. He flashed the yellow card and I was furious, but we had the consolation of winning the game 4-0, and 10-0 on aggregate.

Following hot on the heels of the home and away wins against Valetta, Souey signed Oleg Kuznetsov, a genuinely world-class defender from Dynamo Kiev. Sadly he got a serious injury early on and that curtailed his appearances for Rangers to just a handful while I was at the club, which was a shame, because Oleg could have gone on to become a real Rangers legend as he was just 27 when he joined and should've been at his peak.

One of the main issues when he signed was his inability to speak English, which certainly restricts a player in the normal 'bedding-in' period. If you can't communicate with your team-mates then you can't join in the banter, which might seem trivial, but it's the dressing-room banter that helps build the team spirit and it's not something you want to be left out of. I think it's so important to learn the language because there is also the communication on the park to consider, and listening to the manager before games. Football is a universal game, but there still needs to be a degree of communication between players.

I remember we played St Mirren at home and won 5-0. Oleg was outstanding and strolled through the game. He was picking out all these tremendous passes from the back. I remember thinking he was that good he could've played on his own at the back and we would still have won!

It was a game that stuck in my mind as I was asked to play on the right-hand side to accommodate Pieter Huistra on the left. We absolutely battered St Mirren on both flanks and got our just rewards in front of goal. I managed to score twice, and get the man of the match award, but I was still keen to get back to my more natural position. But here's the thing: I was predominantly right-footed, but enjoyed playing on the left wing. Tony Morley, who I replaced in that position at Villa, was also a right-footed left-winger – and I always took penalties with my right foot.

Around that time we were due to play Aberdeen at Pittodrie and I remember thinking there was no way the match was going to be on as the rain lashed from the heavens on the journey to the Granite City. When we got to Pittodrie, and walked out on to the pitch for a look around, we could see it was quite clearly waterlogged. Imagine our surprise when we were told to get changed as the match was to go ahead. A few of us had been half hoping it might be off as we were due to head straight down to Sunderland after the full-time whistle for Ally McCoist's wedding! The match ended 0-0 and neither side seriously threatened to score. As soon as it was finished we were straight into the dressing room – and promptly threw Ally into the bath with his suit on. He shouted, 'I'm drier now than I was out on the pitch!' Off we went down to Sunderland, where a great time was had by all.

On the back of that match we had the Skol Cup Final against Celtic to look forward to and, as usual, the build-up was pretty intense. Old Firm matches were always important but cup finals were extra special. As it turned out, we played really well on the day and goals from Richard Gough and me ensured we won the cup. The icing on the cake for me personally was the man of the match trophy. We enjoyed another trophy success but if the truth be told, I would have given up the Skol Cup for success in Europe. Once again we had crashed out of the competition, this time to Red Star Belgrade, and it was a major source of frustration that we hadn't done better in Europe during my time at Ibrox. I always believed the European Cup to be a true gauge of where we were as a team. We had proved we were the best in Scotland, so it was disappointing not to be in a position to replicate that success on the European stage.

It is a great feeling winning any cup competition but it would have been extra special to have won a European trophy or even made it to a final. The irony for me is that, not long after I left Rangers, they came very close to making it to the Champions League Final. I remember visiting Ibrox not long after their fantastic ten-match unbeaten Euro run and a few of the guys slagging me off for missing it. In my opinion, part of the reason for our failure in Europe was that we struggled to bridge the gap between playing, say, St Mirren on the Saturday and then Bayern Munich the following midweek. There was a huge gulf between many of our Scottish league opponents and some of the teams we came up against in the European Cup.

In November of 1990, we posted a good 4-2 win at Motherwell, but I was forced off at half-time with a groin injury, and once again it looked like I might miss the forthcoming Old Firm game at Celtic Park. Thankfully I was passed fit for the game and we went on to win 2-1 in a rip-roaring contest. We definitely held the Indian sign over Celtic at that point and we must have gone into most of these games as favourites to win, despite the venue. There was a funny aside to that game, although I didn't find it too funny at the time. When we arrived at Parkhead, I discovered that the kit man had forgotten to pack my boots and I had to wear a pair that were quite a bit too small for me. I ended up with swollen toes the following day but the two points – and win bonus – more than made up for it. I just thought I'd mention it in case anyone thought I looked like a ballet dancer that day!

One thing I always tried to do was mind my own business and just get on with my football, but that wasn't always possible. On one occasion, I did an interview with the football magazine *Match* and they quoted me as saying Scottish football had little to offer except a place in Europe. Not true. What I did say was it would be beneficial to Rangers if Scottish teams were part of a British league, as playing the likes of Liverpool and Manchester United week in, week out would have helped prepare us better for European matches. A British league would offer a higher standard of competition and therefore we wouldn't be at such a disadvantage when we took part in the European Cup. But the article was turned on its head and they made out I was having a pop at Scottish football, when in fact – apart from the early days of the racist abuse – I didn't have a bad word to say about the game up in Scotland. There's no doubt I found it difficult to adjust when I first arrived at Ibrox. The pace was quicker and the game perhaps more physical, but there was a lot of good football played in Scotland. The only part of the interview that was factually correct was the bit where I said the standard of some of the pitches was very poor. A few of them simply weren't up to scratch and there was no way you could play entertaining football on bumpy and uneven pitches.

It was also said I had criticised the strength of the Scottish league, saying there were only four teams capable of winning the title and that the financial security, along with European football, were the only attractions for me. Not strictly true, because it was a similar case south of the border where just about the only sides who could mount a serious title challenge at that time were Liverpool, Everton, Spurs and Arsenal, along with a couple of others who had an outside chance of success.

A couple of weeks before Christmas, I was once again having to give too much of my attention to an inaccurate press report and, if the truth be told, I was becoming a little sick of the distractions. This time there were accusations that I was set to leave Ibrox to try and further my England career. I was so annoyed that I slapped a ban on speaking to journalists south of the border who, for one reason or another, seemed hell-bent on perpetuating the myth that Scottish soccer was inferior and that I couldn't wait to escape my personal hell. Rubbish. Yes, I was still waiting on my chance to play for England, but the decision to play in Scotland was mine, and mine alone, and I was determined to stand by that choice. I was enjoying it in Scotland and maybe some journalists down south couldn't accept that the world of football didn't just revolve around England.

It bothered me because so much of the story had been twisted. The guy asked if I thought playing for Rangers had affected my international chances and I said, 'I don't know, maybe,' and he put it down as a yes. The English reporters seemed to be the main culprits in distorting what I had to say, and I decided enough was enough. Although I had enjoyed playing with Villa, as far as I was concerned I was playing with better players at Rangers, in front of bigger crowds, in more important matches, and with more pressure than I would ever have faced down south. I was also fielding the same, tired old questions all the time. It had become boring. It's my belief that you have to be content in what you're doing and I certainly was. I was happy at Rangers and the supporters were great with me. I didn't need much more.

Things were going well, but when we played St Johnstone in December I missed a golden opportunity to grab my first competitive hat-trick for Rangers. I scored twice and then missed a penalty which denied me that elusive treble. But I was still enjoying a real purple patch in front of goal, and the two against Saints meant I had scored eight goals in 11 Premier League games, and was ahead of McCoist, Johnston and Hateley in the scoring charts. While it was great for me personally, it was also fantastic for the team because we had a lot of firepower up front and all four of us were capable of finding the net. Of course, the other three were better finishers than me, although I would keep telling them that the scoring charts didn't lie!

Mind you, I'm sure the other guys were looking on in awe when we played Celtic in the new year's game at Ibrox – and I scored straight from a corner kick! We won 2-0 that day and were good value for the points, but my goal was something else. I remember scuffing the kick as I went to take it, and the wind carrying it straight into the net. Mind you, the goalkeeper has to take a lot of the blame even though it was a really windy day. I was delighted, though. I didn't care how they went in.

It was a bit different from the goal I scored at Tannadice just before the end of 1990. We had won another hard-fought game and, after I chipped the keeper from outside the box, Souey said my goal had been worth the admission money alone! We all like to receive a little praise now and again, not to fuel the ego but because it can make you feel good about yourself if for some reason you're feeling down.

Throw in a win at Tynecastle and we were soon five points clear of Aberdeen, with Celtic languishing in sixth place on 18 points, a massive 15 points behind us.

And there was a special award waiting for me at the turn of the year when I won the Youngers Tartan Special Player of the Month accolade for December. It was special, because it was presented by a guy I had admired for many years. Willie Johnston had been a terrific player for Rangers, even scoring a couple of goals in the club's European Cup Winners Cup triumph of 1972, and I had watched him in action when he spent time at West Brom and Birmingham City. He was such a talented winger. I was too young to have played against him but he was certainly one of my favourite players to watch. I was speaking to him after the presentation and he told me I was doing a terrific job in the Premier League, which made me happy.

A lot had been made of my failure to get into the England squad under a couple of different managers, so when I heard that Nigel Spackman – who was as English as me – was called up for the Scotland squad for the friendly against the USSR at Ibrox, I was tempted to delve into my family tree to see if I could find a Scottish granny. I was desperate to play international football at that time and saw it as a natural progression from performing every year in the European Cup. I think my surname is of Welsh descent but if only my name had been Mark McWalters I would have been delighted to turn out for Scotland.

Nigel was included in the Scotland squad as his grandfather was from Edinburgh, but sadly he was forced to withdraw from the pool when the English FA complained about his inclusion. At that time, you only qualified to play for an alien nation if one or both birth parents had been born in the country that was selecting you. The grandparent rule wasn't introduced until 1993.

Ironically, England boss Graham Taylor decided to venture north to watch the Rangers v Dunfermline Scottish Cup tie at Ibrox – while I was laid up in bed with chickenpox! Talk about bad luck. Mind you, playing for England was the least of my problems while I had that horrid virus. It was the worst time of my life and I can honestly say I had spots on every conceivable part of my body. It was horrendous. It was the time of the Gulf War and I was watching the coverage on TV when the phone went. It was Walter Smith and he was calling to give me some good news: I had been picked for the England B squad, and that definitely gave me a lift. In fact, I felt so good that I decided to head over to Ibrox and play against Dunfermline. It's amazing what some positive news can do – but the Rangers doctor chased me and told me not to come near the stadium as chickenpox was highly contagious. I took it on the chin, but at least I was delighted to finally gain recognition from the England manager. But try telling Mo Johnston that everything in the garden was rosy as he somehow managed to contract the virus and I recall him blaming me for passing it on by coming into training to try and prove that I was fit so I would get picked for England. He was furious, and after struggling with chickenpox for a while I could completely understand why.

I had made my debut at 19 for the England under-21s and won 12 caps, with the last coming against Italy in 1986, so it had been quite a wait for further recognition. My main focus was then on getting fully fit and making it into the team. The worst scenario would've been to get into the England squad and not play.

I was soon heading south to meet up with the rest of the party, and I shared the train with a large contingent of Welsh rugby fans who had been in Edinburgh for the international at Murrayfield. When I met up with the rest of the guys in Swansea there were a few familiar faces, and guys I had played alongside for the under-21s. Playing for your country, in my opinion, is a gauge as to how well you're doing in your career. Playing for England is the pinnacle. Everybody wants to be at the top of their chosen profession and turning out for England means you're almost there. But I was still adamant that it was what I did for Rangers that was most important. If I didn't play well for them, I wouldn't be in the international picture. The easy part was getting into the squad or team; the hardest part was staying there.

When I played for the England B team against Wales at Swansea's Vetch Field, it was something of an anticlimax because it was so cold and the pitch was brick hard. In the second half the side I was playing on had a big icy patch running straight down it so it was difficult to do anything constructive.

At least we won the game 1-0 and I played from the start. It was still an honour for me to pull on the England shirt and while the first half went quite well, it was a bit more difficult after the break. Due to the state of the pitch, I didn't see as much of the ball as I would've liked, but overall it was good to be back in the fold. Lawrie McMenemy was in charge of the side, but Graham Taylor was there as well and he seemed quite pleased with my performance.

Around that time I had looked at who had played for England at every possible level and there weren't many who had achieved it. I now had a B cap in the cupboard and all I was missing was a full international appearance. If I could get that one I would be one of a select band of players who had represented England at every level, so playing for the full team became a burning ambition.

After my international sojourn, it was back to domestic bliss and we racked up a tenth successive unbeaten match when we beat Motherwell 2-0 in a Premier League match. It was also Chris Woods's seventh shut-out in a row, which was a fantastic achievement. Chris was one of the best in the business, and was probably underestimated at the time. If it hadn't have been for Peter Shilton, Chris would have won far more England caps.

At that time, we had a great defence, and if the opposition ever breached it, they still had to get past Chris. That was a daunting prospect in itself. He had such an incredible consistency about him.

The following week we hammered Cowdenbeath 5-0 in a Scottish Cup tie and it marked a personal milestone for me. With the score at 4-0, I was fouled in the box and we were awarded a penalty. I grabbed the ball and got to my feet, ready to take the spot kick. Standing in my way were the usual suspects, McCoist and Johnston, but they weren't getting anywhere near it. Eventually Coisty said he would let me take it as I hadn't scored in a couple of weeks, while as usual, Mo was just chancing his arm. There was a reason no one else was getting near it as when I stuck the ball in the back of the net it was my 50th goal for Rangers. It was a great milestone and even more pleasing as I had achieved it in 133 games. Before coming to Rangers I had averaged a goal every three games, but this was a slightly better average.

Although I always liked to score goals, I also derived a great deal of pleasure from creating them, but if any player said they didn't enjoy the buzz of scoring then they were lying. That penalty put me level on goals with Johnston and McCoist at the top of the scoring charts, and when I scored the winner against Hearts a fortnight later, I was the top scorer in the entire league with a dozen goals. That was a pretty awesome feeling.

And then it all seemed to go wrong. Back-to-back defeats against Celtic – in the Scottish Cup and Premier League – threatened briefly to undo all the good work we had done up until then. The first of the double-header, in the Scottish Cup at Parkhead, saw the hosts win 2-0 with three of our players being sent off, including me. Looking back, it was actually quite funny as Terry Hurlock had been shown a straight red card after an altercation with Tommy Coyne. About 10 minutes later, I was given a second yellow by the referee Andrew Waddell, again for an incident involving Coyne, and when I walked into the dressing room, there was Terry sitting feeling sorry for himself. We chatted a little about the injustice of it all and then the door came barging in and it was Mark Hateley's turn to be raging. I looked at Terry, and at the same time the two of us said 'for f**k sake!' and we all started laughing. We had to, or we would have cried. It was just one of those situations. We knew that with three of us packed off for an early bath the team would be struggling out there with eight men, so it must have been our way of coping with it because we certainly didn't find the situation we were in at all funny. On top of that we had lost Trevor Steven to injury after just 19 minutes, and were already without John Brown and Nigel Spackman. We were down to the bare bones. I think I was embarrassed more than anything else because I had let everyone down. There wasn't an awful lot said in the dressing room after that game. We were due to face the same opponents seven days later at the same venue and I think a lot of the lads were already looking forward to the opportunity to make amends, more for our supporters than anyone else.

Sadly, we didn't manage revenge. The three red-carded amigos were suspended, which meant we watched the match from the 'comfort' of the Parkhead stand, and it was a tough watch as we lost the game 3-0. We only had one player sent off this time (Scott Nisbet) but the defeat left us just three points ahead of Aberdeen.

We stopped the rot with a single goal win at Dunfermline, but a draw with Hibs left us just two points ahead of Aberdeen. It was a nervy time. The Hibs match was the first of a three-game suspension in the wake of my red card at Parkhead, and I also missed a 3-0 win over St Johnstone the following week.

It was all hands to the pumps as we battled to save our title – and then came the bombshell news that Graeme Souness had accepted the vacant manager's position at Liverpool. He was scheduled to take over the Anfield reins at the start of the new season, until chairman David Murray intervened and asked him to leave straight away. It was a whirlwind few days at the club and we didn't know whether we were coming or going. It wasn't an ideal time for such upheaval as we had just four league games remaining, and Aberdeen were breathing down our necks.

At first I felt disappointed in Souey for accepting the job, as a few weeks beforehand – when Kenny Dalglish had quit Liverpool, and speculation turned to Graeme as a front-runner for the job – he insisted he was going nowhere. But I soon realised that managing Liverpool was his dream job, and perhaps a natural forerunner to managing his country. So, whereas I could understand why he did it, I was still really sorry to see him go because he was a first-class manager and I knew it would leave a gaping void at the club. I'm sure had it been any other club he would have stayed at Ibrox. If I remember correctly he just walked straight out of the door and that was that. No goodbyes in the dressing room, or tears anywhere else; I found out through watching the television, so you can imagine it came as quite a shock.

I still had one match of my suspension to serve and it was against St Mirren at Love Street. It was Walter Smith's first game in charge and, once again, due to injuries and suspensions, he was forced to bring in a number of youngsters. But it was one of them, Sandy Robertson, who got the only goal, which maintained our two-point advantage over Aberdeen with just three games left to play.

On the subject of Walter's appointment as gaffer, I was delighted for him. We had a great relationship and I always felt he was massively underestimated at the club. He was an integral part of the team and had a lot of input while Souey was in charge. Walter's tactics were always spot on and he would also go around the dressing room just before kick-off giving out individual instructions to players as well as offering encouragement. If Souey had previously lambasted players, Walter would put an arm round you and give you a lift. Walter deserved the opportunity to prove what he could do as his own man and wasted no time in bringing in Archie Knox from Manchester United as his assistant; the transition appeared seamless.

Archie's first involvement was in a match against Dundee United at Ibrox – and I still owe Ian Ferguson a great deal of gratitude for that night. Fergie scored the only goal of the match, which was just as well as I had missed an absolute sitter. With the goal at my mercy I somehow managed to hit it past the post. Try as I might, I still can't erase that memory, which I think will be with me for life!

Two league matches left, two points in front of Aberdeen and just two points for a win. Surely we wouldn't blow it after leading the table all season. Well, stranger things had happened, although they didn't come much stranger than the penultimate league match of the season against Motherwell at Fir Park. Even though we were trailing 1-0 with a few minutes left of that game, the destination of the title was still in our own hands. Had the result remained at 1-0, a draw against Aberdeen at Ibrox on the last day of the season would've been enough to see us bag a third successive title. But we didn't do things by half – and two late goals by a diminutive striker called Dougie Arnott saw Motherwell win 3-0. We now had to WIN our final game due to the Dons having the better goal difference. How had we blown it in such spectacular fashion?

With Motherwell leading 1-0, we were awarded a penalty in the 66th minute when Pieter Huistra was bundled off the ball in the box. I was given the opportunity of drawing us level, but the pressure obviously got to me and I blazed the kick over the bar. It was a horrible moment. That would've been my 13th league goal of the season so maybe I was cursed! I did have a few superstitions which I carried on throughout my career. I always wore my socks inside out, which was one of the little rituals I had. When I was playing for the school team, we always thought the socks looked better inside out, and it was something I continued to do when I turned pro – much to the annoyance of the kit man at Villa, because every time I took off my socks at the end of a game they would always be inside out. But I can't blame the gods of superstition for my missed penalty at Fir Park!

And so to the final game of a long and arduous campaign, and one we knew we had to win. The build-up to the game the week before was massive and I'm sure we were all feeling a little bit of pressure. Aberdeen had a good team and while they had the added bonus of knowing a draw would be enough for them, we had a full house at Ibrox behind us – and that was massive. It was set up to be quite a game.

We were definitely the walking wounded going into that game and Walter was once again forced to shuffle the pack. During the game we lost Tom Cowan when he suffered a broken leg, and Bomber Brown was stretchered off with an Achilles injury. In fact, my hamstring went at around the same time as Bomber's, and to this day he always says to me that I was moaning about a wee hamstring injury while he was still trying to run around with his foot hanging off!

The pivotal moment in the match arrived five minutes before half-time. I got the ball out wide on the left, and checked back before sending in a cross to the back post. Mark Hateley made the leap of his life – outjumping Dons's defender Alex McLeish by about four feet – and bulleted a header past the young Aberdeen keeper Michael Watt. Ibrox erupted and that settled any nerves we may have been feeling. Goals change games and it certainly changed our mentality. It gave us the confidence to press forward – because you can't sit in at Ibrox – and it was important that we held our lead till the break. There was also a definite change in the atmosphere after Mark scored. From playing in front of packed, but tense stands, instead the singing started and the fans were in great voice.

When we ran out for the start of the second period, the noise inside the stadium was incredible: it was bedlam, and when Mark got the second, with roughly an hour played, we knew it was our day. I was quite close to him when he followed up Mo Johnston's shot to smash it into the net and the occasion got the better of me as I planted a big kiss on his cheek. Despite the celebrations, he still found the time to tell me to f**k off, which we had a great laugh about afterwards.

Not long after the final whistle sounded, it sunk in that we had just won the league for the third time in a row. Of course, at that point we didn't know that it was the third of nine in a row, and that we would be going down in history, but the celebrations were still particularly awesome.

Our supporters definitely played a big part in that success, because they were behind us from the word go. There was a lull just before we got the first goal, but Mark's header was the catalyst for the stadium to come alive and the supporters didn't stop singing till they got home that night, if they even made it home!

To be honest, we owed them big time after the shocking 3-0 defeat at Motherwell. We were deflated after that game and desperately wanted to play Aberdeen the following day. So I honestly couldn't see past us winning. I had never seen a bunch of guys so fired up for a game in my entire career. I had been playing for ten years and had never witnessed desire and hunger like it.

Yet again we had been forced to chop and change because of injuries, but it had been the same story all season. I'd never known a run like it. When I felt my own hamstring go in the first minute of the second half, I couldn't believe it, although I managed to play on. I hadn't done that since I was a teenager, but that just about summed up the way things had been going for us. Mind you, it also said a lot about the character of the squad that, with all the injuries and suspensions we'd had, we still managed to come out on top. Without these problems we would have romped the league, but because of them it ended up a bit too close for comfort.

Here's the thing, though: I don't think anybody in the whole of Scotland wanted us to win apart from our own supporters. As an Englishman, I'd never experienced anything like that and couldn't believe it could be that way. But we won and proved them all wrong, and that's what mattered.

If we had lost it would have been the worst day of our lives, but it turned out to be one of the best, although unbeknown to me at that point, it would also be my last ever game for Rangers.

With mum at my family home in the Wirral

Mischa, Marlon and me modelling some of the strips I've worn in my career

My kids, Marlon, Mischa and I at a family wedding

Lining up with Holte
Comprehensive

I loved representing my school

I won the Most Valuable Player trophy while playing with England Youths

On the move with England Schoolboys at Wembley against Wales in 1979 (Getty)

Lining up for England Schoolboys

Winning the English FA Youth Cup with Aston Villa (Getty)

I was thrilled to win the Southern Junior Floodlit Cup in 1981 with Villa (Getty)

My first day at Villa – and I'm on the ball!

With my cousin, Robert, who is in the Guinness Book of Records *for his ball-juggling skills*

Receiving the Bronze Boot from Birmingham Dairies boss Jack White for a top performance against West Brom

I was very proud to play for Villa. This portrait was taken at the start of the 1984/85 season (Getty)

Waiting to get on a plane to fly to Southampton for a game in 1984 (Getty)

Winning the Super Cup against Barcelona was an incredible feeling (Getty)

Taking on Chris Morris on my 1988 debut for Rangers against Celtic at Parkhead (Getty)

With a couple of Rangers Legends, my good friend Davie Cooper, and Willie Waddell (courtesy of the Daily Record and Sunday Mail)

Ray Wilkins was a dear friend of mine. Here, we are pictured together during the Skol Cup semi-final against Hearts in 1989 (courtesy of the Daily Record and Sunday Mail)

Taking on Dundee United's Alex Cleland (courtesy of the Daily Record and Sunday Mail)

Receiving my man of the match award from the pop group Wet Wet Wet

With Richard Gough after winning the Skol Cup Final against Celtic (Getty)

Making the cover of the popular Shoot! *magazine*

Signing for Liverpool– and Graeme Souness

In the Wembley dressing room with John Barnes, left, and Michael Thomas (Getty)

Making the Guinness Book of Records *with record-breaking Liverpool*

Proud as punch lining up with England in New Zealand in 1991 (Getty)

My father played for Nigeria against England

Playing for Swindon Town against Ipswich in 1999 (Getty)

I scored for Rovers in the millennium Bristol derby match (Getty)

With Brazilian superstars Careca and Dunga after playing in a charity match for victims of the tsunami

I enjoyed my time with Dudley Town. This was our team

Part of the Rangers Legends set-up

Playing for Rangers Legends in a charity match for the Lee Rigby Foundation

At the Legends match with Coronation Street *star 'Jim McDonald' aka Charlie Lawson*

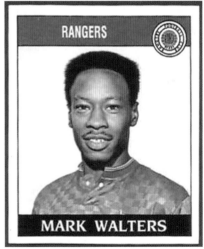

Chapter 13

If the Cap Fits ...

THE first time I represented England at schoolboy level I was made up. There was no greater feeling than pulling on the white jersey and turning out for my country. By the time I joined Rangers, I had played for England at every level apart from the senior side, and that's probably why I always appeared so keen to gain that elusive full cap.

I reckon that had Villa not suffered a terrible form slump in the mid-80s, I would've been picked for England before heading up the road to Scotland. Villa had previously been achieving great things and obviously that had been recognised by the England manager and his assistants, as a number of our players had gained international honours. But our shift from glory days to relegation candidates no doubt had them running for their lives.

I had been a regular in the England youth and under-21 sides and had always performed well for my country. Dave Sexton was in charge of the under-21s when I made my debut in 1983 against Denmark at Carrow Road. We beat the Danes 4-1 that night and I went on to play nine times for the under-21s – and I was never on a losing side.

I played against Denmark (twice), Hungary, Israel, the Republic of Ireland, Romania (twice), Turkey and Italy and I genuinely loved every minute of every game. Going up against teams with different styles always fascinated me and testing myself against high-quality opposition from other nations gave me a real kick.

Dave Sexton seemed pleased with my form for the under-21s and told me I wasn't too far away from a call-up to the senior squad. Bobby Robson had a word too, and said he had been impressed with the way I had been playing under Dave, so I knew he was monitoring my progress. That's exactly what a player wants to hear as it keeps the motivation levels high. But then the downturn in our fortunes at Villa – where my form dipped just as much as everyone else's – soon put paid to any hopes I had at that time under Bobby Robson. We were struggling and I wasn't performing particularly well, so my England chances began to fade. Then I had the shoulder injury and in the remainder of my time at Villa, I didn't deserve to be mentioned as a possible England player and I knew it, but moving to Rangers revitalised me and I soon felt I had a real chance of being selected again. At the start of my Ibrox career, guys like Chris Woods, Terry Butcher, Gary Stevens, Ray Wilkins and Kevin Drinkell were either regularly picked for squads or were there or thereabouts. I used to dream of joining them and the Three Lions every time there was an impending squad announcement. But all those announcements seemed to bring was disappointment.

I remember being overlooked by Bobby Robson for the England v Scotland Rous Cup match in season 1988/89, when I felt I had a decent chance of at least making the squad. In the wake of my omission, there were a few calls from the English press, no doubt looking for a negative response, but as much as I was disappointed I tried to remain dignified. That didn't seem to matter, though, as again I felt I was unfairly quoted. The following day, one headline read, 'Walters blasts Robson!' Really? It couldn't have been further from the truth. It was the manager's job to pick the players he believed were best for England and if I didn't come into his plans then there was nothing I could do about it. I certainly wasn't moaning and telling him who to pick. At that time, I believed there was a feeling in England that Scottish football was inferior, which I thought was ridiculous, but that was the point I was trying to get across. In the late-1980s and throughout the 1990s, the standard of the top clubs in Scotland was very high, which was mostly down to Graeme Souness raising the bar at Ibrox and the others being forced to follow suit. That was my opinion anyway, but why let the 'facts' spoil a good story? Often, when certain members of the fourth estate called, I'm convinced they already had a fair idea of what kind of answers they were looking for. But the facts were I was playing to a very high standard at Rangers, and we were regularly at the right end of the table, often in cup finals and playing in Europe every season, so there was a lot to be excited about. Maybe I was just too impatient when it came to England.

I thought I might have a better chance of playing when Bobby Robson was replaced by Graham Taylor in 1990, probably because we had worked together at Villa and he knew me better. But on one of the few occasions he ventured north to watch me play, we spoke after the game and had quite a frank conversation. I asked him outright if playing in Scotland was hampering my chances of representing my country. His reply was short and to the point. 'I'm not going to lie to you Mark, but if you came back down to England to play your football your chances of playing regularly for England would be better.' He wanted me playing in England but frankly I would never have left Rangers just for that, despite what it meant to me to play for England. I told him I was happy in Scotland and that I would stay and take my chances. For me, it wasn't a convincing enough argument to give up the new life I had made for myself in Scotland and with Rangers.

It was suggested to me a few times that Graham's predecessor Bobby Robson had ignored me a lot, even when I was playing really well, but to be fair to Bobby, England had some great wide players at that time, including John Barnes and Chris Waddle, while the likes of Andy Hinton and Steve Hodge had also done a job for him in 'my' position, so there was an orderly queue forming. I was waiting patiently in line but I knew I was up against it, although I had never shirked a challenge in my life and I wasn't about to start now. But I never lost hope of playing for England, whether I was up in Scotland or not.

Let's say for a moment I had moved back down south. There was still no guarantee I would get a game for England, because the likes of Barnes and Waddle were still playing and weren't all of a sudden going to walk away so I could get in, so I soon knocked that idea on the head. Anyway, things had settled down with the abuse and I was starting to really enjoy myself in Scotland, so giving it all up – and especially taking account of the hurdles I had overcome to get to this point – wasn't an option. I was playing well and if that was good enough for England then great. If not, there wasn't an awful lot I could do about it. I took some comfort from finally accepting that it was more or less out of my hands. I knuckled down in training and concentrated solely on doing well for Rangers.

The whole England thing was shoved to the back of my mind. If it happened, it happened. I genuinely wasn't obsessing on it anymore, and, as soon as I adopted that mindset, a weight disappeared from my shoulders.

And isn't that when things normally happen?

I think it was Walter Smith who informed me that I'd better get myself down south as I had been chosen to represent England in the close season tour of Australia, New Zealand and Malaysia. It was at the end of the 1991/92 season and we had just beaten Aberdeen to win a third successive title, so I was already feeling pretty good about myself. But when the phone rang at home, and I noticed it was Walter, I was puzzled. 'No need for personal congratulations Walter, it's a team game,' I laughed to myself. But when he told me the English FA had been on the blower and they wanted me to hook up with the squad I was delighted.

So delighted in fact that I forgot I was injured. I may have pulled a hamstring at the start of the second half in the match against Aberdeen but there was no way I was going to declare it. I was going on that trip if they had to help me there on crutches! To be honest, it was an opportunity I couldn't turn down and even though I was carrying the injury, I banked on being able to do myself justice when the games actually came around. I knew that if I was honest and said no, I might not get another opportunity.

My family were so happy as they knew how much I wanted it. When I told my Mum, she started crying, and that almost set me off. I was going on tour with England and I was the proudest man alive. We got measured up for our suits and when I tried mine on and looked in the mirror, I was walking on air. Mind you, the heat and humidity on that trip were such that I lost

10lbs in weight, which I couldn't really afford to lose in the first place. But on I walked.

Just being with the squad and entourage was a great experience. We were treated like kings wherever we went and it was at moments like that I realised exactly what representing England was all about.

On the day of the first tour match against New Zealand we were all gathered in the team hotel and waiting patiently on Graham Taylor announcing his team. He started with the goalkeeper, my Rangers team-mate Chris Woods, and went through the defenders. It was getting interesting. He continued, 'Geoff Thomas, Dennis Wise, Gary Lineker … ' Ten jerseys gone. One left. 'And Mark Walters.' Graham had mentioned my name a few times during team talks at Villa, but just hearing him say those two words in that hotel in Auckland was music to my ears.

If I was nervous beforehand, my stress levels shot up a few hundred notches. We were playing New Zealand and I was also a bit worried about my lack of fitness, but the plan was to go out there and play as well as possible. My hamstring didn't go during the game but equally it didn't feel good and I was eventually forced to come off. Hamstrings are peculiar injuries.

The quicker you are the more likely you are to get them, and it's always at the back of your mind that once you're running at full pelt, it could go at any point. The game itself was over quite quickly, and the strange thing was that after all the hype and nerves, it felt like just any other game. Sure, the build-up to my England debut, at least in my mind anyway, had been incredible, but as soon as the whistle sounded I was playing a game of football. It was 11 against 11, and I was desperate to win, which we did. But while we won the battle – I sure as hell lost the war.

After the game, I didn't need any feedback from the manager or coaches to tell me my performance had been underwhelming. I knew the gamble hadn't truly paid off and as far as I was concerned that was that. We had another couple of games on the tour and while I declared myself fit, it was pretty obvious I wasn't 100 per cent, and I didn't play again. I would have loved to have played again but the management team probably reckoned I had picked up the injury playing in the game against New Zealand and I wasn't selected again on the tour. The lads were also doing well and we didn't lose a game so Graham tended to stick with the same team. I got on well enough with the gaffer, we had a good relationship, but I hadn't exactly set the heather on fire and he was just doing his job as England manager.

It was a frustrating time for me but it wasn't anyone's fault. It was fate. When I was chosen for the tour I made the decision to go and I stick by that. To be honest, though, I don't think there was ever a time I walked on to a football field 100 per cent fit. Even at the start of a season, there was usually one niggly, wee injury or another present. For a footballer to be fully fit is a rare luxury. So, I just had to take it on the chin and move on.

The thing is, I did it; I played for England. I always see that as akin to having letters after your name. And there are better players than me who never got the opportunity to pull on the famous white shirt. Take for instance the Aston Villa team that won the European Cup. The likes of Gary Shaw and Dennis Mortimer never played for England, and they were both excellent players, so I count myself incredibly lucky to have managed it.

There were a few guys who did really well on that trip, especially in my position. John Salako came of age and did exceptionally well and I was really pleased for him. Had I been 100 per cent fit then it could've been me who went on to have a good career at international level but sadly it was what it was at the time.

John probably got more chances than he might have because of my injury but he grabbed them with both hands and went on to play more games for England.

I moved to Liverpool not long after making my international debut and thought that once I was a feature in the team at Anfield further international opportunities might follow. After all, like the manager said, I was now playing in England with one of the top teams. What greater stage could I have? I would wait expectantly on squads being announced, but the call never came. And then I had some problems getting into the team at Liverpool and I knew then that my international aspirations had come to an end. I would never become an England regular so once again I put it out of my head and moved on.

First and foremost I always loved winning league championships. My philosophy was that if you were winning titles then you were part of the best team in the country, and that was the most pleasing thing for me. But representing England at every possible level is also a great achievement. Perhaps not my number one priority, but something that made me very proud, and I have the caps as a constant reminder.

The team for my international debut had been an exceptionally strong one. Joining me in England white at the Mount Smart Stadium, in Auckland, were Chris Woods, Earl Barrett, Paul Parker, Stuart Pearce, Des Walker, David Batty, David Platt, Geoff Thomas, Dennis Wise and Gary Lineker.

Gary scored late on to give us the victory, so I can boast of a 100 per cent win record in my England career!

We played three other matches on the tour and beat the Aussies 1-0, New Zealand (again) 2-0 and Malaysia 4-2, with Gary scoring all four goals in that one. He was an exceptional finisher, a bit like Ally McCoist in that he had great anticipation and always seemed to know exactly where the ball was going to land. Coisty wasn't slow by any manner of means, but Lineker was razor sharp in the box, hence the reason he scored so many in important games. I suppose you don't finish top scorer at a World Cup finals unless you're exceptional. More often than not Gary made a 50/50 ball his own by getting there a fraction ahead of his opponent. He won 80 caps for England, and I wasn't in the least bit surprised.

Personally, though, I had fulfilled a dream, and I'm so happy that I did.

Chapter 14

Answering Souey's Call ... Again!

MY contract at Rangers expired along with our third successive championship and before signing a new deal I was keen to see if there were any other options on the table. I wanted to survey the landscape, so to speak. That was all, nothing sinister. At that point I hadn't heard anything from any other club, and was simply keen for a sit-down chat with my agent to discuss moving forward. When Rangers chairman David Murray spoke to me about signing a new deal at Ibrox, I'd had NO contact from Graeme Souness or anyone else connected to Liverpool, so there was no tapping or jiggery-pokery going on.

Mr Murray said to me, 'Mark, I want you to sign the new contract, and I think you will regret it if you don't.' I told him I probably would sign on again but I was just keen to see what kind of opportunities were out there. Don't get me wrong, Rangers were fantastic to me; they looked after me really well and any hesitation was absolutely nothing to do with the club, just purely down to me.

I had been given an extra week or so off at the start of pre-season training because I had been away with England, and it had given me time to think, but I was soon back at Rangers and training in anticipation of the new season. At that point, I didn't see my future anywhere other than at Ibrox.

Behind the scenes, though, and unbeknown to me, Souey had been showing an interest in me. He had taken over at Liverpool and had contacted the Rangers board, and when Walter Smith called me into his office to say that an English club wanted to sign me I genuinely didn't have a clue who it was. Secretly, I hoped it might be Liverpool, and if a list had been placed in front of me with a dozen English teams on it, I would have plumped for Anfield, but something like that was out of my hands. When Walter told me that Souey wanted to speak to me and that it was up to me if I wanted to go down and chat to him, I said I would, but I was still carrying the hamstring injury from the final day of the previous season, and playing for England, etc. Again, I think David Murray believed I had been tapped, and that I was using a fake injury to engineer a move, but it was genuine and I acted honourably throughout the whole process. I drove down to Anfield, met Souey and we had a long chat about his plans for Liverpool, and where he saw me fitting in with those plans, and to be honest I liked what I heard. I agreed to join Liverpool. It was as simple as that. I was familiar with Souey's style, and he was a man who knew exactly what he wanted. He was a born winner and had infused that feeling into the squad when I was at Rangers. When I first went to Ibrox it took me until the next day to recover from the disappointment of any defeat. After working under Souey for a couple of years, I don't think I ever fully recovered from defeat until we were lining up for the next match.

The new season was almost upon us and we didn't waste any time in getting the deal finalised. I'm sure it was very similar to the way I signed for Rangers, when Everton had been interested, but that was that and I was now a Liverpool player. I had gone back down to Anfield and formally signed my contract in front of the press, but while I didn't get much of an opportunity to say goodbye to my Ibrox team-mates, it was a major regret that I couldn't say farewell to the magnificent Rangers fans because they had backed me from day one, just when I needed them most.

It was a big step and one which thrust me even deeper into the media spotlight. That was inevitable, even though I had joined Liverpool at much the same time as Mark Wright and Dean Saunders, and I'd half hoped the other guys might take the lion's share of the spotlight and allow me to slip in quietly without anyone really noticing. But I suppose doing anything quietly at Anfield was nothing more than wishful thinking.

The new three-foreigners-in-Europe rule had just been introduced and that was one of the attractions of joining Liverpool. As an Englishman playing in Scotland, I would've been classed as a foreigner, and we already had a few on the books at Rangers, so there was always the chance that European Cup excursions might be limited. I loved playing European football, so that was a bit of a concern. Don't get me wrong, it wasn't the only reason I left Ibrox, but it was a contributory factor.

In hindsight – and I'm not going to lie – David Murray was right. I did regret leaving Rangers, sooner than I could have imagined. In fact, the moment I scribbled my name on the Liverpool contract I started to wonder if I had made the right decision or not. It wasn't a case of suddenly getting cold feet at joining a club with a massive reputation, but I had been happy at Ibrox and had carved out a great life for myself in Scotland. I worried that I might have acted in haste.

Don't get me wrong, the prospect of winning trophies with Liverpool thrilled me so much. When I signed for them I felt I had a great opportunity to be successful in Europe, while at Rangers there was the prospect of spending extended periods on the bench during those big European nights.

At the time, my gut was telling me Liverpool, and I've always tended to follow my gut, but looking back I was perhaps damned if I did, and damned if I didn't. It was a hell of a difficult decision, but I had to choose one or the other, and all I'm saying is perhaps I chose the wrong one.

Yip, you've guessed it, I was one confused guy!

Going to Anfield wasn't about chasing the money as Rangers had offered a better deal than Liverpool. The two clubs are similar in so many ways: both huge with massive fan bases. Perhaps Rangers have a more far-reaching fan base than Liverpool, as Rangers seem to have supporters' clubs in every corner of the globe, so I suppose the main difference was in the level of competition the clubs faced each week on the park. The general standard of player was probably better in England. There were also more teams in England capable of giving Liverpool a tough game. Liverpool have won more European trophies than Rangers, but the Ibrox club have won more league titles than any other club in the world, so there certainly wasn't an awful lot between them.

Obviously the amount of money in the English Premier League nowadays is way above anything that exists in Scotland, and most of Europe for that matter. It's ridiculous, but money talks. The contrast now is far greater than it ever was back then, the days when many top Scottish players were earning their living in England and the Scottish national team was qualifying regularly for major finals. Sadly that isn't the case anymore.

But I had signed for Liverpool and obviously it was a privilege to play for one of the world's leading clubs. The decision was made so I knuckled down and worked hard in order to make the move a success. Regardless of whether or not I had made the right decision, Liverpool had shelled out £1.25m, which was an awful lot of money, so I owed them. To be honest, I tried not to let such a big price tag affect my game too much. The way I saw it, I had few excuses to fail. The clubs involved had valued me at that price but I just wanted to get on with playing.

But the sum involved immediately made it so different from my time at Villa. There, I was the local boy who hadn't cost the club a penny and therefore, if I failed, no one had lost much. I had also longed for the time when I would be treated like most other players, instead of the local lad made good. That time had arrived.

I made my competitive debut for Liverpool on the opening day of the 1991/92 season against Oldham at Anfield, replacing Steve McMahon after 65 minutes and gaining my first win bonus when John Barnes scored a few minutes later to give us a 2-1 victory. It was the perfect start.

My first start in the league came at Kenilworth Road in a 0-0 draw against Luton Town, in front of 11,000. The atmosphere in my first Merseyside derby a couple of weeks later was completely different. We won that game 3-1 and the crowd were right behind us from the first minute till the last. It was another match to savour and enjoy. The atmosphere was incredible, but a different incredible from the Rangers-Celtic games, certainly the ones I played in, which seemed to be a lot more serious. I'm not saying the whole Liverpool-Everton occasion was very friendly but it seemed to be more about the football than anything else.

Seven days later, I scored my first goal for the Reds in a league match at Notts County. It was a tough game and we were 1-0 down at the break. However, Ronny Rosenthal scored with 20 minutes remaining and then, with time running out, we were awarded a penalty. Despite having players like Ray Houghton, Steve McManaman and our new £3m man, Dean Saunders, on the park, I was entrusted with spot-kick duties and tucked it away.

That win put us second in the league and all eyes turned to our next match to see if we could take over top spot. For me, I had to treat it just like any other game, even though I would be coming face to face with Aston Villa – the club I had supported as a boy – for the first time in my career. The match was played at Anfield and I scored our equaliser from the penalty spot. Kevin Richardson had opened the scoring for Villa but when Ronny Rosenthal was pulled down inside the box, just before half-time, I was again handed the ball. I didn't give much thought to our opponents and fired home. Later that night, I was sitting at home thinking about the match and it felt strange having just played against 'my team'. But football was my job, and there are few friends in business, although you can't just stop liking a team you have supported since you were seven. Mind you, one of the reasons I moved to Liverpool was because winning the top-flight title was always an ambition of mine. In saying that, I also wanted a European Cup winners' medal and a regular place in the England side. You don't always get what you want in life but I felt I had a better chance of achieving these ambitions with Liverpool.

The following season, we travelled down to Villa Park for a league match and the place was packed out. It ended up quite an afternoon, with six goals and one of the worst misses I've ever seen – up close! David James played the ball long down the field and it was missed by a Villa defender and collected by Ronny Rosenthal, who took it round the keeper. With the goal gaping, and just ten yards out, Ronny tried to stick it in the empty net but to the astonishment of everyone in the ground, he hit the bar and the ball was cleared to safety. It was an incredible miss.

I was getting slaughtered by the Villa fans every time I touched the ball so when I put Liverpool ahead two minutes before the break, I went over to the home supporters and did a little dance, which made them extra mad – and then Ronny goes and misses that sitter! If he had scored we would probably have won the game but it wasn't to be. Dean Saunders (who had by then moved to Villa) came back to haunt us by scoring twice, and even though Ronny eventually got a goal – and an ironic cheer – late on, we lost and it was the Villa fans who had the last laugh.

If I'm being honest, Villa's away support was kinder when I scored the penalty against them at Anfield. They were cheering me, which was quite different to the home fans. I know a lot of fans go to the home and away games but they always seemed a bit more forgiving on their travels.

When the draw for the first round of the 1991/92 UEFA Cup was made, Liverpudlians watched on expectantly. Kuusysi Lahti were hardly a household name, but for Liverpool they might as well have been the most famous club in the world, as the first-round tie represented the club's first taste of European action for six years – since Heysel. English clubs had been banned indefinitely from Europe, which was later reduced to five years, although the Reds had an extra year tagged on at the end. For a club who had been European champions four times prior to Heysel, it was a lengthy absence from the continent's premier competition. On game night, it was no contest. We thumped the Finns 6-1 at Anfield and Dean Saunders scored four times. The tie was over.

Winning against a Finnish team in Europe was all well and good but we had to sort out our league form, and next up was Sheffield Wednesday. It was a must-win game – and we were only in September! We drew the match, lost the return match in Finland against Kuusysi, but still went through, and then drew 0-0 with Man United. To be honest, this wasn't the way I had envisaged things going at Liverpool. I was at this massive footballing institution but we were going through a really bad time, and the press and supporters let us know it. There was no hiding place.

The next round of Europe was soon upon us and we were drawn against French side Auxerre, with the first leg away from home. Bossed by Guy Roux, Auxerre turned us over at their place and we were fortunate to escape with a two-goal deficit. Sure, we were a much-depleted side and injuries were threatening to ruin our season, but perhaps it also showed up a lack of strength in depth in the squad. In fact, we could easily have been 3-0 down, as I remember playing a short back-pass which was intercepted, although thankfully Bruce Grobbelaar made a great save.

Before the second leg, Terry Butcher brought his Coventry City side to Anfield and while it was great to see the big man again we had a job to do and thankfully managed to scrape a 1-0 win through Ray Houghton's superb goal. But losing to Port Vale and Crystal Palace – both at Anfield – hardly set us up for the return match against Auxerre. Nevertheless, 23,000 supporters paid to watch us attempt to overhaul a two-goal deficit – and they were treated to a five-star performance by everyone in a red shirt that night. The lads were brilliant, and it was easily my best performance of that first season. The match was played 24 hours after Bonfire night, but by all accounts I turned in an explosive 90 minutes which helped us overturn a 2-0 deficit to progress to the next round. With Anfield just half full – perhaps because our supporters hadn't expected us to get through – we set about warming up the audience, and they were soon fully behind us.

We managed to conjure up one of those great European nights at Anfield, like our predecessors had done so many times before us. We got off to the perfect start when Jan Molby put us in front from the spot after just four minutes. Mike Marsh ensured the aggregate score was level at the break, and we pounded Auxerre for the entire second half. But just when it seemed we might have to settle for extra time, I scored what proved to be the winner to put the seal on a great night. I was told by a family member, sitting in the stand, that when my shot went in, the guy next to him jumped up and started punching the air. That 'fan' was John Aldridge, a real Liverpool legend!

The atmosphere at the match was extra special. The entire ground willed us on to victory – especially the Kop – and there is no doubt their influence played a major role in us getting through. Sometimes the old cliché of the 'twelfth man' is overused, but in this case it's the perfect way to describe the contribution of the fans.

Young Jamie Redknapp had made his European debut in France, while the likes of Mike Marsh, Steve McManaman and Steve Harkness also proved that if you were good enough you were old enough. All four lads were given opportunities due to our injury situation and proved that the Liverpool academy was producing good young talent.

Just before Christmas, Brian Clough brought his star-studded Nottingham Forest side to Anfield and we turned in our best domestic display of the season. We were up against a top side but our fans were due a performance. We played well and won 2-0. Just before the game, Souey unveiled Arsenal's Michael Thomas as his latest £1.5m signing, which perhaps spurred us on to victory.

Prior to the victory over Forest, Dean Saunders had all but destroyed Swarovski Tirol singlehandedly in the third round of the UEFA Cup. He scored five of our six aggregate goals to send us through to the last eight. Deano had also scored four in the first round, so he was on fire.

When I was a kid, one of the most popular annuals around was the Guinness Book of Records. I was lucky enough to get a copy every year and would read it cover to cover, fascinated by the weird and wonderful records, like the world's longest eyebrows or the biggest ever pitchfork! So with Christmas looming, everyone at Anfield was delighted to get a visit from Norris McWhirter, public face of the Guinness Book of Records, and star of television's *Record Breakers*, presented by Roy Castle, which brought us live attempts at breaking random records each week. Norris, and his brother, Ross, would pop up on the show to present certificates to those who had managed to claim a record. It was compulsive viewing for this young and wide-eyed boy from Birmingham. So, when Norris turned up at Anfield to acknowledge Liverpool's haul of 18 titles as the most won by any English football club, it took me back to my childhood, and I enjoyed a chat with him after we'd had our photos taken for the press. It was a real blast from the past.

The beginning of 1992 was special for the club. It was our centenary year and a whole host of events were planned to mark such an important milestone. One way in which the players could help make it extra special was to pick up where we had left off, and extend our seven-match unbeaten record into the new year.

Nowadays, the FA Cup seems to have lost much of its charm for some of the leading clubs. Perhaps they have far too much invested in the moneybags Premier League to worry about risking their big-name players in pursuit of a domestic trophy. But in my day, the FA Cup was magical and EVERY club desperately wanted to win it. We were no different at Liverpool and our quest to win the handsome trophy started off with an inauspicious 4-0 win over Crewe Alexandra at Gresty Road.

In the fourth round, we faced a tricky tie at Bristol Rovers, where a Dean Saunders goal earned us a replay back at our place. I wore the famous number nine jersey that afternoon, and we knew we were in a cup tie. The hosts raised their game in front of the TV cameras, but even in the replay, in front of 30,000, we just scraped home 2-1. Portman Road, Ipswich, was our next port of call and again we were forced to settle for a share of the spoils on an afternoon when both defences came out on top. In the replay, Souey went with me again in the number nine jersey as opposed to the great Ian Rush, and we won another tough contest 3-2, after extra time.

In the sixth round, we were drawn against Villa, at home, and after another narrow win, this time thanks to a Michael Thomas goal, it was clear that if we were going to make it all the way to Wembley, we were certainly doing it the hard way.

Sandwiched either side of the FA Cup match with Villa were home and away UEFA Cup quarter-final ties with Italian side Genoa. I felt we were unlucky to lose 2-0 over in Italy, but the defeat – and lack of an away goal – would make our task at Anfield a tough one. It had been a hard shift in Italy, although we didn't play too badly. I was up against Brazilian World Cup winner Branco for most of the night and would like to think I gave him a few problems before having to go off late-on with a hamstring injury. When the second leg came round, I was still out injured but we had John Barnes back from injury and I knew we had already overcome a similar scoreline to KO Auxerre. Sadly, we lost the tie at Anfield and our European dream was over for another year.

We still had the semi-finals of the FA Cup to look forward to, and we were well aware of how important it was to win something in our centenary year. When the draw was made we were paired with a very good Portsmouth side, and the tie was scheduled for Highbury. The game ended 1-1 after extra time, and it was on to Villa Park a fortnight later for the replay. Even though I had been away for a few years, I didn't feel like a stranger walking through the players' entrance that night – especially as we had played Villa in a league match at Villa Park just 48 hours before the cup tie. But we travelled to Birmingham without our manager, who was in hospital recovering from a triple bypass operation. Souey had been rushed to hospital just hours after the first game. I know that he watched the match on TV, and I can only imagine the hell we put him through as once again it was a goalless stalemate at the end of 90 minutes. On a personal level, it was something of a frustrating night for me as I was left to kick my heels in frustration on the bench. I had been desperate to do well on my return to Villa Park but didn't get the opportunity to come on until there were just three minutes of extra time remaining. I remember sitting there willing stand-in manager Ronnie Moran to throw me on earlier. Thankfully we won 3-1 on penalties, the first time a tie had been decided in this manner. I remember it causing uproar among the press, with one paper even praising Portsmouth for 'accepting the most sickening of defeats in a gracious manner'! Pompey scored just one of their four kicks so I wasn't called upon, but I had been ready, willing and, hopefully, able!

We were in the final, where we would face Second Division Sunderland, and were overwhelming favourites to win the cup. Between the semi-final win over Portsmouth and the final, we had five league games to negotiate and we did so with mixed success. A goalless draw at home to Leeds was followed by a morale-sapping 4-0 loss at Arsenal. We then drew 1-1 at Nottingham Forest and I played up front alongside John Barnes and Ian Rush, which was a pleasure. Our penultimate league match was against old rivals Manchester United at Anfield and a packed house saw us win 2-0. Ian Rush and I got the goals which put us sixth. It also ended any hopes United had of winning the last-ever old-style First Division title, which Leeds would win by four points.

We moved on to the final fixture against Sheffield Wednesday at Hillsborough, where Ian Rush and Jan Molby returned to the starting line-up and I played on the right wing. It was a decent rehearsal for the cup final just seven days later and, despite drawing 0-0, we retained sixth spot in the table.

As soon as the final whistle sounded in Yorkshire, all thoughts turned to the FA Cup Final and Wembley. I was looking forward to it all week, but as we counted down the days and hours till 3pm on the Saturday, I had the feeling I wouldn't be involved. Something was gnawing away at me, and sadly my fears were confirmed when I was handed the number 12 shirt. Souey had decided to bring Michael Thomas in from the cold and I suppose his decision was vindicated as Michael scored just two minutes after the break to give us the lead. Rushy scored the second in our 2-0 win. The Liverpool supporters in the 80,000 crowd were going crazy at the final whistle, but inwardly I was gutted not to have played any part. Of course, you have to be professional about it and paint a smile on your face, but knowing I had played in most of the games to get us to Wembley, missing out on the showpiece match was a sore one to swallow.

But I wanted to be happy for my team-mates, as we had just won the FA Cup and I knew it was a huge achievement. Anyway, I didn't ever want to be one of those bad apples who cast a shadow over the dressing room, so I pretended to be happy. Mind you, there is a photograph of Michael Thomas, Rushy and I on the celebratory open-top bus going through Liverpool and it paints a different picture. Sometimes it's too hard to hide.

To be honest, I was still struggling to accept it the following week – with the season over – and I even contemplated moving on. You might think that's a ridiculous reaction, but that's how disappointed I was. You soon know whether or not you're fully in the manager's plans, judging by how and when he uses you in matches. I was aware of my place in the pecking order, hence the reason I considered leaving. I've never been one to sit around and take a wage. I would rather earn my corn, but while it had crossed my mind, I knew the sensible thing to do was try to get over the disappointment and enjoy the close-season break.

That's exactly what I did and when it was time for pre-season training, I was raring to go. It was also the dawning of a new era as the 1992/93 campaign would be the first under the guise of the Premier League. It was exciting and something to look forward to.

Days after we reported back to Anfield, I had a beaming smile on my face, but not because I was fully over the disappointment of missing out on the FA Cup Final. I was standing next to Bruce Grobbelaar while the official 1992/93 team photograph was being shot. We were there for a while as the photographer tried to get everyone to stand po-faced, but there was never a snowball's chance in hell of that happening with Bruce next to me. If I remember correctly, it was much the same at the start of every season at Ibrox with Ally McCoist and Ian Durrant winding everyone up. Say cheese!

And then there was the irony to end all ironies. As FA Cup winners, we would start the new season with a Charity Shield match against Leeds – at Wembley Stadium, and I played the full 90 minutes in what BBC commentator John Motson described as the most entertaining Charity Shield match he had ever witnessed. Sadly we lost 4-3 with Eric Cantona scoring a hat-trick for Leeds, but it was still good to get a run-out at Wembley, although in all truth, while the Charity Shield might be a glamour curtain-raiser, as far as I was concerned the real business didn't ever start until the opening league fixture. For us, that meant a trip to Nottingham Forest and once again I was in the starting line-up.

I had enjoyed a good pre-season with the squad 2,000 miles up in the Tuscan mountains at Il Ciocco – just like I had done with Rangers – and I was fully prepared for the long season ahead. I wouldn't say the disappointment of missing out on the

FA Cup Final had completely dissipated, but the hunger was certainly there to make a go of it, and I truly wanted to make something of my Anfield career.

The match at the City Ground is now etched in history as the first live televised Premier League game on Sky Sports, but while it's always nice to have played your part, I would much prefer we hadn't lost to a Teddy Sheringham goal, because the feeling as we headed home that evening was of the same old disappointment. Premier League or English First Division, losing was something no one enjoyed.

When I look back at that season, it was ground-breaking in so many ways, but live television changed the way an entire nation viewed its football. To this day we still have many games that kick-off at 3pm on a Saturday, but no matter the time or day, there is always live football on the box, whether it's British, European or from wherever. When we played in that historic first televised match, on a Sunday at 4pm, I don't think any of us could've envisaged exactly what would follow.

The following Wednesday evening, we hosted Sheffield United and I was both delighted and honoured to score Liverpool's first-ever goal in the Premier League (especially after scoring the club's last-ever goal in the old league). We were 1-0 down to a Brian Deane strike when I picked up a pass from Ronnie Whelan 20 yards out. I hit the ball with everything I had and thankfully it flew into the corner of the net and the fans went wild. Paul Stewart scored a debut winner. Naturally I was proud as punch as I left Anfield that night with a win bonus and a little piece of history for company.

The goal against United was my first of the season and I was desperate to get back to the scoring form I had showed at Rangers. Six goals in my first season with Liverpool simply wasn't good enough, especially as I had raised the bar during my time at Ibrox, and I had no excuses. I don't think it was any harder to score in England than it was in Scotland, so I knew I needed to improve on that front. At the start of the season, the manager had told everyone they were on a clean slate, and that whoever did the business for him would be rewarded with a run in the team.

With John Barnes still out with an Achilles tendon injury, there was extra pressure on me to deliver consistently and my form was pretty good in the opening games, which included a thumping 6-1 win over Apollon Limassol in the first round, first leg of the European Cup Winners Cup at Anfield. Just over 12,000 bothered to turn up but those who stayed away missed Ian Rush score four times, which meant it was safe to say we were through to the second round.

And there were 12,000 hardy souls present when we hosted Chesterfield in the second round of the Coca-Cola Cup. I'm still not sure if the size of the crowd was a good thing or bad, but we certainly put our supporters through the mill that night. They witnessed Chesterfield go 3-0 up, and sure, we may have been without many first-team regulars, but we should still have had enough in the tank to win the game – especially at home, but we battled back to get a 4-4 draw. Had we lost it might have gone down in history as one of our poorest defeats ever, and NO player wants that on their CV.

We were facing another crisis, especially when we lost at home to Wimbledon, and next up was Sheffield Wednesday. My old mate Trevor Francis was in charge of the Owls, while Chris Woods was their goalkeeper, so it was good to see some friendly faces. But we had business to attend to and scraped a 1-0 win. We had to do so without our record signing, Dean

Saunders, who had left to join Aston Villa just 15 months after signing for us. It was a strange one. We had slipped into the bottom half of the table and needed to find a solution to our problems sharpish.

The next round of the Cup Winners Cup dredged up some good memories for me when we were drawn against Spartak Moscow, with the first leg scheduled to take place in the Russian capital. I had scored there for Villa, but any hopes I had of an action replay were dashed as we lost the game 4-2. It was also a night when Bruce Grobbelaar was sent off and David Burrows was forced to go in goal as we had used up our quota of subs. Spartak scored two really late goals when it was 2-2 and suddenly a solid draw away from home was a two-goal loss.

I was injured playing against Tottenham a few days before the return leg, which we lost 2-0, so we were out of Europe early, which seemed something of a default setting for me!

We would go on to have a really inconsistent season, firing six past Spurs and five past Crystal Palace, but losing to the likes of Wimbledon and Southampton, and looking on in horror as Coventry stuck five past us at Highfield Road. It was frustrating at times, but it wasn't all doom and gloom. A fortnight before Christmas, we were up against Blackburn Rovers at Anfield. Kenny Dalglish had only been out of football management eight months and it was a huge surprise when it was the Lancashire side who tempted him back. He was given a few quid to spend and it didn't take him long to turn Blackburn into a real force. This was a couple of years before they would shock English football by winning the league, and a packed Anfield roared us to victory. I was delighted to score twice, with Alan Shearer grabbing a consolation for Rovers in between. My second goal that day was probably my best in a red jersey.

Midway through the second half, Jamie Redknapp played a great ball to me and I cut inside David May and unleashed a cracking drive into the top corner.

But any good work was undone just seven days later when we lost heavily at Coventry. We did manage to string together a run of three league wins in March – just the second time we'd done so all season – but the highlight of the campaign for me, personally, came the following month when we thumped Coventry 4-0 at Anfield, and I became the first Liverpool player to score a hat-trick in the new league set-up. It was another record to savour, as it was difficult enough for a centre-forward to score a hat-trick, never mind a wide player. That made the achievement all the more satisfying; it was the only treble scored by a Liverpool player in domestic competition all season. In fact, I had been fretting about a lack of goals since before Christmas, so to get three in the same game was fantastic. The first was an acrobatic volley, the second a chip from 25 yards which took the keeper by surprise, and I wrapped things up with a penalty. A few days later I set one up for John Barnes before scoring again with another penalty as we beat Leeds 2-0 so it was a decent end to a tumultuous season. We finished sixth again but to be 24 points behind champions Manchester United was unacceptable for a club our size. Ironically, Villa were runners-up.

On a personal level, I had enjoyed my best season in Liverpool colours, scoring 13 goals from 44 appearances, but there was disappointment in the cup competitions as we crashed out of both the FA Cup and League Cup earlier than expected.

My second season at Liverpool had been enjoyable, and probably the only time I really felt part of the team. There was a lot of competition for places at Anfield and I had to fend off a few team-mates for the jersey, so it was tough. But my wife and I were settled in the Wirral, which was just a short commute to the ground and training centre, which is always an important factor. Liverpool was very much like Glasgow in the respect that it is a football city. The young guys are only interested in three things: football, women and drink, although I'm not sure in what order!

Mind you, I would be lying if I said I didn't cast an envious glance a couple of hundred miles north to Ibrox Stadium. The season just finished had seen the start of the new Champions League, although the competition had started off as the European Cup for a couple of qualifying rounds before morphing into two groups of four and a final, which was the inaugural Champions League. And it did as it said on the tin. Every club taking part were champions of their country.

Probably not too many people outside Glasgow paid too much attention when Rangers beat Danish side Lyngby in the first qualifying round, but when they drew Leeds in the next, everyone sat up and took notice. It was a bona fide Battle of Britain and I didn't miss a moment of the action. Not many folk down south gave Rangers an earthly of beating the English champions, but they didn't just beat them on aggregate, they beat them home and away. It was quite a feat and I remember thinking what I would have given to have been part of it.

And then Rangers went on to the group stages where they were paired with Marseille, CSKA Moscow and Bruges. They remained unbeaten throughout the six group matches and only lost out to Marseille by virtue of a single point. I tried to watch all their matches and I was gutted for my ex-team-mates that they missed out a Champions League Final against Milan.

Chapter 15

Out of Favour
at Anfield

DESPITE playing just over 80 competitive games for Liverpool in my first two seasons, there was still a part of me which didn't feel like a regular member of the side. Crazy, I know. Perhaps that was down to the manager rotating the squad, an inconsistency in my performances, or a bit of both. I'm not sure. I always remember reading a quote by Souey when I signed for Rangers, something along the lines of, 'Flair players tend to be inconsistent, but that's just the nature of that type of player. When Mark is on his game he is devastating.' Perhaps the type of player I was did lend itself to a degree of inconsistency, but it was never for the want of effort on my part.

During my third season at Anfield, I was in and out of the team – more so than the first couple – and played almost as many matches for the reserves as I did the first team. It was frustrating, and a big part of the reason I would eventually call my decision to join Liverpool in the first place 'the wrong one'. I started off the season in the team for the opening league match, against Sheffield Wednesday, and we won, comfortably, 2-0. I then missed out on a couple of matches before being brought back and dumped on the bench for games against Spurs, Leeds and Coventry. Mind you, a certain teenager had barged his way into the first team and taken it by storm. Robbie Fowler wasn't hanging about, nor going anywhere soon. He was in the team to stay and within his first few games had scored all five goals in a League Cup tie against Fulham, and grabbed a hat-trick in a league game against Southampton. I'm not sure there was a youngster who had announced himself on such a big stage so spectacularly. Robbie was a sensation from the word go and as a local lad, the Kop loved him.

The Merseyside derby at Goodison would be my last start for a while, and even then I was hooked seven minutes into the second half. It was demoralising. Mind you, playing in front of very few spectators for the reserves was in itself a demotivating experience, so I was getting used to the feeling. Near the end of January I was called back into the first team and we edged Manchester City at Anfield. I played well and was hoping it might kick-start a run of games, and I was right. But the repercussions of my next appearance had dire consequences. We had drawn 1-1 with Bristol City in an FA Cup tie at Ashton Gate, a match which had originally been abandoned due to floodlight failure. We were still confident going into the replay and with players like Barnes, Rush, McManaman and Redknapp involved we had every right to be. But a single swish of Brian Tinnion's boot led to one of our worst results in a long time. It also led to Graeme Souness vacating the hot seat. And while Souey's decision to quit left us all in shock, it wasn't entirely unexpected as the loss to City had marked a new low for the club. Liverpool supporters were no different from those at Rangers. They demanded a certain level of performance and result, and the Bristol game fell way below the acceptable. As we were trooping disconsolately off the pitch at the end, our supporters stood to a man applauding, but the praise wasn't for their own, it was our opponents who were lapping up the cheers. Liverpool supporters have always respected effort and good play and the City players were in their element that night. And fair play to them.

In three years in charge at Anfield, Souey had just a single FA Cup to show for his efforts, and he received criticism for his transfer dealings and man-management. I reckon most of the flak was unfair. Graeme taught me a lot. He was a legend as a player and when you command respect like he did it's half the battle. But managers will always be judged on what they win, especially at a club like Liverpool, so I can understand why people might think differently about him. He brought through a lot of great young players like Fowler and McManaman, although perhaps he was guilty of splitting the team up too quickly and making too many changes too soon after his appointment, but I'm sure he was keen to put his own stamp on the team.

Near the end of his tenure, Souey wasn't picking me for the team all that often so we weren't exactly going out for dinner, but I was still sorry to see him go as I had a lot of respect for him. But the bottom line is I wanted to play first-team football and I waited patiently to see who the new manager would be and if I would be in his long-term plans.

When Roy Evans was appointed as Souey's successor, I was delighted for him as he was a really nice man; some might say too nice, though, as some of the players took advantage of his good nature and were regularly turning up late for training, and that included a couple of the so-called 'Spice Boys', the new crop of young players racing through the ranks, some of whom – perhaps because they were still teenagers – didn't really have much time for authority. I've always believed that discipline is so important in football and sadly I noticed a decline when Roy took over. In my opinion, if the players don't respect the manager, then it's always going to be a struggle to gain cohesion and win anything.

What happened next with Roy and I was really strange. In the wake of the Bristol City debacle, and a changing of the guard, a few of us probably expected to be on the sidelines for a while, but in my case it was the opposite. Roy's first game in charge of the Reds was a 2-2 draw with Norwich City at Carrow Road. I played the full 90 minutes and again the following Saturday as we lost heavily at Southampton, thanks in the main to a Matthew Le Tissier hat-trick. In our next three matches, I came on against Leeds, played the full 90 at home to Coventry and came off the bench again at Blackburn. For the first time in my Liverpool career I felt I was getting a good run at it, and I seemed to be an integral part of Roy's plans. What I will say is that I don't think I was ever 100 per cent suited to the way Roy set up his teams to play. He preferred to use his wingers as wing-backs, getting up and down the flank (which wasn't a problem) and tracking back with opposition attackers and getting the tackles in. I had done a pretty similar job at Rangers on occasions, but I wasn't a wing-back. I was an attacking winger who liked to take defenders on, get crosses in and score goals now and again. It's as simple as that. I wasn't being awkward, but it just wasn't me. That said, I was desperate to make a success of my time at Liverpool – as I have done everywhere I have been – and I wanted to do well for Roy, personally, as I had a lot of time for the man.

Sadly, though, my appearances in the team didn't so much dry up after I came off the bench at Blackburn, as stop altogether. The next match was a Merseyside derby against Everton at Anfield and these were the type of games I loved playing in, but the name 'Walters' wasn't in the starting 11, nor was it next to the three boxes containing the substitutes. Walters was sitting in the stand that afternoon along with 44,000 fans. I was sitting there with my suit on and I was gutted, and even though goals by Rush and Fowler won us the game, I found it hard to smile. Of course, I was delighted for our supporters and my team-mates, but I was gutted inside at missing out on such an important game, especially as I was just starting to find my feet in the team, and hadn't been playing too badly.

A similar fate befell me for our next game, a 2-1 win over Chelsea at Anfield, and by the time the players were preparing to face Arsenal at Highbury, I had already spoken to Roy and he agreed it was best that I go out on loan for the rest of the season. Do you understand how that feels, knowing that you're surplus to requirements having given it your best shot? Being a part of Roy's first five matches in charge had offered no more than a false dawn. I had looked upon it as acceptance by Roy, but the reality was somewhat different. Each manager likes to come in and stamp his authority on the squad, bring in new players (as Souey did) and get rid of some of the old guard, especially if they were deemed to be the previous gaffer's 'men'. But Roy was in a different situation. He had been Souey's right-hand man, and knew every single member of the squad inside out. Of course he would have his own ideas about players, and perhaps want to implement a different system, but he also knew exactly what I could do, which is why the early run of games offered me false hope.

I was in the latter stages of the third year of my five-year contract, so at that point I didn't think running down my contract was a viable option. I was on the cusp of my 30th birthday so time was of the essence. I wanted to be playing football and not trudging back into the reserve team and the Pontins League, so I was pleased when I discovered that Stoke City had been monitoring my situation at Anfield. They noticed I hadn't been playing regularly and made enquiries about taking me on loan for the rest of the season; Roy left the decision up to me. Joe Jordan was in charge at the Victoria Ground and the club were playing in the First Division so while it wasn't the Premier League, it was still a very good standard and I decided to go for it. Oh, and Stoke was just up the road from Birmingham.

Just before heading off to join Stoke, Roy offered me a one-year contract extension, which I declined. I reckoned I would have been as well at Scunthorpe United than Liverpool. If you're not playing regular first-team football – which didn't look like it was going to happen any time soon at Anfield – then I should start to look around for something else. What was the point in signing a new contract to play half-a-dozen games for the reserves and then twice for the first team? It still baffled me a bit though, why Liverpool would offer me an extension if they didn't want me. Looking back, it's easy to get caught up in the moment, and when you haven't played for a few weeks, you start to believe you're not wanted. It gets inside your head. In hindsight, perhaps it wasn't that big a deal and maybe I jumped the gun. But regardless of the reasons, I decided to go to Stoke. It was the end of March and there were about ten games to go. I was determined to get as much game time as possible before the end of the season.

Two days after arriving at Stoke, I made my debut in a home match against Crystal Palace. We lost 2-0 and I was gutted, but at least I was back in the groove and with Palace being runaway winners of the league, maybe it wasn't such a disaster after all.

Our remit was to try and get into the play-offs and our main rivals in that respect were Tranmere, Derby, Notts County, Wolves, Middlesbrough, Charlton and Bristol City, the latter being our next opponents. We managed what we couldn't do at Liverpool and beat City 3-0. It was a good start in our push for a play-off place, although the wheels came off a little when we lost to Birmingham City – yes, them – at St Andrew's the following weekend.

Despite losing just once in our last seven league games, we missed out on the play-offs by just four points. Our defensive record stood comparison with our rivals but we just didn't score enough goals, and perhaps that was down to the club allowing Mark Stein – who had scored 13 goals by October – to join Chelsea midway through the season. Had Mark remained at the Victoria Ground, the club might just have been playing Premier League football the following season.

When I was at Stoke, our kit man was a guy called Neil Baldwin. He had special needs and was later the subject of a very moving film. His story was incredible as he had been given the job by Lou Macari after apparently badgering the Stoke manager for ages. 'Nello' was fantastic around the dressing room, but the lads would wind him up and ask him what he thought of me, and his ready-made answer (pre-ordained by my so-called mates) would be, 'Oh Mark, he's f****ng crap!' and everyone would fall about the dressing room laughing. Nello was brilliant at keeping everyone's spirits up and he was loved so much at the club. I had a lot of time for him.

I managed to score a couple of goals for Stoke but my time at the club ended on the last day of the season with a 2-2 draw against Luton Town. Of the ten league games I played, we won four and drew three. I thoroughly enjoyed my time in the Potteries.

One of the biggest things I miss as a retired footballer is matchday, and I had missed it enormously at Liverpool when I was in and out of the side. It was so frustrating training all week and preparing for Saturday's match, only to find yourself on the bench or not even in the squad, but I got that back at Stoke as I was playing every week. Training was a necessary evil and I eventually kind of got used to it, as it was a means to an end, but matchday was my biggest love. Arriving at the ground, heading into the dressing room to meet the rest of the lads, and the banter right up until kick-off and then the game. That was it for me; that was all I needed.

But it was time to head back to Liverpool and see what awaited me at that famous old club. Despite spending a large chunk of the season on loan at Stoke, I was still disappointed I hadn't managed to get more game time at Anfield, and it was frustrating not to have scored for Liverpool that season. I had still played 20 times for the Reds, and with the likes of Barnes, Rush, Molby and even Fowler ahead of me in the penalty-kick queue, scoring from 12 yards hadn't even been an option. I took a fair few penalties in my time, mostly because I loved scoring and it was a great way to boost my goals-to-appearances ratio. Many of them were pressure penalties, and I didn't always succeed in scoring. But my penalty-taking philosophy was simple: hit it hard and hit the target. And I wasn't scared of missing. I have videos of both Pele and Maradona failing from the spot, so there was always an excuse for me. One thing I never got was the shakes when either the penalty was awarded, and I knew I was on spot-kick duty, or when I was taking my run-up to hit the ball. I must just have been that kind of person. I remember taking one for Liverpool against Villa, and standing between me and glory was Nigel Spink, my former team-mate at Villa Park. Nigel knew me inside out, but he might also have known that I was very much a spontaneous penalty taker, and always followed my feelings at that moment (which helped that day as I scored). I had no pre-ordained notion that I was going to stick it, for example, low and hard to the keeper's right. It was a case of in the moment as far as I was concerned. I would pick the ball up, place it on the spot, have a look at the goal and the keeper and then decide. It was a good philosophy to have, especially with the advent of live televised football, where keepers and coaches would be able to study penalty takers much easier.

Sadly I still remember my first ever penalty only too well – as it ended in complete disaster. I was at Villa and we were playing Leicester City, and when we were awarded the spot kick I keenly offered to take it. Perhaps a bit too keenly. The older players let me go for it but I missed by quite a bit and fled the scene immediately! Gordon Cowans and Allan Evans wouldn't let me anywhere near the responsibility after that but a couple of months later, with neither playing that day, I stepped up and scored. Hopefully they were watching from the stand.

When I went to Rangers, we were playing Celtic one afternoon and we were awarded a penalty. A few team-mates in close proximity put their heads down and hastily departed the scene – a bit like I'd done after missing against Leicester – but I stepped forward and scored. Let me tell you, if ever there was pressure to score a penalty kick, it was in an Old Firm match, but thankfully it was on target and firmly struck. I didn't look back after that.

Chapter 16

On the Move

MY PENULTIMATE season as a Liverpool player was another mixed bag. It started off with a month in the Anfield reserves playing in the Pontins League and trudging around grounds performing to a couple of hundred folk ... and the occasional dog. Mind you, it was still preferential to sitting on the bench as an unused sub, or taking my seat in the stand proudly wearing the club blazer and tie. To be honest, nothing beats the feeling of signing for one of the biggest clubs in Britain, and one of the biggest in Europe, but if you ain't playing ...

And then the phone rang, and it was Graham Taylor. Nope, he wasn't calling me up for England, but he had just taken over as manager of Wolverhampton Wanderers and wanted me there on loan. To be honest, I wanted to play football so I asked Liverpool if I could go and thankfully they agreed. Graham also landed my Anfield colleague, Paul Stewart, who had cost Liverpool £2.3m when they had signed him from Tottenham Hotspur just two seasons before. Personally, I was delighted with the move to Molineux. I was back with Graham and Wolverhampton was just half an hour from Birmingham.

I was looking forward to getting started, and once I did, the fact I was happier at Wolves soon started to show in my play. I felt as though I had been given a new lease of life. Graham's philosophy of getting the ball on the deck and passing it was also right up my street.

We were due to play Tranmere Rovers just a couple of days after I signed and I remember arriving at the stadium in plenty of time for the Saturday afternoon kick-off and feeling like an excited kid as the manager read out the team. I was in, and when I looked around the dressing room we had some formidable players. I would be charged with supplying the ammo for the likes of Steve Bull and David Kelly – both international strikers – and that was enough to get the juices flowing. We also had Wolves legends like Neil Emblen, Andy Thompson and Mark Venus, who had played around 1,000 games between them for the first team. Perhaps it sounds a bit dramatic, but I fell in love with football again in the Black Country.

I certainly enjoyed my debut, as we beat Tranmere 2-0, which put us third in the table. Wolves have always been a well-supported club with fans as passionate as any, and after a dodgy start to the season they had good reason to cheer as we were again moving in the right direction. In the next game – a midweek encounter with Southend – we scored five times without reply. Suddenly, we were top of the table and there were lots of smiles around Molineux.

I remember the fourth goal against Southend well. I received the ball wide on the left, cut inside and attempted quite an audacious curling shot, which I was delighted to see nestled in the far corner. In fact, ten days later I did exactly the same thing at Portsmouth as we came from behind to grab the points. We won the first five games after I joined Wolves, and it was only a draw at Chesterfield in the cup which halted our great mini-run.

Sadly, my introduction to the Molineux side coincided with the death of a Wolves legend, the most famous player the club had ever known. Billy Wright died at the age of 70 a few days before I joined, and it was immediately clear how much the supporters revered Mr Wright, as an area directly outside the ground quickly turned into a colourful shrine to the first player ever to be capped 100 times by his country. Before the match with Tranmere, an impeccably observed minute's silence was held to remember Wolves's favourite son.

One of my new team-mates was Darren Ferguson, son of Sir Alex. Darren had started his career with his dad at Old Trafford, but moved to the Black Country when things didn't work out in Manchester. He played on the right-hand side of centre midfield but just after I signed he was switched to the left, and we teamed up well together. We were also on the same page when it came to the way we viewed the game. I remember him saying he didn't like playing too wide as he didn't see as much of the ball as he did when he played in the centre, and that was definitely a view I shared. It could be quite lonely out on the wing at times and you had to be patient and permanently switched on.

Mind you, one place I didn't think I would be playing when I joined Wolves on a temporary basis was in Europe – but I didn't reckon on the Anglo-Italian Cup! That season, Wolves were in a section alongside Ascoli, Lecce and Venezia. When I signed, they had already won over in Lecce, which is in the south of Italy, and lost narrowly at home to eventual finalists Ascoli. I was included in the squad for the trip to Venice and we knew that only a win would be enough if we were to progress in the competition. We arrived in Venice the day before the match, and on the morning of the game a few of us went for a stroll through the city centre. I remember thinking how incredible it was that many of the streets were made out of water! It was the first time I had seen anything like it since Birmingham was hit with terrible flooding when I was a kid. Seriously, though, it was a beautiful city but one aspect which wasn't so pretty was the smell of stagnant canal water.

The Anglo-Italian Cup was designed as a glamorous fixture-filler for second-tier clubs from both countries, but I didn't realise just how much apathy the Italian public had reserved for the competition until we turned up at the Stadio Pierluigi Penzo to find barely 750 souls in the vast stadium. The backdrop to the game was a ghost-like atmosphere, but Mark Venus gave us the lead (I always thought 'Venus scoring in Venice' was quite funny!) although they equalised before half-time. In the second half, a young lad called Christian Vieri scored the winner. Yes, the same Vieri who would go on to become the world's most expensive player when he moved from Lazio to Inter Milan. He was a bit of a handful for our defenders that night and I suppose it was only a matter of time before he removed the shackles and found the net.

A further aside to that game was the appearance of another Venezia youngster called Paolo Vanoli, who was a full-back. Ten years later he would sign for Rangers, but not until he had won a pile of honours in his native Italy with the likes of Parma and Fiorentina.

I made 11 consecutive appearances for Wolves before signing out and heading back to Anfield. To be honest, I had hoped to make the move permanent but Graham didn't try to make it happen so once the loan had expired I was on my way back north. It was the end of November and to be fair to the manager, he had Tony Daley in the squad and he played in the same position as me. Tony – who was coming through the ranks at Villa while I was there – was injured and that was why Graham had signed me for a spell. Sadly for Tony, he didn't ever manage to play regularly, due to injury, but by that time the gaffer, being forced to prioritise, had set his sights on a couple of new defenders with the cash he had available. I was also the wrong side of 30 and the chances are Graham wanted to bring in younger players. Still, it was disappointing to be told 'Thanks, but no thanks.' During my time with Wolves, we were consistently in the top four – and even led the table at one point – so I toddled off happy with the job I had done.

The week I left Wolves, Graham signed Don Goodman from Sunderland and Dutchman John de Wolf, previously with Feyenoord. The signing of de Wolf, for £600,000, was an interesting one. The towering centre-back was immediately installed as captain, scored a hat-trick just a few games in and then suffered a knee injury. Graham Taylor left at the end of the season to return to Watford, and Mark McGhee was installed as gaffer. The story goes that McGhee wasn't too happy with the Dutchman and selected him for the reserves. De Wolf apparently took exception to this and refused to play. He was on the next plane home.

For me, it was back to Liverpool and I decided, once again, to try and fight for a place in the first team. I didn't want to be languishing in the reserves for the second part of the campaign so I worked ever so hard in training to impress Roy Evans. I was an unused sub for Liverpool in the League Cup Final win over Bolton Wanderers, and while I was disappointed, I wasn't surprised. I knew the script by that time and with my contract running down, I knew I would be leaving relatively soon. I sold my house in the Wirral and rented a place and decided that even if I was offered a new contract, I wouldn't be signing it.

But if season 1994/95 was stop-start as far as Liverpool were concerned, the following one was more of a, well, stop, as I didn't play at all for the Reds. I kept myself fit by playing in the reserves for the first part of the season and if I wasn't involved on a Saturday afternoon I would work on my own to maintain a decent standard of fitness. It's funny because people who knew me early in my career would never have believed that I would actually grow to love training. It had been the bane of my life for so long. I also believe that's why mentally I have always been a bubbly person, because I think people who keep fit have less mental health problems. Some of my ex-team-mates who I have come across later in life, and who perhaps haven't maintained their fitness, have had psychological issues to deal with. I played for more than 20 years and I think my level of fitness helped me come to terms with coping mentally the day I called time on my career. I don't care who you are but it's really difficult to go from playing in front of 50,000 folk one Saturday to looking round garden centres the next. That's what quitting playing feels like and it's a big knock. I can completely understand why folk like Gazza really struggle to adapt to life after football.

You're living in a bubble and people adore you, and even if you aren't completely adored, they still tell you how wonderful you are. It's a real shock to the system when it all stops, and it took me at least two years to go to a game again. I'm thinking to myself, 'I can do better than half these guys, I should be out there instead of them,' and this wasn't me being nasty or vindictive, just frustrated and unwilling to accept that my career was over. It's only after two or three years you accept it's over and try to move on to the next chapter.

But back to season 1995/96, and just before Christmas I was becoming increasingly frustrated at a lack of game time; first-team game time. That was the reason that when I got a call from an old team-mate, I treated it with the respect it deserved. During my last two years at Villa, I'd had the good fortune to play with Simon Stainrod, who was an incredibly talented forward capable of doing things others could only dream of. Don't get me wrong, Simon was a regular footballer who gave his all for the team, but I recall reading about a goal he famously scored from the halfway line, straight from kick-off, while he was playing for Falkirk. He was that type of player. We got on well at Villa, and we both left the club at the same time. I headed to Scotland to play for Rangers while Simon made the short trip up the M6 to sign for Stoke. He then had a couple of seasons in France. Once we had left Villa, though, our paths didn't cross again until many years later when I was running down my contract at Liverpool. Mobile phones were all the rage and one day a number which I didn't recognise popped up on the screen. It was Simon, and the conversation went something like this:

'Hi Mark, it's Simon Stainrod, how are things?'

'I'm good, Simon, yourself?'

'Yeah, good mate. Listen, I know things aren't going too well for you at Liverpool at the moment and I was wondering if you would be interested in coming and playing for me.'

To be honest, I didn't have an earthly what Simon was up to and who he was with, so I had to ask.

'What are you up to at the moment, Simon?'

'Sorry mate, I'm manager at Ayr United, in the Scottish First Division. How do you fancy coming up to play for us?'

'How about I give it some thought, and get back to you ASAP? I just need to think about my current situation and work out what's best for me at this moment in time. I'll get back to you, promise.'

At that time, as I had done throughout my entire career, I just wanted to play first-team football. I knew there was a good chance I would be playing every week at Ayr United and there was a certain amount of appeal. I wasn't massively up to speed on the fortunes of Ayr, but I was mindful that Simon was looking for a decision sooner rather than later, and after weighing up all my options I decided I would give it a go, but decided to sleep on it and call him back the next morning to accept his offer. Next morning, though, I was having breakfast, and my mind drifted back to my time at Rangers. I was playing for the best team in Scotland and anything else, I believed, would be a backward step. I know Ayr United were playing in a different division from Rangers, but there was the potential for the clubs to meet in a cup competition, and the thought of playing against the team that had supported me so much during my time in Scotland proved the deciding factor. I rang Simon up to tell him thanks, but no thanks. I was pleased with the decision I made. No other Scottish club could ever come close to the love I have for Rangers and so it was best that I only ever played for one Scottish team – and that was Rangers.

But while I was pleased with my decision, it didn't help my immediate problem. And then I heard a whisper that Southampton were interested in me, but unlike the moves to Stoke and Wolves, they wanted me on a permanent transfer. Liverpool eventually agreed to let me go on a free and I signed for Saints in January 1996. It represented something of an inglorious end to my time at Anfield, but in many ways I wasn't surprised, and it was even a relief to get it over with.

Once again, though, it was a bit of a mixed bag for me at Southampton. I enjoyed playing again, and, while I was happy to be back in the Premier League, this time I was playing for a club at the other end of the table. Because of that, I was more often than not playing as an auxiliary full-back.

And then there was the manager, Dave Merrington. There is no point in beating about the bush here, but I couldn't stand him. There aren't many managers I came across that I disrespected. You can like or dislike a manager but when you have little or no respect for him then there is a problem. I didn't like the way he went about his business, so that was an issue for me virtually from the start.

Apart from that, Southampton is in a lovely part of the world and I really liked being based there. But come the beginning of April I knew I had to leave. I just couldn't put up with it anymore, and it was probably the worst decision I ever made because two months later Graeme Souness was announced as the new manager and I would love to have played for him again. Who knows, I might even have been able to coach under him. But that's the way football works at times. At Liverpool I decided to stay and run the clock down, while at Southampton I did the opposite and missed out on a potentially excellent opportunity. Don't get me wrong, he might not have been interested in my coaching proposition, but I guess we will never know. But we got on very well and I think it might have been a goer. That said, football is full of ifs, buts and maybes.

Right from the beginning, I didn't take to Merrington. I found him ignorant and I simply didn't like him. I remember one day in training he singled me out for 'banter' and said something like, 'Come on Mark, you'll never win anything training like that. Not even an egg cup!' I didn't often challenge managers but I offered to take him to my house and show him my display of trophies and medals – and that just wasn't me. I felt he was trying to take the piss in front of the lads and I decided to defend myself. We didn't ever have any kind of relationship and that was a pity.

A highlight of my time at Southampton was getting to play alongside one of the most talented players ever to kick a ball. Matthew Le Tissier was a wonderful footballer, but he also has to be one of the most laid-back guys I have met in my life. When we were travelling to play in a game, whether it was an important league match or cup tie, he looked as though he was turning out for a Sunday league team. He literally looked as if he didn't give a f***. And then you would see him in training and he would sidekick the ball harder than you could kick it. He had that languid style which was obviously very effective, but the most important thing at Southampton was that the team had to revolve around him, and that certainly isn't a criticism. It was the only way it would work, and boy did it work.

We would go for a pre-match meal and we would all be having beans and toast, you know, something which we could digest quickly, and there would be Matt tucking into half a chicken! But I think his nickname was Le God because they revered him down there, and on form he was unplayable.

Apart from the manager, it was an enjoyable time and I got on well with all the lads. In fact, I loved Southampton so much I could have settled down there. For a start, the weather was quite a bit better than it was in the north of England or the Midlands, but I simply couldn't have put up with the manager. I was at that age when I wouldn't say I was financially secure, but

I knew that I wouldn't starve if my career ended the next day, so I didn't have to indulge him. It was a pity, though, because football is a great career, although it just shows how one or two individuals can spoil it for you.

If Matt was the biggest character at Southampton then there were many more at Anfield, and I think a few thought they were in charge. You always get that in a dressing room, and Liverpool was no exception. I loved John Barnes to bits but he could be very argumentative, and I felt he had far too much to say at times. As a person, John is unbeatable, and obviously he was a fantastic footballer, but his dressing-room comments were just a bit too much for me. I wouldn't say he bullied Roy Evans but I felt he put his personality on to him which in turn undermined him a little bit. In fact, he was on Big Brother earlier this year and I'm sure he was voted off for being too argumentative. I was watching the programme and he seemed to be putting his opinion across too aggressively, and I was sitting there laughing, and thinking, 'That's John down to a tee.'

During my time at Anfield I was probably closest to John and to Michael Thomas. I got on very well with both lads and we used to socialise together quite a lot. I also liked Mark Wright and Dean Saunders. In fact, Dean and I were staying in the same hotel when we initially signed for Liverpool so I used to see a lot of him and we got on really well.

Ian Rush was another big character but he was different to John Barnes in as much as he knew when to chip in with his tuppence worth. If he ever tried to undermine the manager then I didn't notice, or perhaps he did so in a more subtle way. Sadly Roy Evans was too soft, unlike Souey, who could handle the big names quite easily. As the complete centre-forward, Ian Rush probably has the edge over the others I played with, although when we played together he maybe wasn't as prolific as he had once been. His goal ratio had dropped, perhaps because Liverpool weren't at the top of their game at that point. But one part of his game which really impressed me was his defensive side. He was brilliant at intercepting balls from opposition defenders and I lost count of the number of times he broke up play and started off an attack for us. Ian was like our first line of defence, and that's why I'd give him the edge over Gary Lineker. Mind you, I didn't play alongside Gary that much, although I've seen him play many times. Ian Rush's all-round game was first class. When I was at Rangers there was talk of Souey signing him from Juventus. He would've been a great signing for Rangers and an absolute sensation in Scotland, although sadly it didn't come to anything.

When I was at Liverpool, the likes of Robbie Fowler and Steve McManaman were just forcing their way into the first team and the gaffer simply couldn't ignore them. They were both fantastic players and our fans loved them because they were local lads. They were quite a few years younger than me so I didn't socialise with them, but we got on fine at the club. Robbie went on to become one of the club's greatest-ever goalscorers, while Steve ended up at Real Madrid. Enough said.

Bruce Grobbelaar was a real character, there is no getting away from that, but I thought he was a far better goalkeeper than many gave him credit for. I understand he was well known for his gaffes and his outrageous personality, but he had great strength of character and if he made a mistake he didn't allow it to get to him and would inevitably bounce straight back. He was such an authoritative presence and would come out and collect the ball and work well with his defenders, which I like in a goalkeeper.

If anyone was destined to become a keeper in life, it was definitely Bruce. Both of his parents were goalkeepers, his dad keeping goal for a team in Rhodesia (now Zimbabwe), while his mum was a net minder for one of the top hockey clubs in the country. He would talk of how he had goalposts erected in his back garden when he was six, and how BOTH of his parents regularly tested him by taking shots at him! Off the park he was always up to something and he would regularly wear a fancy-dress mask to training. I suppose his nickname, 'Hound Dog', sums him up perfectly. In fact, he tells the story of how he joined Liverpool. Apparently he was struggling to get a work permit to play in Britain and ended up with Vancouver Whitecaps as a result. When it was established that his great-grandfather was British and had served in the Boer War, he was granted a permit. Former Liverpool manager Bob Paisley, following up on reports from his scout, travelled to Vancouver to speak to Bruce. The conversation between manager and player went something like this:

Paisley: 'Would you like to play for Liverpool?'

Grobbelaar: 'Yes.'

And Bruce insists that was that. No more questions, no protracted negotiations, just a shake of the hand and 'I'll see you at training.' Bruce and I were never close socially, but we did get on very well as team-mates and he was always quick to put a smile on your face.

I still have a lot of great memories of my time at Liverpool, and while I probably should've stayed at Rangers, I don't really regret joining them, if that makes sense. But playing is what turns me on, and if I'm not playing then I'm not happy, and life's too short to be unhappy.

Chapter 17

Enjoying My Football Again

JUST before leaving Southampton, I started to look around at potential new homes. I knew I didn't have a long-term future at the Dell, so I sifted through a list of the clubs I thought I could make an impact at; clubs which were also within a certain radius of Birmingham. One which stood out from the crowd was Swindon Town, who were in the First Division at the time. The manager at the County Ground was Steve McMahon, a former team-mate of mine at both Villa and Liverpool, so we knew each other well. I rang him up and told him my contract was expiring at Southampton and that I was extremely fit and still full of enthusiasm. I reckoned I could do a good job for him at that level and he took me at my word and gave me a contract. Destination number seven on the Walters CV was Wiltshire.

It was good to meet up with Steve again. I liked him. He could be quite abrasive, but I knew him well as a person and we got on absolutely fine. In saying that, a few of the other players didn't appreciate his style of management and there was often a bit of friction around the place, but I didn't have any issues with him. His man-management style could've been a bit softer, but Steve was a young gaffer at the time and was also on a learning curve.

I hit the ground running at Swindon and was soon enjoying my football again. After my time at Liverpool, where I had been in and out of the side, and the spell at Southampton under Dave Merrington, it was like a breath of fresh air. Some folk reckoned I was inconsistent at Anfield but opportunities there had been few and far between. Maybe my performances weren't good enough but I don't think I was ever given the game time I needed to build up a true level of consistency. I was never a wing-back and didn't feel entirely comfortable with the system Roy Evans played. That's probably why I relished my time at Swindon so much. I was playing as a winger and I was enjoying the job of taking on full-backs and supplying the ammo for our front men.

When I moved to the County Ground I was going through a divorce so a change of scenery definitely helped. It was kind of therapeutic for me, as training was good and I was enjoying the banter with the lads. Apart from the stress a separation brings, I didn't have too much to worry me off the field. Our marriage had been going through a real rocky patch and we had virtually been living separate lives. We hadn't seen an awful lot of each other and felt the best road to take was to go our separate ways and make it official. This had all been going on while I was at Southampton and into the close season, so by the time the new campaign was about to get underway I was more or less free to concentrate solely on my football.

At first I rented a flat in Swindon, but after a while I decided to put down some roots and bought a house in Solihull, where I live to this day. It's less than ten miles from Birmingham and, even though it was still a fair jaunt to the County Ground, it was a good base for me. Door to door, it took me two hours to drive, but around six months to get used to the drive! On the night before a game I would stay over at a hotel, but in the first few months I had a succession of hamstring problems and I was really struggling to deal with the travelling. The distance was bad enough, but wasn't the main issue. The roads were really busy and were often subject to delays and slow traffic. It was a frustrating drive. There was one occasion when I decided just to drive down on the day of the match because I wasn't fully fit and didn't think I would be playing. However, when I got there, Steve took me aside and asked if I could play as he was struggling badly for personnel. I agreed to give it a go and I actually played very well. There were no issues with the hamstrings during the game and from that day onwards I ditched the hotels and drove down on the day of the game, and I did that for the remainder of my contract. It even marked an upturn in my form and people would speak to me after a game, saying they couldn't believe I was going through a divorce as I was playing really well. I suppose football was my escape.

During my first season at the County Ground, we landed a couple of plum cup draws – although both were away from home. We had knocked Wolves and QPR out of the League Cup and our reward was a third-round trip to Old Trafford. We actually gave a good account of ourselves but lost 2-1 in front of 50,000. I had obviously played at Old Trafford a few times but it was good to go back there with Swindon and not disgrace ourselves. The likes of David Beckham were playing for United that night. In fact, with a little more luck we might have nicked a draw and taken them back to our place, which I'm sure would've made our treasurer very happy.

It was a slightly different story in the FA Cup. We were paired with Everton and I'm afraid we weren't at the races and lost 3-0. Mind you, it was still a good experience for some of our younger players. Our kids had been doing well and helped us to a decent, mid-table spot until a late-season collapse saw us finish just a few places above the drop zone. We were playing in what is now the Championship and at one point it looked as though we might just kick on and land a place in the play-offs, and perhaps even a spot in the hallowed land of the Premier League.

We had a great start to the league campaign in my second season at Swindon and were top of the table heading into November, but after hammering Oxford just before Christmas, we managed just three wins from our next 26 league games, and that was simply unacceptable. It was probably only our good start – and getting points on the board early in the season – that prevented us from taking the drop. As it happened, Manchester City and Stoke City were among those who failed to escape the trapdoor. But as if our poor league form wasn't bad enough, crashing out of the FA Cup to non-league Stevenage Borough was the final ignominy for the club. There was a lot of talk about Steve losing his job in the wake of that game, but the chairman Rikki Hunt stood firmly behind him.

However, the inevitable happened at the start of my third season. We failed to register a single win from our first five games, scoring just three goals, and the calls for Steve to be sacked started to gather momentum. But the chairman insisted he wouldn't sack him, and Steve refused to resign. We picked up a bit and consecutive derby wins against Bristol City and Oxford helped steady the ship. But this was followed by a 5–2 defeat at Portsmouth, and when Watford won 4–1 at the

County Ground the fans staged an on-pitch protest, sitting in the centre circle at the end of the match and shouting for both Steve and the chairman to quit the club. That was it for Steve and he decided enough was enough and tendered his resignation. It was sad to see it reach such a critical stage, but when results aren't going your way the manager's head is always on the line. Steve had given it his best shot while working under severe financial restraints. Of course, the players were far from blameless.

Jimmy Quinn was his replacement and unfortunately we didn't really hit it off. I felt right from the start that Jimmy believed I was after his job, which wasn't the case. I remember saying something during training one morning and he flipped his lid. It was a completely innocuous comment but he took it the wrong way and snapped back at me, saying, 'If you don't want to do things my way then just go back to the changing room.' I responded by saying, 'If you want me to go and get changed, I will,' and off I trudged to the sanctity of the dressing room. I think he also took the nip with me as I had said some good things about Steve, like how I thought he had been unlucky with results, etc. I felt I owed Steve something as he had taken me on at a time when my life was in a bit of turmoil and really helped me out, both on and off the field. I wasn't seeing my children regularly, which had a big effect on me, but with football obviously still an important part of my life at that time, Steve gave me the opportunity to keep playing and stay sane. I was always grateful for that.

That said, Jimmy was still way off target if he thought I was after his job. I admit I did have a desire to break into coaching, but I definitely didn't want the manager's job at Swindon. And anyway, it would have been too big a step too soon.

That third campaign at Swindon wasn't the greatest for the team, or the club. We finished 17th in the table and gave our supporters very little to cheer. To be fair to Jimmy, when he came in, he steadied the ship a bit, starting with a good win over Huddersfield, and then just one defeat in the next five, which included a hard-fought draw at Birmingham City. Iffy Onoura and I were scoring a few goals and we were giving some of the bigger teams in the division a going over, but we tailed off again and a 6-0 loss at home to Ipswich was a particularly hard defeat to take. I managed 11 goals overall but it was tough to see our average crowd drop almost 4,000 to just over 6,500 from the previous season. When the fans vote with their feet in such big numbers, someone somewhere has to sit up and take notice.

My final season with Swindon was a bit of a non-starter. The Robins were struggling financially and administration came calling in November. They were around £4m in debt and were reportedly losing £25,000 a week. The chairman resigned and a number of staff members were made redundant. It was a bad time all round. In fact, so bad it was suggested the manager wasn't allowed to pick midfielder Robin Hulbert for any more games as one more appearance would trigger a £25,000 payment to his parent club Everton under the terms of his transfer a couple of years beforehand. As far as I'm aware, Robin played 29 games for us before being transferred. If true, that's how tight a financial ship Swindon were steering at the time. The club did eventually find a new backer but it was too late to prevent relegation.

Finding out about the financial problems at the County Ground didn't really surprise me too much, because in the three and a half years I was there, I think we were only ever paid on time on a handful of occasions. The wages were usually a week or a month late, but it was something we had come to expect.

My time was up in the November. As the rest of the country was preparing to welcome a new millennium in just a few weeks, the clouds of gloom had settled over the County Ground and the administrators were working overtime in a bid to prevent the ship from permanently sinking. As I expected, I was part of the financial cull, which was designed with just one thing in mind: survival. Not First Division survival, but survival for the club, and to that end, thankfully it was successful. Sure, it meant the team had to take a hit by dropping a division, but in the grand scheme of things that was nothing. Swindon Town had been around since 1879 and it was imperative that a club with such a rich historical heritage wasn't lost to the town.

Swindon is a nice little club and will forever have a place in my heart. We were never going to do anything special, like win major trophies, but it was friendly enough and I was happy there. I believed I would finish my career at the County Ground; I couldn't see myself playing anywhere else. Our training ground was a stone's throw from the stadium and directors like Mike Spearman would regularly pop in for a chat. It was that kind of club. I remember Mike telling a reporter, 'Mark's skills are unbelievable, the fans love him and he is an immense asset to this club.' When you hear things like that from a member of the board it definitely makes you feel wanted.

When I left Swindon I was at a bit of a loose end so I called the Aston Villa manager John Gregory to ask if I could train with the team just to keep myself ticking over, and in the hope that another club would come along and offer me a swansong. It was only a few miles from my home in Solihull so I was hopeful John would agree. Sadly he didn't and I was really disappointed when I was told he had refused my request. We ended up falling out over it, although we have made up since. I'm not saying for a moment that Villa owed me anything, but they were my club and I had been associated with them for many years so I felt it was a poor show. Villa had about 17 acres of training ground and all I wanted was a little corner. I could've gone and trained in a local park but I wanted a tiny share of the banter and camaraderie which I could only get by training with a group of footballers.

I was still determined my career wouldn't end in administration and even at the age of 35, I still felt fit enough to do a job for someone.

We were halfway through the 1999/2000 campaign when I received a call from an old Villa team-mate of mine, Garry Thompson, and what he had to say was music to my ears. Within an hour of hanging up, I was in the car and driving the 90 or so miles down the M5 to have talks with Bristol Rovers. Garry was assistant to Ian Holloway, and I think both guys realised I had looked after myself well and they offered me an 18-month contract, which I was delighted to sign. We were already halfway through the season, so I was keen to get the boots back on and start playing again.

Bristol is a football-mad city and that showed in the passion of the Pirates' supporters, who backed the team home and away, even though we were in the Second Division. Ian was player/ manager at the time and, while he was just starting out on his managerial journey, he was learning quickly. He was incredibly well organised for such a rookie boss and knew the game inside out. He was also a fantastic character to be around, and his fitness was exceptional. I remember he slaughtered one of his players in training for being out either the night before or two nights before a match. Ian went on about fitness and looking after yourself, etc., but he also gave the guy an opportunity to redeem himself, and told him that if he could beat his personal best time for running round the perimeter of the training field he would let him play in the game. The guy was super-motivated and did beat his time, and Ian was true to his word. Ian's mantra was as long as you put the work in, and did the business during games for him, then you could play hard. I had an awful lot of respect for him and also really liked him, because he is a fair guy. It's disappointing that he has never achieved a lot more than he has as a manager. I know he had success at Blackpool, and took them to the Premier League, but I expected him to be a fixture in the top flight as a manager. He is that good.

In my first (half) season at Rovers, we narrowly missed out on the play-offs, finishing seventh, and would definitely have been good enough to have played in the First Division had we been promoted. Sadly, we went backwards the following season and were battling relegation for most of the campaign. Ironically we were locked in a battle with Swindon Town to see who would join Oxford United, Swansea City and Luton Town in the bottom league. Cambridge United were also involved in the three-way scrap to avoid the trapdoor, but we ended up the fall guys and, even though we had a far better goal difference than the Robins, they had one point more than us, and that proved crucial.

Ian Holloway had already left the club by that point, with Garry Thompson placed in charge. Garry held the reins until former England striker Gerry Francis was unveiled as the new gaffer. It would be Gerry's final appointment as a manager, but prior to arriving at the Memorial Ground (for his second spell in charge of the Pirates) he had managed at clubs like Queens

Park Rangers and Tottenham. Sadly it didn't work out for him second time around though, and he lasted just five months.

That season, 2001/02, was probably the biggest rollercoaster ride I had endured in football. At one stage, we looked as though we were a good shout for the play-offs, but as injuries took their toll – and Gerry resigned before Christmas – we slid down the table at an alarming rate and just managed to fend off relegation to the Conference League by a single place.

It was certainly an inglorious manner in which to end my 21-year career in the senior game.

We had a few good strikers during my time at Rovers. The likes of Jamie Cureton, Jason Roberts and Bobby Zamora were all capable of sticking the ball in the net, but it was Bobby who really caught my eye. So when I got a call from Ian Culverhouse, who I'd played with at Swindon, and who was now assistant manager at Brighton, asking about Bobby, I had no hesitation in giving him a glowing report. Bobby hadn't been playing regularly at Rovers, and had perhaps fallen foul of strict disciplinarian Holly, but when Ian Culverhouse asked if I thought Bobby could do a job for him at Brighton I said yes. He certainly had the ability, and went on to have a great career, also playing for England on a couple of occasions. I think Ian Culverhouse had initially been put off because of Bobby's brushes with Holly, but Bobby only liked a night out and the things that thousands of other young guys enjoyed, but once I explained a few things, and that his football head was spot on, he was more than happy to take him – and I'm glad he did because Bobby had too much talent for it to be hidden away. In fact, every time I see Bobby he always thanks me for speaking up for him.

I had a really good time at Bristol Rovers and wouldn't have swapped it for the world. I even had the opportunity to coach the reserves in my last season, but when Ray Graydon was appointed manager he put an end to it, which was a big disappointment for me. He said he was bringing in his own men and that I was out. Ray was a Villa legend, but that meant little to me at that point. Perhaps he was another guy that thought I was after his job, even though I was happy coaching the reserves. It seemed ex-Villa men had something against me at that time!

My contract was about to expire at that point and I spoke to Ray about signing on again. I said he could amend my contract and that I would do without the appearance money, just straight wages, but he said no. He obviously didn't want me around and that was his prerogative, so I emptied my locker and left. It was a disappointing end to an enjoyable spell but at least I am still held in high esteem at the Memorial Stadium, and I'm regularly invited back to take part in social evenings and as a guest of hospitality. I had a great rapport with the Rovers supporters and they were always 100 per cent behind me, so you will never hear me say a bad word about the Pirates.

I have one other special memory of the Memorial Stadium and it came at the end of my second season with Rovers. After the final home game, the players were invited on to the park to take a lap of honour. I had my kids with me and Mischa was about seven, and Marlon a couple of years younger, but they accompanied me on to the park and both had a ball. Mind you, they both said the crowd were making an awful noise! After the game, we went for something to eat and Mischa said to me, 'Daddy, I thought it was quite funny when all the supporters were chanting your name.' It was definitely one of the cutest things I had heard.

Chapter 18

Back to Villa

WHEN the final whistle sounded at Bristol Rovers, I was adamant I wouldn't let the grass grow under my feet. I had heard all the stories about ex-pros turning to drink or gambling to while away the long hours, or seeking a thrill to replace the buzz of playing football. I was determined it wouldn't happen to me, so the only thing on my mind was finding something to do at three o'clock on a Saturday afternoon, something that didn't involve garden centres or supermarkets! Thankfully I didn't have too far to look. One day, ironically while I was at the supermarket, I received a call from former Bolton Wanderers and Scotland striker, John McGinlay. John had moved into management with non-league Ilkeston Town, and after some short formalities, he asked if I was interested in turning out for his side. He'd heard I was finished at Rovers and that I might be looking for a team. He was both right and wrong. First of all, I had retired, but even though it was the close season, I was already missing it. It's difficult to explain the attraction to someone for whom football hasn't been all-consuming most of their life. It was definitely that to me, so after some thought, I agreed to give it a go.

One of the first things I'd done after leaving Bristol had been to ring up Brian Jones to see if there was anything going in the coaching department at Villa. Brian was the guy who took me to Villa as a kid and if anyone could get me back in then he was the man. I was keen to stay involved in the game and after playing at a good level for just over 20 years I felt I had something tangible to offer. Perhaps 'putting something back' is an old cliché, but I genuinely felt that was what I wanted to do.

Brian put me in touch with a guy called Steve Burns, who was assistant director of the Villa youth academy at the time, and he agreed to give me a start. The 2001/02 season had just finished and I was asked if I wanted to wait until the start of the new season, or begin straight away. I chose the latter as I was keen to get going. It was a part-time post, but not a straight 9am till 3pm gig; the hours were all over the place due to the age groups I would be working with.

During one of my first conversations with Steve, I told him I wanted to keep playing, and that I had agreed to turn out for Ilkeston Town. He insisted I wouldn't have time to play, but what I did was tell John McGinlay I wouldn't be able to train with him midweek, but that I would still play on a Saturday afternoon, and he seemed okay with that. I also mentioned to him that I understood completely if me just turning up on a Saturday afternoon to play would cause ructions with the rest of the squad, and that all he had to do was let me know and we would work something out.

I started with the under-9s at Villa so you can imagine how different an experience it was from every other single experience I'd had during my time in football. The first thing I had to do was discourage this 'pack' of youngsters from chasing the same ball everywhere it went, as positions meant little to the young children. It was certainly a challenge.

I was the only coach at the academy who had played league football, bar Gordon Cowans, of course, who was full time. I would have loved a full-time position at the club and I would have invested so much of myself in it to try and bring kids through the system. If anyone knew that side of Villa it was me. I still had strong feelings for a club I had supported fervently as a kid. But I knew there weren't too many full-time positions available so I got on with my job and hoped that one day Steve would like what he saw and keep me in mind if a permanent position came up.

I worked my way up through the age groups over a five-year period and like to think I had a great rapport with the kids I was working with. Initially, I didn't think I would enjoy the job, as I had never once seen myself teaching kids so young, youngsters taking virtually their first steps in the game. But I grew to love it and I like to think I taught them a thing or two, and always offered loads of encouragement. By the time I had taken my age group through to the under-15s, though, two full-time positions had already come up, but had gone to others who, I was told, were friends of Steve, which I wasn't too happy about. I've always felt jobs should be given out on merit, although in football it seems to be more about who rather than what you know.

When I had finished with the under-15s, they wanted me to start coaching the under-12s again. I felt that was a retrograde step, as I had learned my trade and wanted to keep progressing up the age-group ladder, not head back down the 'snake' again. I wanted to coach the youth team but they were adamant I take the under-12s. All I wanted was a fair crack at the whip but I didn't feel I was getting it. I had spent five years coaching at Villa and felt I had made good progress. I had obtained my UEFA 'A' Licence and helped many young players along in the game. Seeing them develop and become better players had been incredibly rewarding.

Something I always tried to do when I started coaching was instil confidence in the forwards. Even if I didn't really fancy them that much I always tried to talk them up, because without confidence they wouldn't try anything in the last third of the pitch, and that's exactly where you need your flair players to be on their 'A' game. I thought back to a match I had played for Rangers against Hearts at Tynecastle. Yes, 'that' match. I remember our keeper Nicky Walker kicking the ball out, and watching it head my way, to the left wing. I controlled it and flicked it past defender Hugh Burns in a single movement. I had done it a few times in training but only once in a match in England, and that was for Villa. The time I attempted it at Tynecastle, it almost led to a goal. That was all down to confidence, not just in myself, but also the confidence my manager had in me. If I had been low on self-assurance, the chances are I wouldn't have tried it, because there were just so many things that could go wrong. But it proves how important confidence is for a player, and probably more so for a forward. The main point of coaching is to find the best way to impart your knowledge on to the youngster, in a way that he or she understands clearly. The other important factor was for me to make those young players feel good about themselves. If I could succeed at both then I had done my job.

A few of the kids I helped develop, such as Gabriel Agbonlahor and Luke Moore, went on to make the first team, which gave me a lot of satisfaction, but I was never given any feedback from Steve or anyone else to suggest I was a good coach or a bad one so I decided it was time to move on, as career progression didn't look like it was on the table. Never for a moment did I think that, because I had played for Villa, and the likes of Rangers and Liverpool, should I be given preferential treatment, because decent players don't always make good coaches. All I wanted was an opportunity to fail, or at least be given a reason why I was being overlooked for a certain position. Not too much to ask.

When I look back at my career, and think of all the different managers I played under, and inevitably their different styles of playing, I always come back to Rangers, and Graeme Souness. The role I was given at Ibrox was different from most others I filled. Souey gave me more of a licence to roam, whereas at Villa I was more or less stuck rigidly to the left wing. That said, our game plan at Villa relied heavily on width when Graham Taylor took over, so we had to be in our proper positions more often than not for the plan to work. At Rangers I had more of a free role and could come in off the wing from time to time. I felt the shackles had been taken off and Souey was clearly proved right as I scored more than 50 goals for him in three and a half seasons.

In my opinion, playing with better players definitely makes you a better player. When I was a coach at Villa, Gareth Barry was doing really well and was on the radar of both Liverpool and Manchester City. Villa were desperate to keep hold of him and he asked me for a quiet word one day as he was looking for advice. He had been at Villa 11 years and reckoned it might be time to move on, certainly if he wanted to step up to the next level. I told him that if he wanted to improve, he had to be playing in the Champions League both with and against better players. I reckoned both clubs were a good fit for him, although it was advice I probably shouldn't have offered as I was working for Villa. Unfortunately, the manager at the time – Martin O'Neill – heard about our little chat and I'm afraid that probably put the kybosh on me progressing while Martin was there. The thing is, Gareth is a lovely guy and when someone like that asks my advice then I'm always going to give it. Perhaps Martin didn't appreciate my background as a Rangers man, and obviously with him being on the other side of the fence, that could've played a role in any decision he made, although that's just a thought. I think my advice was sound, given that Gareth eventually went to Manchester City, but not until a long and protracted move to Liverpool had fallen through, and he had been stripped of the Villa captaincy by O'Neill. But despite taunts from sections of the Villa support, Gareth publicly thanked the fans for their tremendous support during his time there. To my knowledge, he has the highest number of appearances in the Premier League, which is a phenomenal record to hold. He had a great club career and has played more than 50 times for England, so I think he more than deserved his move.

Funnily enough I made more progress as a coach at Villa when David O'Leary was manager, and was even invited to take a few sessions with the first team. Sadly, though, nothing more long term came of it and I was soon back with the kids.

As far as playing had gone, it had definitely been my intention to stop after leaving Bristol Rovers. You do start to feel the old legs going and that's generally the main reason for your descent down the football pyramid. I had thoroughly enjoyed my career, but when John McGinlay got on the blower I was up for delaying my retirement by a year or so. He seemed happy enough with the 'non-training' arrangement and I knew my appearances would be limited, but I was still keen to give it a go. Ilkeston Town have been around since 1945, and are based in Derbyshire, so it was a case of playing for them when my coaching duties allowed. As it turned out, I was only able to make three competitive appearances for Ilkeston, so my time at the club was indeed limited. Mind you, I scored on my debut against Bath City and celebrated that goal just like the rest. I loved scoring and whether it was in an Old Firm game or a Midland League match against Bath it didn't matter. It was a goal, and it was a special feeling. Mind you, this goal was quite special, even if I say so myself. One of our defenders broke out of the box with the ball and played it to me around the halfway line. I 'out-paced' the Bath City midfield and defence (yes, even at the age of 37!) and ran around 50 yards with the ball before scoring. I didn't quite need oxygen by the time I had despatched the ball into the net, but it did take it out of me! Sadly it wasn't the winner as the game ended one apiece.

Ilkeston Town were dissolved in 2010, although I believe a new incarnation has emerged, so the town still has a football club. Despite limited involvement at Ilkeston, I had enjoyed the experience of playing again, even though non-league football can be quite unforgiving. But I certainly wasn't put off and when the manager of non-league Tividale got in touch, I turned out for them a couple of times. Again, circumstances dictated I could only stay for a short while, but I was soon joining my THIRD club of the season when Willenhall Town asked me to sign. The manager was a friend of a friend, and a big Villa fan as well, and I was off to try my luck in the Midland Alliance League.

Willenhall is close to Walsall, so it was local to me, but again I found it difficult as the manager, who was a well-intentioned lad, messed me about a bit. I was still coaching at Villa so I couldn't train with Willenhall, but I was rushing away from Birmingham after the kids' team game on a Saturday morning to get to Willenhall, or wherever they were playing, in time for my game, but I would get there and the manager would say, 'Mark, I'm not going to play you today,' and I would be left watching from the sidelines. I did say to him, 'Look, it's absolutely fine if you don't pick me because I haven't been to training, or I've been playing shit, but can you please just let me know even that morning because I'm not going to struggle to get to games just to watch.' Sadly, it didn't seem to make any difference so I gave it up and that looked to all intents and purposes like the end of my football career. Not before I had scored a few goals for Willenhall, though, and there is one game in particular that stands out, probably because it epitomised what most people might view as a 'typical non-league game'. We were playing Chesham United at their place and it had been a decent game. We were 3-2 down with less than five minutes to play when one of our lads slipped and landed on top of the ball. An opponent steamed in and started kicking lumps out of him. He was taking these big swipes at him to try and free the ball. It wasn't as if our guy was trying to waste time, as we were losing. Next minute, just about every player on the field was involved in a mass brawl, like *Gunfight at the O.K. Corral!* Once the melee had calmed down, the referee sent off both players who were involved in the initial flashpoint – and booked just ONE other guy for his part in the mass brawl. It was a bonkers decision, but the fight had fired up our guys and we ended up getting a draw.

After playing for just six clubs in more than 20 years, I had just gone through three in one season! Along with coaching at Villa, and a job I had with the English FA, it was probably my busiest ever season in the game. But if you're thinking that was that, and that I gave it all up and didn't touch non-league football again with a bargepole ... then you're wrong.

A few weeks before the start of the new season I got a call from a friend who asked if I was fixed up for the new campaign. I said I'd retired ... again, even though I hadn't really given the subject much thought, but just like the coach of Beeches Colts all those years ago, who refused to give in when my Mum insisted her son didn't play football on a Sunday, my friend asked again, and I signed for Dudley Town. And I'm glad I did as it was easily my best experience of playing non-league football. I thoroughly enjoyed my time there, so much so in fact that I stayed for a couple of seasons.

I remember sitting in the dressing room before the first game and the manager pulling me to one side, saying, 'Mark, I'm not going to try and tell someone like yourself how to play the game. Just go out there, play wherever you want and enjoy yourself.' And you know something, this guy might not have been Sir Alex Ferguson or Jose Mourinho, but he certainly knew how to get the best out of people and he spoke a lot of sense. I did exactly as he suggested and had a ball. I was still coaching at Villa but I was playing almost every week for Dudley and it was a great way to wind down my career. Near the end of the second season there, I picked up an injury and decided to give it up. The thing is, the injury didn't come in the rough and tumble of non-league, but while playing for Rangers Legends in an indoor competition. I had knocked the ball past Kenny Black and he just completely smashed me. The bang on the shoulder was a bad one and I got carried off. The upshot was I couldn't coach for a fortnight, and I knew I had a decision to make.

The non-league football was also quite tough, and while I was getting about £60 a week playing for Dudley, I knew another injury – and more enforced time off from coaching – would see me in a spot of bother at Villa, so for that reason only I decided to call time on playing. I was about 40 anyway and reckoned I'd had a great innings.

I still play the odd charity match but I've slowed down so much now that it's noticeable and I couldn't play competitively, but I've long since accepted that and it's fine. When I reached about 45 or 46 I couldn't believe how much my body had changed, in terms of not really doing what it was asked. Any time I play in a charity match it's like slow-motion football. I still play squash and racketball and I enjoy that, but I play it on my terms, and at my pace.

When I was playing non-league I definitely felt like I was a target. The good thing about being given a free role, though, was that I could go wherever I wanted on the park, so it meant I wasn't up against a big bruiser of a right-back for the entire match. Mind you, there were a few occasions when guys went right over the top on me, or left a boot in, and it led to a few confrontations, and me inevitably telling them a few home truths. When you come up through the ranks in football, you soon learn to look after yourself and that was something I put to good use on many an occasion in competitions such as the Midland League. That said, the bruisers were definitely in the minority. There were a lot of good, clever footballers playing in that league and most of the teams were well organised with good set-ups.

When I decided to give it up, though, it was definitely the right time. If you don't listen to your body, there will only be one loser.

Chapter 19

All Good Things ...

FOR all the wonderful things I achieved in my football career, the greatest prize I have is my children. Mischa and Marlon are my world and I'm so grateful and thankful to have them in my life. Mischa is the older of the two and was born in 1993, while I was at Liverpool. Marlon followed two years later.

Mischa wasn't my first child, though.

When any couple get married, the hope is you will be together for the rest of your life. Tracey and I were no different, but for a footballer, sadly, the reality doesn't always come with a happy ending. You can be away from home for such long periods of time, and because you spend so much time with team-mates, bonds form and you tend to act differently around them than you would with your wife.

When I was at Rangers, Tracey and I were engaged and we were very happy. We were married in the summer of 1990, immediately after the season had finished, and everything was great until I moved to Liverpool just over a year later. Tracey liked it in Scotland but was equally happy about the move to the Wirral, where we set up home. That was when tragedy arrived at our front door. Tracey discovered she was pregnant and we were both so happy. The pregnancy went full term, but sadly it wasn't to be and our daughter, Yasmin, didn't make it. It was a horrendous time for us. Yasmin died in the April, and would've been our first, so that put an enormous strain on our relationship because people handle tragedy differently. I immersed myself in my football to try and deflect from what I should have been doing, and that was grieving properly and supporting Tracey. Naturally I still tried to be there for her, but was that enough? I'm not sure.

You never fully get over losing a baby and at the time I couldn't sleep for ages. The mental and physical pain was just awful. It was torture, but I'm sure it was even worse for Tracey, as she had been carrying the wee one for nine months.

The experience taught me a lot of things, but one specific lesson I learned was never to judge another player if he doesn't perform at a specific time, or with a specific club, because you don't know what is going on in his life. Sometimes people look perfectly happy on the outside, while inside they are struggling to cope with their personal situation.

Tracey and I went on to have two beautiful children and I couldn't be happier with them, but nothing will ever make up for the loss of our first child. I was numb for god knows how long. At the time you do your best to get through it, no matter what it takes, but there is no doubt it affected my football.

I had another four years at Liverpool, but within that period there were loan spells at Wolves and Stoke, and six months at Southampton, so you can already see the amount of moving around I was doing, while for the most part, the family were settled up in the north-west of the country. When Tracey and I eventually split we had moved back down to the Midlands. I recall we had a heated debate at the time about buying a house in Solihull. She was against it, and I realise now it was probably because she was planning on leaving me. I ended up buying a house there within a year of us breaking up and I still love the area.

The break-up wasn't down to just me, or Tracey, there was definitely blame on both sides. I was still playing football and travelling about here, there and everywhere. I was away from home a couple of nights a week minimum, and commuting was taking its toll. My career had taken me to Southampton, and then to Swindon, and in the interim period, my wife and I had grown apart. She wanted to go left, and I preferred right. It was as simple as that. The kids were only six and four at the time, which was far from ideal, and even though they are very resilient, it still had a profound effect on them.

Our house was relatively big – I was living upstairs and Tracey was downstairs – and when she came home I would be going out, so we had become like passing ships, especially in the last two or three years of our marriage. It's never nice, or easy, splitting up from your long-time partner, but sometimes it's unavoidable and it was eventually for the best that we went our separate ways.

One thing that saddened me, though, was when Marlon told me many years later that he still remembered vividly the night he, Mischa and Tracey left the marital home, and recalled me and his mother arguing about it. He also said his mother had told him they'd only moved out as the house was being renovated and that when it was finished they'd be moving back in. He said he was distraught a few months later when he asked if the house was finished yet and was told they weren't going back.

The break-up of my marriage naturally left a big void in my life. I was also moving club at the time, which for a footballer coming to the end of his career is quite a big deal. The clock is counting down and you don't know if this move will be your last, or, worse still, if the previous one was your last. I was feeling really down; I would've said depressed, but knowing what depression is now, it wasn't that serious, although it felt like it at the time. It was certainly tough.

Equally, knowing I still had my career was a big help as it proved to be the perfect distraction. People would ask why I was still playing. The answer was simple: I didn't know anything apart from football and my philosophy was that while I was still fit and enjoying it why should I stop?

I was offered a player/manager role at non-league Nuneaton when I was coming to the end of my career, but knocked it back because I knew I would have to stop playing sooner than I'd wanted to, to concentrate more on management. But then a wonderful opportunity presented itself. I was contacted by a friend of a friend about going to America to play. The kids were still relatively young but Tracey and I had split up so I had no alternative but to turn it down because I knew I wouldn't see my children. I was trying to break that cycle of the way my father had behaved when I was growing up. I didn't want to be like him. At the same time it was a great opportunity to go over to the States, play for a while and then start coaching. It was far easier to get a coaching role over there compared to the UK so it's the type of opportunity I would have relished had the family still been together. I've always looked upon the States as one of the best countries in the world and it might have been nice to settle there, but the moment I realised it would mean only seeing the kids a few times a year it became a complete non-starter.

Players are often advised to play as long as they can, as you're a long time retired, but I worried if by playing too long, perhaps I might be affecting my chances of getting a coaching job. Looking back, I did the right thing by playing as long as I did. Had I stopped playing in my mid-thirties, I reckon I would just have been out of the game longer.

When a footballer finally calls it a day it's pretty scary knowing you have very little to occupy your waking hours. Football is like an extension of school: you're with your mates, enjoying good banter and taking the piss, and then it all comes to an end. Just like that. If you don't want to take the next logical step and become a coach, there are a lot of hours to fill each day, and you need to do something.

Lots of people told me that coaching was the next best thing to playing, so I threw myself into it and received my qualifications, but it didn't take me long to realise it was actually nothing like playing. If you can grow to love coaching then it can be a good career but it's not for everyone. For me, nothing comes remotely close to playing football for a living.

Of course, one of the positive aspects of retirement was the time I would be able to spend with my children. I am extremely proud of how they have got on with their life and made something of it. My son Marlon enjoyed football when he was a kid but attending a rugby-playing school was perhaps always going to work against him. He was actually very good at rugby but again he was playing just for fun. In fact, any time I watched him play football he always seemed to be in goal. I thought to myself, 'He can't be related to me. I couldn't head the ball never mind catch it!'

But if Marlon wasn't ever going to stick with football, I was glad to see him take part in rugby, because in my experience if you're active in sport as a youngster, you generally keep fit all your life. I coached for the FA and in most of the schools I went into I would have to say that the levels of obesity were very high, often as much as 30 per cent of the kids, and that isn't good at all. So, football or rugby to him were just hobbies while he was studying to be a lawyer. Mind you, now that he has his degree in law, which he got in 2017, he has changed tact and decided he would like to work in medicine, so it's back to university for him. He is academically very good so I think he will soon lay down his marker in that field.

My daughter Mischa has also qualified as a lawyer, but thankfully she has decided to remain in this field while her brother goes off chasing another degree.

When the kids were growing up, I vowed I would always be very close to them, probably because of the non-existent relationship I'd had with my father. I made sure we always went on holiday every close season, even when I was out of contract after leaving Southampton, as it was the only quality time we had together. For the remainder of the year, while the kids were at school, I was preparing for games or away with the team.

When Mischa was just three weeks old, Tracey and I took her to Peter Huistra's wedding, which was daunting as just 18 months previously we had lost a child, so whenever Mischa moved, or if there was a lack of movement, we were worried in case there was a problem. Marlon was a totally different baby as he would cry a lot and was always moving around, so we knew he was okay. He would keep us up half the night, whereas Mischa was a quiet baby. It was only when she got to 18 months and started walking that I truly felt that what had happened to Yasmin probably wasn't going to happen to Mischa.

One of my favourite times with Mischa was a holiday we had near Nottingham at a place called Center Parcs. Tracey was carrying Marlon at the time so Mischa and I enjoyed a fantastic two-week, all-inclusive break at the complex which had some great swimming pools and lots of outdoor activities. Mischa also had her first proper swimming lessons there.

When I was coming to the end of my career, keeping fit was incredibly important to me. If the kids were staying over at the weekend we would all be up on the Sunday morning and doing a warm-up together before taking part in some exercises – and then breakfast!

It was then off to the cinema with Mischa, Marlon and a few of their cousins. Inevitably, no matter how good or bad the film was, I would look across and see six children all fast asleep in their seats, and folk would look at me as I was sitting there on my own, laughing my head off and it probably wasn't even a comedy! Mind you, my first thought would be, 'Well, that was a waste of an afternoon!'

I still see my kids a lot, and that's so important to me. In fact, my daughter has moved in with me as she wants to work in the Birmingham area, and also wants to be near her grandparents. And my son is hoping to win a place at the University of Warwick so it looks like I will be seeing a lot more of him too. I have a great relationship with Mischa and Marlon. I think they appreciate what I went through when they were younger, and I think they now know of the times when their mother made it very difficult for me to see them. Sadly, I eventually had to take her to court in order to get access and perhaps that's one of the reasons I have a real bond with my kids. In fact, there was even a time when Tracey moved back up to the Wirral after the court had granted me access, and that made it doubly difficult for me to see them. That was a bad time in my life. But my priority was always to ensure they were a part of my life; anything else was never an option. Sadly it has taken years to get to the point we're at now where I can see my children freely.

While I was trying to eke out a living in coaching, a member of my extended family was starting to make a bit of a name for himself in the game. My nephew, Reece Wabara, is my stepbrother's son and I used to enjoy going to see him play, especially as he looked as though he had what it took to succeed in the game. I remember getting him a trial at Villa when he was 12 or 13 but he wasn't quite right at the time and it didn't work out. He was a good athlete and physically very strong but his touch wasn't quite there, so he went to Walsall, and that was when he started to make progress. He was 16 when Manchester City picked him up and he was there for six years – three in their academy and the other three as a pro. Sadly, he only managed to play one first-team game, replacing Pablo Zabaleta from the bench against Bolton. He did also represent England at under-19 and under-20 level, though.

He was part of the England squad at the 2011 Under-20 World Cup, which was held in Columbia. The likes of Jack Butland and Saido Berahino were in the squad but it turned out to be one of the most bizarre campaigns involving an England side at the finals of any big tournament. England were drawn in Group F alongside Argentina, Mexico and North Korea, and somehow managed to draw each of their three group games 0-0, which I suppose was good for defenders like Reece, but bad news for supporters who might have gone out to Columbia looking to see some goals. The group match against Argentina, played in Medellin, drew a crowd in excess of 40,000.

England qualified from their group as the highest ranked third-place team and were drawn against Nigeria – who Reece also qualified to play for, because of his grandfather – in the knockout round of 16, but lost 1-0. So they flew home having failed to find the net in four games.

Here's the thing, though. Reece's dad was really into cars and I think my nephew inherited his love of smart vehicles. When he was a teenager he was paying about five grand in car insurance, and perhaps the likes of Man City didn't think his head was in the right place, although that's just my opinion. Technically and physically he was very good, but they let him go and that surprised me. While on the books at City, they loaned him out to Ipswich, Oldham and Doncaster Rovers. He played plenty of games for all three, with his winner for Oldham against Liverpool in the FA Cup an obvious highlight. When his contract at City was up, he signed for Doncaster. He was there a full season and played over 40 games, but decided to move to Barnsley, then Wigan and finally to Bolton Wanderers.

I couldn't understand why he was moving around so much, because it certainly isn't good for a player. You want to settle somewhere and see what you can achieve. But then I got a call from Gavin McCann, who I knew from his days at Villa. He was a coach at Bolton, and he said to me, 'Can you have a word with Reece for me please, Mark? Can you ask him to hire a car to drive to training? He's turning up in a Rolls Royce with tinted windows!' It was ridiculous, of course it was, but I was picturing Reece driving into the car park at Bolton in his Roller, and the manager turning up in a Volvo. Don't ask me why.

I then spoke to Patrick Vieira – a coach at City – about Reece, not long after Patrick had gone on record as saying Reece was one of the most improved players at City, and that he had a real chance. I met Patrick at one of the veterans' tournaments and I asked him how Reece was getting on. His face fell and he answered, 'You know, Mark, there is something that just isn't right.' As I said, City released him and he had a string of clubs after that, so quite clearly something wasn't right.

That something was an internet clothing company – called Manière De Voir – which was becoming one of the fastest growing companies around, and Reece had started it while he was at Manchester City. I'm sure he had some tough choices to make, but when Bolton released him he apparently turned up for his final day in a £250,000 Lamborghini! Let's be honest: even if your company is doing well, you still don't turn up in a car worth a quarter of a million pounds. It's not exactly a good way to endear yourself to folk. I have told him many times that being a professional footballer is the best job there is, and that one day he will regret the decisions he has made. I don't care how well his company is doing; there is nothing to compare with playing football for a living. But he's very single-minded, and I would rather he was that way than down on his luck. He will be 30 in a couple of years and he won't be able to get a club. You don't get many opportunities to be a footballer so he might look at it as an opportunity lost. Mind you, I'm only looking at this from a footballing perspective. What Reece has achieved with his company is out of this world, and I'm so glad that his business has been successful. I think part of the issue is that he has had success in both fields relatively early, and the amount of hours it takes to succeed in both is probably greater than the 24 there are in any one day, so something had to give, and it was his football.

One of the first things I did when I quit playing was to go back to college – to learn Spanish. It wasn't because I thought the first club on the blower to offer me a coaching job would be Real Madrid! Once I had come to terms with having to train every day as a kid and maintaining a good level of fitness throughout my career, I knew that I would keep that going into my 'retirement'. But a few people had mentioned I would also have to keep my brain active, and that learning a language was one of the best ways to do that. So I enrolled at college and learned Spanish. It took me two years to kind of learn the lingo, and then another two to learn French – as my mate lives in France – but ten years on I'm still not that great, although I can get by in both languages. In fact, I still take one lesson a week, and my brain feels fine! It apparently gives you a decent chance of keeping dementia at bay.

I suppose I was a bit paranoid about having nothing to do when I quit playing, so when I was told the English FA were looking for ex-players to take their coaching programmes into schools I thought it was right up my street – although I have eagle-eyed former Arsenal and West Brom player Brendon Batson to thank for ensuring I had a shot at the job. Brendon was working at the FA and he rang me one day and said, 'Hi Mark, I've just noticed you've sent in your CV for a job at the FA. Is that right?'

I said, 'Yeah, I think what they're doing is great.'

'Right,' he replied. 'It's just that all your CV covers is work you've previously done for television!'

I had done a bit of punditry work for TV, especially when I was at Bristol Rovers, so I had two CVs. One for coaching and the other for media work, and guess which one I'd sent in? Thankfully Brendon was on the ball so he told me to send in the right one and he would make sure it was seen by the right eyes. He was true to his word.

I got the job and started in 2007 and I worked with the FA for around five years. We would start off by going into schools with a tailored programme for the children, help them with their session plans and then run a skills centre in the evening for the kids who had a better chance of making the grade. Effectively it meant everyone was involved, regardless of skill level. It was ideal because there is nothing worse than seeing a youngster stuck on the sidelines because he isn't as good as some of the others.

Ultimately, though, I wanted to work at a league club with professional players, although my brother always gives me a hard time for not putting myself out there enough. He would constantly be at me to network more, even to go out and see a couple of games a week and get my face known at all the local clubs.

He wanted me to let them know I was job hunting and see where it took me, but I would look at the fixtures in the paper and if I didn't fancy any of the games I wouldn't go. I was acting like a supporter, wanting to be entertained, while my brother was looking at it purely from a business point of view. Of course, he was right and I was way off the mark. Even now, friends will call and ask me if I fancy going to watch a specific player, and I don't mind doing that, but please don't make me watch a rubbish game! I know it sounds awful but I love football played the right way.

Things have cooled off for me nowadays, but there was a time, right after I stopped playing, when I was never at home. I was out of the house seven days a week. In the mornings, and some evenings, I was coaching for Villa, and in the afternoons I was working for the FA. Saturdays I was playing non-league and on a Sunday I was with the Villa kids. I had gone from being a professional footballer, where you basically 'do jack', to working seven days a week.

Nowadays, I sometimes wonder why I couldn't get a job in coaching, and while I'm not suggesting there was anything sinister at play, there is definitely a problem when it comes to clubs hiring black coaches. When I look at the number of black footballers in the professional game in England, it's something like 30 per cent. Then I see how many black coaches there are, and it's less than two per cent. I would like to think there isn't a problem with colour, but the statistics suggest otherwise. I've met a few black guys who aren't interested in coaching, just like there are a number of white ex-players who don't want to go down that road, but there are loads of black guys who would relish the opportunity to work in the dug-out but simply can't get an opening. In America they have a scheme called 'positive discrimination', whereby a certain number of black players have to be interviewed for positions.

Ideally we would all like to get a job on merit but the stats are so bad there just has to be an issue somewhere, and it needs to be addressed. An entire generation of potentially successful black coaches has already been lost because there is little hope of them ever securing a position. Being white, or black for that matter, doesn't mean you will be a better coach than the next guy, and there are also a lot of great coaches around who perhaps never played at the top level. It's just about giving everyone a chance and seeing who emerges as the better coaches, because our game – and society – needs that right now. If I'm being honest, my chance has probably gone, but I would have loved an opportunity to fail. That's all I ever asked. And the jobs I would be prepared to do now are different, so my chances are more limited. When I stopped playing, I was coaching young kids at Villa, but I wouldn't do that now. It would need to be at a certain level.

Luckily I've owned some properties since I was in my early twenties, and I've had agents looking after them virtually full time, from finding tenants to getting any repairs done. But I've eased them out over a period of time and now do everything myself. I have places in Birmingham, London and Lancaster. The latter was my son's doing. He was all set to go to Lancaster University, so we identified a property and I almost bankrupted myself buying it. But a week before I was due to sign the contract, he decided he wanted to live in town with his mates. We were a good bit down the road on the property so I decided to go ahead and buy it anyway. In hindsight, it was more profitable to get another tenant in because no doubt my son wouldn't have been paying rent! It has worked out well for me so I'm glad Marlon was the catalyst for me purchasing that particular one.

When I was 22, Tottenham were showing a lot of interest in me so I went as far as buying a property in North London, thinking that I might need to live there if and when the move was completed. I like London, but the move fell through. I still went down a lot to visit family, perhaps even once a month, going out or visiting, and looked upon the property as an investment even though I have never actually lived in it. I let it out now and everything has been going smoothly, apart from when the boiler broke and I had to source an engineer as quickly as possible, but I don't mind looking after things as it keeps my mind active.

This might sound quite self-obsessive but if I'm being honest, one of the things I missed most when my career ended was the attention and adulation. Most players do. I don't think there is anyone out there who doesn't like being praised for a job well done, or being told they were a good player. Any kind of praise is always welcome, and it's far better than being told you're crap. I've been called both and I know which I prefer. There is no better feeling than scoring a goal in front of a big crowd, or playing your part in an exhilarating performance. Looking back, I'm not surprised there are many players who find it difficult to accept their career is over and that the adulation has come to an end. A lot of players either don't plan for the future or they think the time will never arrive when they have to hang up their boots. Luckily I had family to remind me that football isn't for life, and that I would still have to think about what I wanted to do when the day finally arrived. Well, it did arrive, although I still get a chance to pull the boots on now and again thanks to my association with the Rangers Legends team. Probably the reason I still do so – and play with injuries like a swollen knee – is because it's not really an option to turn down the chance of playing 'one more time' at Ibrox, in front of a big crowd, and seeing all the lads again and having a bit of banter like the old days. It's priceless.

I think the first Legends match I played in was in 1999 in the Hong Kong Masters. In the lead-up to that competition, I had decided to bury the hatchet with my father. I felt the time was right as I had children of my own and I wanted them to meet their grandfather. I took them round to his house, but there was no one in. I tried again: same result. When I called round a third time, which was just before the competition, again there was no answer but I decided to knock on a neighbour's door, to see if they had seen him around, or find out if he still lived there, and they told me he had passed away; that was how I found out. It was a double whammy as I was also going through the divorce.

I got in touch with the organisers of the Hong Kong Masters to tell them about my father's death and they said if I was up to it they still wanted me to play. They also said it would be absolutely fine to fly home early for the funeral. The day before I was due to fly out, I bumped into one of my stepbrothers and I was telling him about my predicament. He told me not to worry and to go to Hong Kong and enjoy the tournament and fly back when I was ready. As it turned out, I flew back for the funeral but didn't get involved in anything to do with the organisation, apart from helping to pay for it.

Knowing my father had passed away had a strange impact on me. All the memories of my childhood came flooding back – both good and bad – and it was like years of those memories suppressed into a few moments. I'd never really had anything resembling a relationship with my father, and I think that was the saddest part of it all. Mind you, there was one final insult to contend with. When I had decided to take the kids to meet my father, I had to get the address from a family member. I didn't even know my own father's address. Imagine the shock when I discovered it was a house I had been in and out of when I was a kid. It had belonged to the parents of one of my childhood friends, Taju Forlarin (remember the dinner-money scam?). When we were younger, I would go round to Taju's house, and maybe nick the odd cigarette off his mum. Imagine my horror when I discovered my father had bought the house and moved in with his 'other' family. Isn't that ironic? It really pissed me off. It was in Newtown, literally 500 metres from where we had lived.

Obviously I am eligible to play for Villa, Rangers and Liverpool Legends, and I enjoyed them so much it got to the stage where I would play for anyone who asked! I left Villa at the end of 1987 so I hadn't seen a lot of the lads for the best part of 12 years, so playing was a great way of keeping in touch with them; I also thought it might help me get a job in football. There is an excellent social side attached to the Legends, as inevitably we all go out for a few drinks, which can sometimes – no, make that always – turn into a bit of a session.

Earlier this year was a classic example of how hectic it can be. I played at Ibrox in a Legends charity match on the Saturday. Seven days later I was back in Glasgow for a nine-in-a-row dinner at a swanky hotel, and less than 12 hours after that finished I was in Portsmouth for another Rangers Legends match against Pompey, for the Lee Rigby Foundation. It was hectic, but enjoyable and very worthwhile.

When you get to my age, it's inevitable you will be carrying some sort of injury, but you still go out there and do your best. Listen, when you've been a pro footballer, pride kicks in – yes, even at this age – and won't allow you to accept anything other than a thoroughly decent performance.

The Legends match at Ibrox in March also gave me an opportunity to see some of the guys I get on best with, like Charlie Miller – even though we never played together. I also had a long chat with Ally McCoist, and it was great to see Walter Smith, who was very good to me when I left Ibrox, and who always welcomes me back with open arms. In fact, I still say to the guys that I left Ibrox far too quickly. But I had a dilemma at the time. Do you turn down what was the most successful club in Britain at that time, Europe-wise? In hindsight, yes I should have, but in fairness to Walter, he has never held that against me. I'll always be grateful to him for that.

It's strange, but when we all get together again we talk about the things we got up to when we played for Rangers, probably things I can't discuss here! The only guy that was missing the last time I was at Ibrox was Durranty, due to his position as assistant manager at Dumbarton. They were playing in a cup final on the same weekend, which was great.

I didn't think I would finish the Legends game but I wanted to be there, speak to the staff, walk the corridors again and see the photographs on the walls. Everything about Ibrox is magical. It's one of the greatest places on earth and Rangers are such a special club. But the whole Legends scene is fantastic, and it isn't all about the football. It's about renewing old acquaintances, meeting the supporters and trying to put on a show. The moment you walk through the front door at Ibrox the memories come flooding back.

Even to this day I'd say the two things I still miss about football are matchday and banter with the lads. Bar that, I have to accept everything else. Obviously I'd love to still be playing, but retirement comes to everyone. The banter, though, you just can't get that anywhere else and it's only when you finish you struggle to handle not being involved because it is a big wrench not to have that banter and people taking the piss about your clothes, haircut or whatever. It's such a big part of your life for so long. When I stopped playing non-league football I didn't know what to do with myself for ages on a Saturday afternoon, I was really at a loose end. For a while I even went shopping! In the end you think to yourself, 'Get a grip, man,' get something worthwhile to do and within a few months you get out of it, but some people can't, and I understand that. Say, for instance, you've had a short career, perhaps because of injury; I can see why some guys might turn to drink or drugs, looking for something to replace the highs they had as a footballer. I was very fortunate to have a long career, and a good 23 years as a professional, but it was still quite a gap to fill when I eventually quit. If I was working with the PFA, one of the things I would do is give players coming to the end of their careers help with making the transformation back into civilian life, for want of a better term. It's certainly needed.

So that's it. My football career, over in the blink of an eye, but boy was it fun while it lasted.

Epilogue

To Those We've Lost

NOTHING is forever; not football, not even life itself. And never has that been more greatly illustrated than with the friends and former colleagues I've lost since beginning the task of writing this book. In most jobs, colleagues are exactly as it says on the tin. Occasionally, new friendships are formed and can last a lifetime. Football is different from most jobs in many ways, but it's a little easier to form good, lasting bonds with team-mates as you spend so much time with them, and you also have to rely on each other so much when the chips are down.

During my professional career with Villa, Rangers, Liverpool and the other clubs, I found making friends quite easy, and I've maintained many of these friendships to this day. But when fate intervenes there isn't an awful lot you can do.

When I started out on my career at Villa I received a fair bit of abuse. It was tough at times, but perhaps youthfulness played a small part in helping me through it. Getting through it was one thing, but accepting it was a completely different ball game, and the credit for the latter has to go to just one guy, Cyrille Regis. He was the main reason I played on. While he was with West Brom I witnessed him suffer a terrible barrage of abuse at Villa Park one afternoon, but no matter the ferocity or volume of the taunts, he simply shrugged his shoulders and got on with the game. It was as though nothing could penetrate the barrier he had put up. Deep down, though, I'm sure he was hurting badly, big guy or not. But he would flash that endearing smile and laugh it off. I really looked up to Cyrille, and I would think to myself, 'If he can do it, so can I. I'll take it on the chin and get on with it.' Sadly, I knew players who weren't able to cope with it and they ended up quitting football after a short time. So that was my dilemma: be like Cyrille, or give it all up. It was my choice; that's the way society and football was back then and nothing was changing quickly. I had a decision to make and I plumped for the former, as quitting a game I loved simply wasn't an option.

When Cyrille passed away in January of this year from a heart attack it shocked me to the core. I had spoken to him a couple of weeks beforehand and he gave me some great advice about a business opportunity I had been considering. He was a fantastic man and even right up until the end he was still inspiring me.

When we lost Cyrille I didn't just lose an ex-footballing friend and mate; we all lost a very special man, someone who had paved the way for black footballers in this country. Someone who had taken the abuse for all those who would follow him. He had taken that abuse and batted it straight back to its perpetrators. Words are insufficient to describe what Cyrille sacrificed for so many. He was a genuine legend and will never be forgotten.

When I left Villa to sign for Rangers, one of the biggest thrills for me was getting to play with some incredible players at Ibrox. Among them were Trevor Francis and Ray Wilkins; two superstars of the game, and two guys who made me feel so welcome at Ibrox and helped me settle in.

Ray arrived at Ibrox just a few weeks before me but when I first walked into the Ibrox dressing room, Ray already looked at home. It was as though he had been a Rangers player his whole life. He was very comfortable there. But he wasn't just my friend at Rangers; he also helped look after this young English lad, far from home and on his own. At times I had my fiancée for company, but when I was on my own Ray took me under his wing and that is something I will never, ever forget. Here was a guy I had looked up to throughout my career going out of his way to make me feel at home. What a gentleman.

When I heard he was unwell earlier this year I was praying he would make a full recovery. Sadly that didn't happen and he passed away just seven days after suffering the heart attack. I was numb. Ray was only 61 years old and was taken from us when he still had so much left to offer life. I for one will never forget him; he was a great footballer, but above all he was the perfect gentleman.

Guys like Ray don't come into your life all that often, but the same could be said about a lad I renewed old acquaintances with at Ibrox. His name was Neale Cooper and he was a lovely lad. We initially met at Aston Villa and became very friendly, because it was really hard, nay, impossible, NOT to like Neale. He is undoubtedly the funniest man I ever met in football, and had gags for every occasion. Don't get me wrong, he took his football as seriously as the next guy, but he had a wicked sense of humour that endeared him to me almost immediately.

Neale had come down from Aberdeen and obviously knew our manager at the time, Billy McNeill, very well. I'll never forget him making up a hilarious song about McNeill's tenure at Villa Park, which was a disaster to say the least. During our limited team talks, the manager would say, 'Mark, I want you to get down the left and get a cross in. Bingo! Gordon, you do such and such. Bingo!' So, Neale made up a song called The Bingo Rap and sang it at the Christmas party and everyone was in stitches. He had captured the manager's style perfectly. McNeill wasn't there to hear it, which is probably just as well – for Neale! When I read last year that Neale had suffered a heart attack it shocked me to the core. I phoned him and we had a good chinwag about the old days and he assured me he was fine. He is the kind of guy you could speak to for hours, so you can imagine the old ground we covered during the conversation. There aren't too many tales I can tell about Neale, but I recall one time in Italy, while I was at Rangers and we were at the Il Ciocco training camp. The gaffer allowed us to go out for a few drinks one evening and, being footballers, we stretched it to the limit. Most of us could barely walk as we headed back to our quarters to go to bed. But as we walked into the dormitory, we saw Neale lying next to the minibar – which he had quite clearly mistaken for the toilet! Seizing his opportunity, Mark Hateley whipped one of the bed sheets off Neale's bed and used it as a giant nappy, which he put on Neale. It was one of the funniest sights I had ever seen.

I also remember being on a tour of Jamaica while with Villa, and we were having a night out in Kingston. Martin Keown was with us at the time and he and Neale were indulging in a little light-hearted banter. At least that's the way it began. We'd all had a few drinks and so the 'banter' quickly descended into mud-slinging, with one giving as good as the other – until Neale called Martin 'pizza face', due to his bad skin. That was the line. Martin pounced on Neale and before long they were rolling around scrapping. Within seconds there were a couple of armed guards heading our way and we had to break up the brawling pair before anyone was arrested, which thankfully we managed to do.

Neale and I got on so well and when he signed for Rangers I was delighted. I hadn't seen him for a while but it was like we had spoken only the day before. But that was Neale, he was a lovely guy and a great laugh, so you can imagine how shocked I was to hear that he had died suddenly – and at the age of 54. I felt so sorry for Neale's kids and family. It's no age at all.

I've lost three former team-mates and friends this year, but their families have lost so much more. It has been a horrendous year in that respect, but the three guys I've mentioned will certainly never be forgotten. While they were with us, their stars shone too brightly for that to ever be an option.

To Cyrille, Ray and Neale. Rest easy fellas.